THE SECRET CASTLE

The KEY to GOOD and EVIL

Miguel Hernández-Bronchud

MA (Cantab); DM (Oxon); MRCP (UK)

First edition published 2006

Third Edition © 2019 Miguel Hernández-Bronchud

ISBN 978-0-9957205-7-2

Typesetting & design by
Hamilton House Publishing Ltd

Rochester upon Medway,
Kent.

Printed by
Amazon Print-on-Demand

The Castle

CONTENTS

INTRODUCTION

This book is divided into two parts:

1. **My Secret Castle**: Starting with a brief description, almost like a tourist guide, of what my 'secret castle' at Mora de Rubielos, in Aragon, in Spain, looks like today, following a couple of decades of restoration work that probably saved the building but unfortunately destroyed much of its ancient symbols, I shall take the reader through a personal search of esoteric signs and symbols that can still be observed in the castle itself, dating from the ownership of the Knights of St. John and the Knights Templar, but also in some very early European cultures, like in the writings of ancient Ibers or Etruscans, or in some early Christian dwellings (for example, those in Ephesus), and even as recent as the twentieth the century in Nazi Germany.

By symbols, I refer to any sign, mark or object which may be regarded as representational – of ideas, beliefs, emotions, abstractions, concepts or values. Unfortunately the code that might help us to understand such ancient 'esoteric symbols' as remain to us, has been totally or partially lost, and unless a 'Rosetta Stone' of symbolism is found in the future, our interpretation can only be speculative.

Modern traffic signs, for example, are understandable to most of us and are universal because they give us warnings and directions to make car driving safer. But, what exactly runic or alchemical symbols, early Christian or masonic marks, meant to initiates or small groups of disciples or followers a millennium or two ago, is open to question. Esoteric knowledge is traditionally restricted to initiates and is usually transmitted verbally, or by secret signs, tokens and passwords. Hence the difficulty in understanding the meaning and power conferred by this type of teaching.

2. **What happened to our grand-parents?** When one looks back at the twentieth century, and at its first half in particular, so rich in political and violent turmoil ending in a Second World War which cost some 50 million lives and shaped our present world, one inevitably asks the reasons for such turbulent, disorderly and uncontrolled behaviour. What kind of forces acted upon our grand-parents and their generation? Besides rational forces, it became clear to me during my investigations that irrational passions and fanatic ideas were the main motors of these painful historical events. This

is why several 'esoteric' groups or societies are also briefly discussed, in the context of Nazi Germany. Ideas and beliefs that led to bizarre and still not fully explained historical episodes such as the solo flight of Rudolf Hess to Scotland in May 1941, when Hitler seemed so close to total victory in Europe. His mission and exactly what happened to him remain an enigma.

An enigma is any puzzling question, person, thing, or circumstance which cannot be properly explained or understood. This is often because the truth has been deliberately hidden, or even destroyed, to protect or maintain the privileges of the powerful. History is full of enigmas and several are reviewed in this book from a personal perspective based on many years of research. Mystery is slightly different from an enigma, because it is impenetrable, the cause or origin of the question or concept is hidden to our human minds or impossible to understand. Thus, for example, the nature of divinity, the knowledge of Good and Evil, and our own fate are mysteries to us. In this book I use anthropological, psychological, philosophical and even theological arguments to interpret and to try to understand all of the enigmas and mysteries encountered in my historical and biographical research.

PREFACE

Children live in a world of their own. Time passes in a different way; reality and fantasy are often mixed up; there is no clear purpose in life except for enjoyment and pleasure. But there is also curiosity and mystery. As a child, I had a 'Secret Castle', which I am only just now beginning to understand. It was awesome and yet attractive, good and yet evil. It made me feel and think of strange energies. A real but 'Secret Castle', somewhere in one of the most remote parts of Spain, in what used to be the ancient Kingdom of w.

I knew it was there, in the village of Mora de Rubielos, for I had seen it many times with my own eyes during my summer holidays. I knew it meant something painful to my mother and maternal grand-parents, but it was something so painful that they were ashamed or afraid of telling me. It was something which they kept secret until I became an adolescent. But then, when I was finally allowed to visit the interior of the place, I started to find other secret symbols, and hidden energies in that very same castle, whose meaning and true purpose I was only just beginning to grasp, at the age of forty-seven. Feelings of 'Good' and 'Evil' were communicated to me, and still are communicated whenever I visit the castle. I am not superstitious. I am, by profession, a cancer physician and a scientist, and I certainly do not believe in ghosts. But very often reality is even more rich and imaginative than fiction. Ghosts and supernatural beings can be considerably less interesting that some real human beings. This book will give many examples of this truth.

Neither my father nor my mother liked to talk about the history of our family. Their past and their childhood was taboo. As the eldest of their four children I was more aware than my brothers and sister that this conspiracy of silence was due to something painful and terrible in their past. This silence increased my curiosity and my own will to try to understand what really had happened to them. It gradually became evident that it had to do with our Spanish Civil War, in many ways a prelude to the Second World War.

When my father, for example, decided to leave Spain in 1963 for political reasons and we moved to the city of Turin, in northern Italy, my life changed dramatically. I still remember vividly how, at six years of age, I saw the Alps from the train that was taking us, my mother and my sister and my younger brother, to a new life, where my father was already waiting for us. He had promised that although the weather was going to be colder than in sunny Spain, and the days darker, we would enjoy something which in Spain was then forbidden. Something that was, according to him, the most important aspect of life, apart from health. This something was understandably difficult to comprehend and fully appreciate for a six year old boy: he meant **Freedom**.

My father said that in Italy one could speak without constraint about politics, religion, ideals, and being Catalan or Basque (among other things), and fearing nothing. But, again, what can a six year old boy say about that?

While helping my mother to carry our heavy luggage across the French-Italian border, at a railway station in the Alps, all I could say was that 'I had never seen mountains so high, with snow at the top, looking more like clouds than mountains…'

No doubt my parents' excitement, and the obvious stress that this change brought to our lives, undoubtedly impinged upon my subconscious mind, and made me feel that **Injustice** can be, and often is, part of life. It is the dark side of things. The glass half-empty; the flip-side of the coin; the cause of much despair and unhappiness.

This type of feeling, and an increasing awareness of human cruelty and evil, were further enhanced and reinforced by a number of events in my childhood and early adolescence. One of them was becoming close friends with my school-mate, at the *Liceo Classico Massimo d'Azeglio* in Turin, with Renzo Levi, only son of Primo, a chemist and writer who is now becoming increasingly well known outside Italian and Jewish cultural circles.

Levi survived Auschwitz, the Nazi concentration camp, and in 1946, after his liberation by the invading Russian troops, he wrote a wonderful but rather sad book entitled: *If this is a man*.

This book can be briefly summarised in a little known poem also written in 1946, entitled *Shemá*, which I later translated from Italian into English as follows:

'*Shemá* :

You who live secure
In your warm houses,
You who find coming home in the evening
Your food hot and friendly faces-
 Consider if this is a man
 Who works in the mud
 Who doesn't know peace
 Who fights for a scrap of bread,
 Who dies for a yes or for a no.
 Consider if this is a woman,
 Without hair and without name,
 Without strength any more to remember,
 Her eyes empty and her womb cold
 Like a frog in the winter.
Meditate that this has been:
I commend these words to you.
Carve them in your heart
When at home, when on the roads,
Going to bed, arising:
Repeat them to your children
 Or may your house collapse
 May disease cripple you
 May your offspring turn their backs on you.'

Primo Levi

I can have little doubt that all of these events in my early life encouraged me to confront the evil side of human nature with courage, and to fight evil even of a non-human nature. Hence, at the age of seventeen, in London, in 1974, I committed myself to choose my profession as both cancer researcher and cancer clinical doctor. Because cancer shows the 'malignant side of nature', the real and changing face of Evil, being, as it still is, the origin of much human suffering and sorrow.

 To understand History and Philosophy a little bit better, I decided that besides reading as many relevant books as possible, I should gradually uncover the hidden past of my family, and the real nature and true 'engines' of Human History.

I must warn the reader, that what I have found in History is of great complexity, and will require both patience and motivation, as well as considerable parallel thinking and a certain level of cultural background, to follow and comprehend the various chapters of this book. For this personal research has reinforced my intuitive views that History is not linear, that is to say, going from one event to another, but rather random or chaotic. Moreover, it is always relative, written by the victors rather than by the losers, and it is driven by passions rather than by rational arguments. The real forces that shape human history and our fate are so complex and unpredictable that it is hard not to perceive the interaction of supernatural forces, of Good and Evil, fighting each other like angels and demons, as they do in mythology, religions and great works of art.

Frequently, in History, unprecedented facts that seem at first sight to change significantly or even drastically the course of political, social, religious and economic events of the world end up having relatively little impact on History. A fairly recent example of this could be the first human landings on the moon in the 1960s. They were, no doubt, the result and great achievement of technology and a natural ambition to reach even beyond our natural limits, but they have not changed our history as such. On the contrary, small events that often pass unnoticed to contemporaries, or are not so widely publicised, can some times have long-lasting consequences. For example, when Jesus was born, in extreme poverty, in Bethlehem, Judaea, in the days of Herod the king, few could have imagined the birth of a new religion, and the subsequent developments of Christianity.

I have also realized that civilization cannot be taken for granted. In the same way as life on earth has witnessed dramatic changes and several mass extinctions (for example, the dinosaurs that disappeared from our planet some 60 to 65 million years ago), Human History is fraught with examples of great powers and civilizations that have also become extinct for ever: the ancient Egyptians, the Babylonians, the Persians, the Greeks, the Romans, the Byzantines, the Mayas, the Aztecs and many others. They all ruled large tracts of land, created their own social and philosophical rules, their arts and sciences, their religions and beliefs, and yet all that may be found of them is ruins, inanimate objects and translated texts. Empires too are ephemeral: in modern times we have witnessed the birth and death of the Spanish Empire and the British Empire, to give just two examples with which I am reasonably familiar. Nothing is permanent. Nothing is absolute. Nothing is stable for ever. The only constant is change.

History often is chaotic and irrational. Chaos theories are mathematical models developed to explain complex and often unpredictable events, like weather forecasts, traffic jams, turbulence phenomena and stock exchange fluctuations. No models have yet been invented to explain History. If Leonardo da Vinci is right when he said that everything in Nature, including the mountains or clouds, takes its shape from the forces that act upon it, then historians and political leaders should find out which forces act upon History. All I can conclude in this book is that irrationality, as well as rationality, are the essence of the forces that shape the destiny of nations and individuals alike.

I beg the reader, to persevere with me, as a panorama of seemingly unconnected facts and characters is reviewed, as if from a bird's eye view, starting from true facts, people and events that I have had the fortune, or misfortune, to experience myself. These seemingly unconnected facts, in many ways, have turned out to be connected, not always necessarily as 'cause and effect', but certainly influencing each other and changing human matters such as politics, businesses, religions, philosophy and science.

This is why I decided to write this book, essentially a philosophical essay based on History, in a 'non-fictional essay format', rather than in a 'novel format', because what I found and studied were neither fictional characters, nor invented facts, but real historical people and true facts. Some of the 'protagonists' of this book are famous people, like Winston S. Churchill, Rudolf Hess or Adolf Hitler, for example. Others are perhaps less familiar save to experts in their own fields, such as the Grand Master of the Order of St. John, Don Juan Fernández de Heredia, Sir Steven Runciman, Rudolf von Sebottendorf, or Ernst Bohle. Still others will be entirely unknown to most people, such as my own grand-parents and ancestors.

I have based my search on visible and palpable facts; books, documents and references which are reliable and established. But whenever facts and documents have been found to be missing, or it was clear that they had been deliberately manipulated, I have been guided by friends with special knowledge or training, and by a certain 'compelling intuition'. Reason is a much more recent invention of Nature than passions. This is why in The Secret Castle, the reader goes backwards and forwards in history, although the Λογοσ (in the full meaning of the word) is exactly the same all along the book. The 'Logos' is the search for truth.

Let us take an example. To understand the horrors of the twentieth century and modern times a little better, I decided to start from those sources which I ought to know better by which I mean myself and my own ancestors. It is by this method of investigation, and by looking at proven facts and unproven facts, using a 'diagnostic hypothesis', that I move freely but not randomly from early Christianity to the Middle Ages, and from the Middle Ages to Modern Times.

In fact, in spite of considerable study and the help of patient and knowledgeable friends, I still do not have complete answers to all of the questions raised by the Secret Castle. Some of the questions first came to me on my personal visits to the place. But others have been inspired by the many symbols found in the castle, and by my fascination for the Grand Master of the Order of St. John, who lived in the fourteenth century. Surprisingly, I found that many of these ancient symbols were connected not only to prehistoric times in Europe, but also to more recent events, such as the birth and development of Nazi Germany.

Can anybody still believe that what happened in the past, even several centuries ago, is not relevant to the present? Can anybody still think after 9/11, that what happens, for example, in Baghdad or in Afghanistan, is not relevant to what happens or can happen in New York, Madrid or London?

It was and is not, my intention to teach anything to anybody, nor to challenge any current dogmas or beliefs. As a person born in twentieth century Spain, brought up in Italy, and educated in England, who has travelled worldwide, and particularly across Europe and in the USA, I belong to the international scientific community of cancer physicians and researchers. I am neither an academic historian nor a philosopher.

What I do I feel is that history belongs to all those keen to study it, because we are all, willing or unwilling, protagonists of history and thereby direct or indirect witnesses. It has been said that history is written by the victors, not by the losers. Not words alone but true facts, may be manipulated, hidden or confused. The apparent absence of documents does not mean that certain things or events never took place. On the contrary, this absence often means that these things did exist, these events did take place, but that for obscure reasons their mere existence, or whatever evidence there might have been for it, had to be destroyed, denied or suppressed.

There are certain matters that, whenever they can affect the stability of states and institutions, or jeopardise the privileges of the powerful, are better kept in the darkness for ever and ever. For that is precisely where they belong: to the darkness of the human spirit.

If I were asked: 'Why, then did you feel compelled to write this book?' I would not hesitate to answer: 'This book was written because Good and Evil exist, but I find it increasingly difficult to judge people and events'. In other words, I have gradually become aware of my own limitations as a human being to fully understand Truth, and to Judge others. One of the reasons for this increasing difficulty is my increasing appreciation of the complexity of history. Truth and complexity have a lot in common and the simplicity hypothesis, popularly known to us as Occam's razor, needs reviewing. One hundred years ago this fact began to become evident to eminent physicists, with the publication of works on quantum mechanics, Einstein's General Theory of Relativity, Eisenstein's Uncertainty Principle and research into the dual nature of light (photons and waves), to name but a few. Something similar is just beginning to happen in the Biological Sciences. History is no different, and equally complex, as well as equally relative. The final judgement can only be according to God's laws, not those of mankind.

Good and Evil are 'real' entities, no doubt, as life itself is 'real'. But, given their existence, from whence do they come? How do they shape our lives? How can they change the history of mankind? Ask yourself why wars exist and how they come about? What inner forces moved the greatest and most cruel Dictators of the twentieth century? How may Evil be avoided, understood or defeated? What is the relationship, if any, between Almighty God and what we term 'Good and Evil'?

I believe the answers to these questions pose a challenge to our minds at least, if not equally, as important, as finding the real meaning of our own existence. However, let us be realistic. Most people today do not like to 'challenge their minds'. Life is easier without thinking too much. What is the point of finding a meaning to our lives anyway? Perhaps there simply is no meaning to be found.

We read in Genesis, 2:15, that the Lord God took man and put him into the garden of Eden to cultivate it and keep it, and said:

> 'Of every tree of the garden thou mayest freely eat: But of the tree of the knowledge of good and evil, thou shalt not eat of it: for in the day that thou eatest thereof thou shalt surely die.'

The serpent (Evil) said to the woman, Eve:

> 'You surely shall not die! For God knows that in the day you eat from this tree your eyes will be opened, and you will be like God, knowing Good and Evil'

Although, as for any single part of the Holy Scriptures, there may be several interpretations, it is out of question that the 'Knowledge of Good and Evil' can be, according to the Bible, the equivalent of 'Being like God'. We can deduce that this knowledge is not only crucial but absolutely fundamental. To the extent, that when Eve and Adam ate from this tree, God, in spite of his divine compassion and love for what He had created, became so upset that he cursed his human creatures:

> 'In the sweat of thy face shalt thou eat bread, till thou return unto the ground; for out of it wast thou taken: for dust thou art, and unto dust shalt thou return.'

Wisdom is an individual search, and a personal responsibilityfor every decent human being. This search falls within the vast and complex subjects of religion, moral philosophy or Ethics. But Truth is like…

> '…Darkness Visible, serving only to express the gloom which rests on the prospect of futurity. It is that mysterious veil which the eye of human reason cannot penetrate, unless assisted by that Light which is from above.'

One of my first modest academic contributions, while still a medical student at the University of Oxford, was a study in the laboratory of Sir David Weatherall, comparing the evolutionary relationships of human populations from an analysis of their DNA, eventually published in the prestigious scientific journal *Nature* (vol. 319: pp. 491-93, 1986). Our data was consistent with the hypothesis that modern humans, the species we call *Homo Sapiens Sapiens*, originated in sub-Saharan Africa as 'recently' as 100 or 200 thousand years old. Considering that life on earth probably originated some 3.5 to 4 thousand million years ago, or that dinosaurs became extinct some 60 million years ago, it is evident that humans are a very very recent species on planet earth.

History as such, at least in written format, is an even more recent phenomenon: 3.5 to 5 thousand years ago, depending on exact criteria. But even modern history is not taught in the same way in different countries. Born in Spain, while yet the long dictatorship of General Francisco Franco lasted, I was brought up in Italy and educated at university (both Cambridge and Oxford) in England. I can assure the reader that my history books in the same three countries were rather different. Even the same events were often explained from separate and distinct points of view.

I would like to invite the reader to follow closely this personal pilgrimage through history, but not as a person who travels to a sacred place as an act of religious devotion. Rather, I would like the critical reader to share with me the perplexity I felt for so many of the historical events and characters encountered.

'It is so hard to find out the truth of anything by looking at the record of the past. The process of time obscures the truth of former times, and even contemporaneous writers disguise and twist the truth out of malice or flattery.'

Plutarch (*circa* 100 A.D.)

Part I

My Secret Castle

Chapter One

The secrets of the Castle and Church
Of Saint Mary at Mora de Rubielos

Right at the Southern and Eastern limits of the ancient Kingdom of Aragon, bordering with the then Arab Kingdom of Valencia, *El Maestrazgo* (literally 'The Land of the Masters') was, and still is, a rather remote, and little known place. The land is mountainous, and not very fertile. In some aspects, it can physically remind the visitor of the harsh and dry lands in the Middle East, particularly around Jerusalem. It is full of castle ruins, a reminder of the old frontiers with Islam, but also of pre-historic (2000-1000 BC) and Iberian (fourth century BC) remains. The Iberians were the well established inhabitants of the place, at the time of the Roman invasions, and in the North West parts of Spain they had also mixed with the Celts, creating the so-called 'Celtiberic' cultures.

Figure 1
The Castle of Mora de Rubielos. It is not, as is often the case, right at the top of the village nor on its highest point but nevertheless, because of sheer volume and presence, it dominates the rest of Mora.

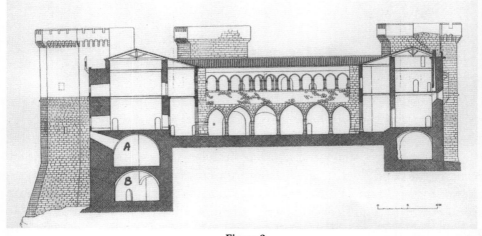

Figure 2
Drawing of the Castle buildings by the Architect Antonio Almagro (1975). On the left is the solid
and robust south-west tower of the Castle where the magic 'winding staircase' leads to the
'bottom chamber' or Temple and it is communicated by passages to two large vaults (one on top
of the other), denoted as A and B in the drawing

Mora de Rubielos, with a modern population of only around two thousand inhabitants, prides itself with a name that can be spelled with three different meanings: *Mora* (a Moorish girl), *Amor* (love) and *Roma* (Rome). In spite of this, there are very few signs left of the Roman and Moorish occupations. Close to Mora de Rubielos, one can find a rather different, but no less beautiful little village called Rubielos de Mora. For some time the frontier between the Christian and the Arab dominions lay exactly between these two villages.

The Castle of Mora de Rubielos (*see* Figures 1 and 2 *above*), which dominates the village, has a rather obscure origin, though some historians argue that it must have been a Moorish castle prior to the eleventh century. The governor of *al-Sahla*, Abd el Malik, is credited with building the first fortress. The Moorish origins of the Castle have been confirmed by very recent excavations (below the courtyard of today's Castle).

As a curiosity, even the legendary though historical Spanish figure of *El Cid Campeador*, during a period of his life when he was at odds with his king (Alfonso VI of Castile), actually took possession of Mora de Rubielos, and even lived there for some months. Contrary to popular beliefs which portray *El Cid*, (real name Rodrigo Diaz), as a champion of Christianity, he was, over a period of several years, both an ally of the Moors and of the Kings of Zaragoza, Almoctader and his son Almuctaman, in particular. Around the year 1076 he received power and money from them to pay for up to seven thousand armed men, and *El Cid* became a real headache to the Christian kings, and to Sancho, King of Aragon and Pamplona, also to Berenguel, the count of Barcelona, in particular. The latter was defeated by *El Cid*, and was imprisoned by him.

Very curiously, there is no direct documentary evidence for the presence of the Templars at the Castle of Mora de Rubielos, though several nearby places are well known to have been Templar enclaves. Some of the best known of these enclaves can still be found in the near vicinity at Iglesuela del Cid, Albentosa, Linares de Mora and Miravete de la Sierra. The fact that no clear evidence for their presence in Mora de Rubielos has yet been found, is intriguing, but it is not totally unusual, considering the fierce repression of anything vaguely connected to the Order, particularly with respect to their Gnostic or esoteric practices, and the deliberate destruction of anything related to the secrets and rituals of the Templars, following their betrayal by the King of France (*Filippe Le Bel*) and Pope Clement V in October 1307.

In any case, it is well documented that the troops of the Christian King of Aragon, Alfonso II, re-captured Mora de Rubielos from the Moors on St. Michael's day, on 29 September 1171. King Alfonso II, like his son *Pere El Catòlic*, who died defending the Cathars at the battle of Muret, and his grandson Jaume I *El Conqueridor*, who eventually re-conquered Islamic Valencia and Mallorca, was always accompanied, in this sort of military and diplomatic enterprise, by his faithful Knights of the Temple, and by their 'brethren' the Knights of St. John.

Furthermore, according to a still remembered and well documented legend, King Alfonso II and his troops, exhausted by a long and unproductive siege of the Moorish town of Mora, experienced a miraculous appearance of the Archangel St. Michael himself, precisely on the eve of St Michael's day, who led the final and victorious battle against the Moors. St. Michael is still celebrated today as the patron saint of Mora de Rubielos, on 29 September, and St. Michael (in the purest hermetic tradition) was the sacred patron of the Knights of the Temple. Several decades later, in 1259, King Jaime I of Aragon (in Catalan, '*Jaume* I') paid tribute to St. Michael, and thanked him for his victory over Islam, and the capture of Valencia (*Reconquista*), returning to this same castle on 23 September of that year and staying at least until October 9.

Indeed, as can be seen in the drawing of the Castle buildings (*see* Figure 2) by the Architect Antonio Almagro, who published his doctoral thesis on it in 1975, the same year that General Franco died, the lowest and deepest part of the building is the most ancient (the darker colour in Figure 2), and which, like the roots of a tree, may well have been in Templar hands for some time, before relinquishing it to their successors, the Knights of the Order of St. John, as is historically well documented from the fourteenth century.

At the opposite corner-end of the Castle building, below a small museum dedicated to the Spanish Civil War (1936-39), we can still find the dungeons, used by Franco's troops at the end of this bloody war. The dungeon was employed to keep and torture Republican prisoners, one of whom was my grand-father Antonio Bronchud (*see* Chapter 7).

Even today, one can find scattered villages in El Maestrazgo full of monuments and ruins that may well date from Templar times, but with no obvious archival documents available to confirm it. Some of them still keep their original names, reminiscent of their original close ties with the Middle East, under Islamic rule, like the little town of Jerica (only twenty miles from Mora de Rubielos).

Traces of Templarism were almost completely eradicated under the influence of the Holy Inquisition, whose rule, in Spain, lasted until the nineteenth century. Between the fifteenth and the eighteenth centuries, showing an interest in Gnostic ideas, or other esoteric practices, made one the object of harsh penalties and punishments which included confiscation of property, or the cruel *Autos da Fé* at the hands of the Inquisition.

For those curious readers who want to see with their own eyes, and touch with their fingers my 'Secret Castle', and the 'Alpha and Omega' key to Good and Evil, the easiest way to get to Mora de Rubielos, if travelling from abroad, is a flight to Valencia International Airport), and from there take the A7 motorway as if going north to Barcelona, then taking the N-234 road at the ancient town of Sagunto towards Teruel (in other words, going west and inland).

You will pass the city of Jerica, dominated by the tower of the church that once used to be the impressive minaret of the local mosque, and when you reach the high plateau of La Meseta, around 1000 metres above sea level, you should turn right and take the smaller A-228 road from Venta del Aire to Mora de Rubielos.

It is not the easiest of trips, but it only takes about one hour by car from Valencia. Once there, the best place to stay is probably the three star, but comfortable, Hotel Jaume I, named after the King of Aragon who re-conquered Valencia from Muslim domination.

Despite its relatively small size, there are a number of interesting monuments to visit in Mora de Rubielos:

a) the Castle: originally under Moorish dominion from the seventh to the eleventh centuries and thereafter thought to have been held by the Templars between the eleventh and thirteenth centuries, and later under the control of the Knights Hospitaller of St John, Rhodes and Malta, from the fourteenth to the seventeenth centuries and who gave it its distinct 'Spanish Gothic-Renaissance' architectural style, somewhere between a castle and a palace. The stone carvings are in reasonably good condition, despite being of a type of sandstone, which will certainly require some expert preservation treatment to enable it to endure the exigencies of time in anything like good shape. Some rather 'sloppy' restoration work has been going on for a couple of decades, since 1975, and some important stone marks or carvings, for example in the various capitals and columns, have been lost for ever. From the mid seventeenth century onwards this Castle belonged to the Franciscans, who also ran their Convent in Teruel (*El Convento de los Franciscanos*, built in the fourteenth century), with interesting operative stonemasons' marks on the walls, again reminiscent, if not identical, to those of Mora de Rubielos.

b) The Church *Colegiata de Santa Maria*, built, or rebuilt, in the early fourteenth century (*see* Figure 3), and full of many similar marks as those which are to be found in the Castle, carved by skilled stone masons who, according to local historical archives, originally came from Geneva and Konstanze in Switzerland.

Figure 3
External view of the fourteenth century Church of St Mary, which was later to become a *colegiata* with a Theological Seminar and over ten clergymen.

5

There now follows a description of the marks chiselled into the walls and the steps that have been found in the Castle and the Collegiate Church of St. Mary. This is simply intended to offer the reader a brief glimpse of what may be seen there, but the best way to find out the truth, is to visit the place. In any case, my present modest contribution can only be interpreted as a first account and regarded as an initial historical approach, as well as an invitation to make further and deeper studies on the subject.

These marks can be seen, in profusion, on the stones from which both the Church and the Castle have been constructed.

The true meaning of these marks is unknown, but I do not believe that they are simply a representation of the 'trademark' of a given mason or a peculiar way to take account of the amount of work put in by every single master builder. These marks can be seen in many other churches, castles, cathedrals and fortresses scattered throughout Europe. Does it mean that they all belonged to the same stone-craft schools? This would be difficult to believe. Why did these experienced craftsmen not mark all of their stones, rather than just a few, with more simple cuts or scratches? Stones next to each other, and virtually identical in size and shape to each other, often bear very different signs, and some parts of the buildings have a significantly greater 'density' or 'complexity' of marks than others.

I have come to the conclusion that these marks possessed an esoteric as well as an exoteric meaning to the master masons who taught their craftsmen and apprentices how to cut them, and where to put them. Neither was this decided by chance, nor only for architectural reasons. Rather, it was decided on the grounds of the 'mystical energy' of the stone, the significance to the building of the site where the stone was going to be placed, and to the message that master architect and his master masons wished to convey to the visitor. They were secret modes of communication, whose code, like an archaic language, has unfortunately been lost, like the freemasons themselves admit in their modern rituals: '… the genuine secrets of a Master Mason have been lost'. The ritualistic answer today as to why these genuine secrets were lost is 'By the untimely death of our Master Hiram Abiff, master builder and chief architect of King Solomon's Temple.

As we enter the Castle after a fairly steep approach, we enter the cloister area, and immediately on the left we find the Chapel, which nowadays has lost all of its original decorations as a result of a big fire in the year 1700 and the damage suffered during the Spanish Civil War. On the floor of the Chapel a hole was found, which is now covered by thick glass. I shall come back to the probable function of this hole which communicates with the levels below.

Immediately to the left of the Chapel entrance, there is a winding staircase going downwards which has only recently been opened to the public. For many years a wall, designed to protect the public from the very slow repair work and excavations still going on at the bottom, prevented any entrance by visitors. Lack of finance and any real interest in restoration work had slowed the repairs almost to a standstill until fairly recently. I first descended the staircase in 1992 with the help of a small torch. Even so, thanks to the darkness and rubble, I barely managed to get safely to the bottom of it. My progress was also impeded by the fragments that had fallen from the roof and on my way up, when I cleared them away, I realized that each of the thirty-six steps of this winding staircase, with the exception of the first three (1 to 3) and the last one (36) had a single mark carved on its vertical face.

This interesting winding staircase was said to lead to the ancient crypt used by the Franciscans to bury their departed brethren. They may indeed have used it for that purpose, but after the Civil War and the early restoration work in the 1970s, all human bones and remains were removed and taken to the local cemetery. At present, there are no signs of buried bodies or any gravestones to be seen. The way they were originally buried is fascinating. The body of the dead monk was draped in his own monastic robes, and lowered with a rope tied round his waist through a hole – still visible in the ceiling of the 'Temple' – down into a large 'grave-pit' excavated under the original pavement of the 'Temple'. This hole almost certainly lined up with the hole above on the floor of the Chapel.

Thus what was essentially an exoteric religious ceremony could have been transformed into an 'esoteric ritual' by the act of lowering the corpse deep down into the crypt. This was probably what the Franciscan monks had learnt from their predecessors in the castle, the Knights of St. John and before them, the Knights of the Temple but with this difference that the Knights probably used this method to lower the live body of the candidate, from the Chapel down to the Temple at the bottom, where a large equilateral triangle in relief on the end wall (*see* Figure 4 *below*), occupied part of their Initiation Ritual.

The marks of the original level of the pavement are still visible on the walls, provided one uses a powerful torch or light source to see them in the darkness. The thirty-six steps lead sequentially to two horizontal and parallel empty Vaults with Gothic Arches. Although there are now a couple of electric light bulbs, the truth is that it takes some time for one's eyes to become adapted to the darkness of the place, and one must walk very carefully in order to avoid any injury. Also a part of the floor of the top nave (A) has collapsed on the bottom floor (B) (*see* Figure 2). Both Vaults lead to two single window small cells (with rather high ceilings), one of which is the base of one of the large corner towers of the castle. This relatively small cell was probably the secret 'Temple' for in it, is a large Equilateral Triangle, whose apex points towards the ceiling, measuring approximately three cubic metres, on the eastern vertical stone wall (see Figure 4). It is unmistakably Masonic, and may date back to the early part of the thirteenth century, belonging, as it does, to the deepest and most ancient part of the castle building. The south-east tower is shaped like the leg of an elephant, with the 'Temple' right at the base, as if forming the foot.

Figure 4
The large Equilateral Triangle on the Eastern Wall of the Temple.

Mysteriously, as shown in Figure 4, the only part missing from this large equilateral triangle is its triangular apex. The reasons are unclear. The highest point of this stone structure may have been damaged, possibly deliberately or not. It has certainly been destroyed at sometime in the last seven to eight hundred years. Another, more speculative but more attractive, hypothesis is that this missing apex was in fact a portable 'All Seeing Eye' that each secret lodge of Knights Templar or Master Masons carried with them, together with their Warrant (in this case, a document that gives justification and authority to a recognised and perfect lodge), and their ritualistic jewels and robes.

Before each ceremony, the appropriate officer of the lodge may well have placed the 'portable apex' at the very top of the equilateral triangle and lit candles in the East, South and West parts of the 'Temple'.

Even a perfunctory view of the winding staircase reveals some exciting findings to the visitor. The first step from the bottom, which bears a mark carved in the stone, is step number four. This depicts a single square (*see* Figure 5). The first three steps (steps 1-3) show no mark whatever.

Figure 5
The Square carved on the fourth step.

According to freemasons, '... the square teaches us to regulate our lives and actions according to masonic line and rule, and to harmonize our conduct, so as to render us acceptable to that Divine Being from Whom all goodness springs, and to Whom we must give an account of all our actions.' But it is also a runic symbol, called Kano or Kaunaz. Kano is a Rune of major blessings. Kano signifies a blessing received and a blessing bestowed. Acceptance forms the foundation for loving yourself. Before one can rebuild one's life, one must accept oneself. Self acceptance forms a beautiful Triangle with serenity and patience. Hence the 'Serenity Prayer':

> 'God grant me the serenity to accept the things I cannot change, the courage to change the things I can, and the wisdom to know the difference.'

I realized immediately that the winding staircase must have a symbolic meaning and that I had to try to find out exactly what it this meaning was. I also realized that the walls of this 'Secret Castle' spoke a wonderful language. All those marks, runic or alchemical or Gnostic' were trying to say things to the beholder, and, what is more, these things were not always the same. For example, any one of those symbols could convey different meanings to the beholder, at one and the same time. The perception of the meaning would be entirely dependent on the beholders specific emotional state. Thus the 'Square' might be interpreted in the strict masonic sense of '… good moral conduct', or in the runic sense of 'Acceptance'.

In the Masonic sense, the square defines our moral conduct within the compasses, which are also present in 'masonic' marks present on some of the stones both in the Castle and in the Franciscan Church and Convent in Teruel. The compasses are used by the Mason to ascertain and determine, with accuracy and precision, the limits and proportions of objects, drawings or parts of buildings. In the speculative sense, the compasses remind us of the '… Limits of Good and Evil and of the unerring and impartial justice of the Creator, Who will reward, or punish, as we have obeyed or disregarded His divine commands.'

In the runic sense, Kano will teach us that it is the gradual acceptance of the feelings and memories of our past that enables us to change. In other words, if, for example, we want this twenty-first century to be definitely better for the world than the twentieth, then we must accept and understand the errors committed in the latter.

In the Oxford Advanced Dictionary of Current English, runes are defined as: '… any letter of an old alphabet used in Northern Europe, especially by the Scandinavians and Anglo Saxons from *circa* 200 AD This dictionary, very briefly, adds that runes are also similar marks of 'a mysterious or magic sort'.

As will be discussed in the next chapter, I have found evidence of a runic alphabet in the written language of the most ancient historical habitants of the Iberian Peninsula, the Ibers, probably used before or at the same time as the old English or Germanic Runes. In fact, similar , but not identical, runes were also used by the Etruscans (*see* Figure 6), the most developed Italian civilization prior to the Romans, and several centuries later, *circa* 700-900 AD, by the powerful Vikings, who colonized great parts of Northern Europe (the Scandinavian countries up to Greenland) and parts of Eastern England.

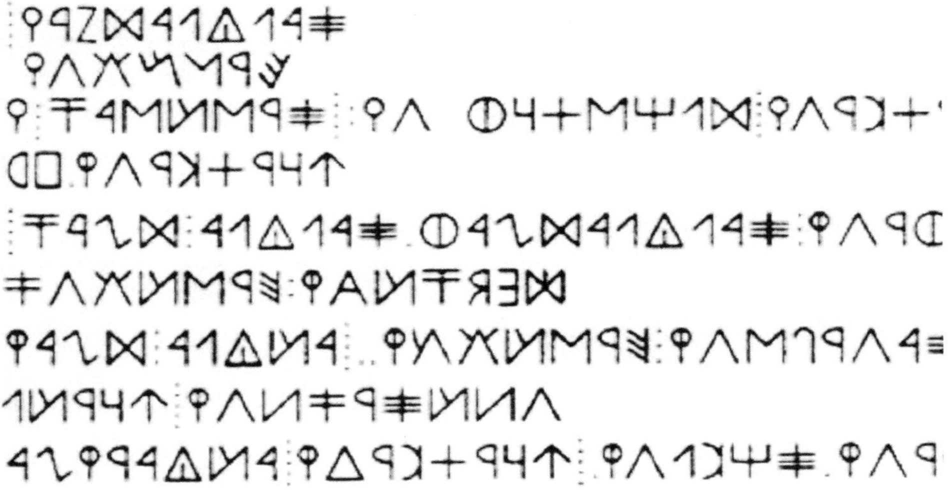

Figure 6
Etruscan text reproduced from a burial place in Tuscany. The percentage of runic elements is high but this language has yet to be translated although several models have been offered (*see* the paper by Jorge Alonso Garcia '*Desciframiento de la lengua Etrusca*' (Editorial Jamal S.A., Barcelona, 1998).

In short, the runes are best known as an ancient form of symbolic graphology formed by sharp separate lines but never curves, for writing or cutting upon wood, metal or stone; but they were also used for their magical properties in divination, oracular casting of lots, invocations and the preparation of amulets and charms. Each individual rune possessed its own name and symbolism over and above its phonetic and literary value.

Although it is widely believed that runes are derived from an indo-european language, and essentially came from the east, my findings and the similarities between the runes and the written symbols of the ancient written language of the Ibers in Spain and the Etruscans in Italy suggest an alternative and ancient pre-historic origin in North Africa.

In a later chapter I shall discuss the tremendous importance of runes in some of the key and occult roots of Nazism, which started towards the end of the nineteenth century (1890-1910), long before the Great War.

Suffice it to say that the Swastika was not only an ancient indo-european symbol but a rune as well, having been used for its magical properties in remote regions of Tibet long before it was used as the most powerful Nazi symbol.

Occultism has its basis in a religious way of thinking, the roots of which stretch back into pre-historic times, and are part of the universal esoteric tradition. As the western world developed without over-much direct exchange or cultural contact with the East, with the notable exceptions of Islamic conquests and those military adventures typified by Alexander the Great's impressive campaigns in Persia and India, the esoteric traditions of the West are inevitably linked to *inter alia*, Neo-Platonism, Gnosticism, Alchemy, Hermetic Treatises, Medieval Magic Spells, Druids and the Jewish Mysticism of the Kabbalah.

Gnosticism properly refers to the belief of certain heretical Christian sects, among the early Christians, who claimed to possess the *Gnosis*, or special knowledge of esoteric spiritual matters, such as the faculty of knowing 'Good and Evil'. The Knights Templar, during their contacts with Islam, the Jews and Middle Eastern heretics, to say nothing of the Manichean and Dualist heresies of the Middle Ages mentioned earlier, had almost certainly been contaminated by a certain degree of Gnosticism, leavened, no doubt, with some of the more abstruse concepts derived from familiarity with the Kabbalah and alchemical practices.

I remember vividly the excitement I felt when, for the first time, I compared the drawings I had made of all of the stone marks to be found at the Castle of Mora de Rubielos and the Collegiate Church of St. Mary with drawings of ancient runes. *A great number were absolutely identical* and the rest could be related to Masonic symbols, such as the Square and Compasses, to certain triangular alchemical symbols, to the Jewish Kabbalah or even to the Israeli Star of David or hexalpha, to cite but a few examples.

A powerful esoteric current of 'Hermeticism' also experienced a degree of revival in the late Middle Ages and Early Renaissance. The Greek texts of the *Hermatica* were mainly written in Egypt between the third and fifth centuries AD, and were a peculiar synthesis of Gnostic ideas and symbols, Neoplatonism and Kabbalistic Theosophy.

Step thirty-six, right at the top, again shows *no mark at all*. This lacuna is in itself is deeply significant. The 'Empty Rune' signifies divinity. Receiving this rune is a gentle reminder to place oneself in the Presence of God each day. When God spoke to Moses (Genesis 20: 4-7), He said:

'Thou shalt not make unto thee any graven image, or any likeness of any thing […]. Thou shalt not bow down thyself to them, nor serve them: for I the LORD thy God am a jealous God […]. Thou shalt not take the name of the LORD thy God in vain […].'

If you find yourself facing a test for which you feel unwilling or unready, make the Divine your strength. What you are is God's gift to you; what you make of yourself is your gift to God.

Step thirty-five shows a new mark (*see* Figure 7) easy to trace, but in itself, both elegant and beautiful. This mark, as far as is known, has never previously been described. Carved on the stone that constitutes the thirty-fifth step from the bottom, it shows an eight pointed star on the left, linked horizontally by a straight line to a simple cross on the right. I believe this referred to the Alpha and the Omega, the birth (represented by the star) and death (the cross) of Jesus Christ. How better to delineate in stone: the beginning and the end? All these matters are explained to us in the mysterious 'Revelation of St John', better known to us as The Apocalypse.

Figure 7
The mark on the 35th Step: the Alpha and the Omega:
I AM who WAS and IS To Come.

According to the fascinating text of Revelations, St. John (or possibly Mary Magdalene) says that while in the Greek island called Patmos, because of '… the word of God and the testimony of Jesus …', the voice of Jesus was heard to say:

> 'Fear not; I am the first and the last: I am he that liveth, and was dead; and, behold, I am alive for evermore, Amen; and have the keys of hell and of death.'

It is another puzzling observation that a similar sign, an eight pointed star linked vertically to a cross of St Andrew can be seen in an eighth century AD MS written and illustrated by San Beato de Liébana, in a remote part of northern Spain called Santo Toribio de Liébana, near the town of Santander (*see* Figure 8).

Figure 8
An eight pointed star linked verically to a cross of St Andrew can be seen on both sides of the river bank in the eighth century. MS by San Beato de Liébana, in the remote Santo Toribio de Liébana near Santander in northern Spain, illustrating the book of Daniel, the prophet.

This MS contains beautiful illustrations of the Book of Revelation by St John the Evangelist , but the figure with the sign described above is an illustration in the Book of Daniel, the biblical prophet who met with three angels, a white one (Michael) and two others on each side of the bank of a river.

The eight pointed star and the cross seen on the thirty-fifth step of the winding staircase in the castle of Mora de Rubielos (*see* Figure 7), looks remarkably like a key. Was this the key to the thirty-third degree, the key to the highest secret in Freemasonry, or was it the 'Key to Good and Evil', the knowledge of whose powerful usage the Gnostics of ancient times guarded so carefully?

Why were there thirty-six steps, rather than thirty-three? The answer is simple: many people believe that Jesus died at the age of thirty-six, rather than thirty-three. Indeed, modern astronomers, emulating their ancient counterparts, have calculated that the appearance of the 'star' over Bethlehem, was that most unusual cosmic happenstance, the triple conjunction of Saturn and Jupiter which occurred in 7 BC, several years before the official birth-date of Jesus. The first three steps required no marks, for they represented the three Craft degrees of Entered Apprentice, Fellowcraft and Master Mason. The thirty-sixth and last step at the top had no visible mark because it was the symbol of divinity, associated with the highest of all degrees. The successful candidate would only have received its pass word, sign and token, verbally, or by touch. These may only be hypotheses but the unexpected finding of this staircase prompted me to try to find an explanation.

The sequence of thirty-six steps (*see* Figure 9), with thirty-two stone marks, one per step from the fourth to the thirty-fifth on the winding staircase, their distribution, the presence of two porch entrances leading to the Nave Vaults, on two different parallel levels, the 'Temple' with its Equilateral Triangle on the East Wall at the bottom, and the geometry and history of the place most strongly suggest that this was a place where some form of speculative ceremony must have taken place, and a secret ritual worked.

Some of the marks on the winding staircase are already well known. Four of them, which may be seen in both the castle and the collegiate church, are identical in every particular, to historic masons' marks to be found in the tower at Chester and the church at Holt, near Wrexham, in Wales.

These two observations go some way to confirming that masons were a truly international organization, free to travel, work and impart their crafts and attendant symbolism around Europe. Itinerant masons would most certainly have been familiar with a profusion of primeval European cultures and symbols amongst which should be included the original Iberian graphology, still largely incomprehensible to modern historians.

In modern Freemasonry, the Ancient and Honourable Fraternity of Royal Ark Mariners, continues to use a ritual, within the Mark Master Masons lodges, that has the equilateral triangle as its centre piece. The lodge is laid out in triangular form, the Commander, like the Master of a Craft lodge, is located in the East of the lodge, with the usual pedestal, on top of which are placed the symbolical Porphyry Stone on which, when the lodge is open, is placed a small equilateral triangle. In the centre of the lodge, on the floor, is placed a relatively large, portable equilateral triangle, flat and with sides approximately twenty-four inches long on the inside, with one point presented to the East for most of the time.

The triangle is emblematical of the sun, moon and stars, but also represents wisdom, strength and beauty. The ritual commemorates the story of Noah who built his Ark to save his family and all living creatures from the great deluge that flooded our planet in biblical times. 'The Supreme Commander of the Universe [meaning Almighty God] fixed His bow in the sky (the magical rainbow) and established His covenant with Noah that the waters should no more become a flood to destroy all flesh'. This modern masonic degree dates from 1871 but, from its content, it is fairly obvious that it was based on a much older ritual and esoteric knowledge.

Ralph Elliott, an authority on the history of runes, believed that it was a Germanic tribe which spread these symbols throughout northern Europe, probably from a starting point in the north of Italy.

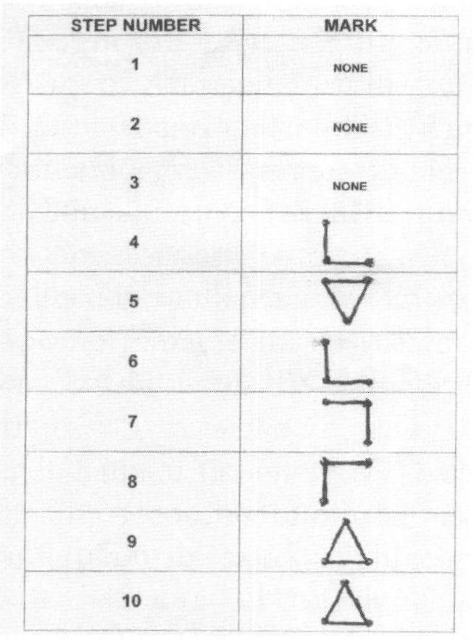

STEP NUMBER	MARK
1	NONE
2	NONE
3	NONE
4	L
5	▽
6	L
7	⌐
8	Γ
9	△
10	△

Figure 9
Marks on the steps from the bottom
of the Winding Staircase (Steps 1-10).

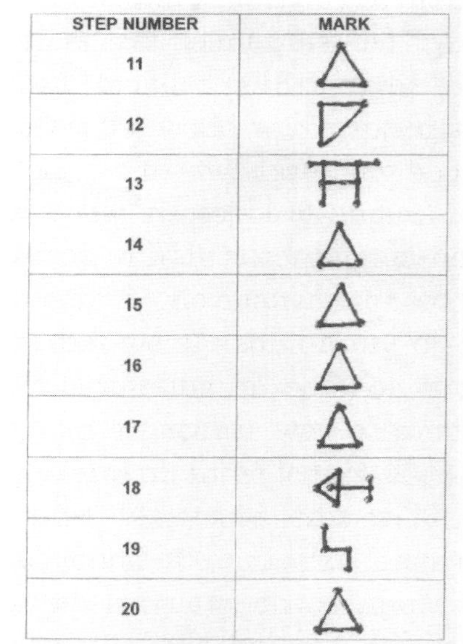

STEP NUMBER	MARK
11	△
12	▷
13	H
14	△
15	△
16	△
17	△
18	⇷
19	↳
20	△

Figure 10
Marks on the steps from the bottom of
the Winding Staircase (Steps 11-20).

STEP NUMBER	MARK
21	 ⌐
22	 ⌐
23	 ⌐
24	 M
25	 ◁
26	 L
27	 Ħ
28	 ←
29	 △
30	 ⊠

Figure 11
Marks on the steps from the bottom
of the Winding Staircase (Steps 21-30).

STEP NUMBER	MARK
31	 本
32	 ▷
33	 ⩔
34	 ⊏⊐
35	 ✳—⊢
36	NONE

Figure 12
Marks on the steps from the bottom
of the Winding Staircase (Steps 31-36).

However, as has already been observed, some runic symbols are identical to the ancient and, as yet, un-translated Iberian graphology which was used, not only in central and eastern parts of Spain, but also in the south of France as well as northern parts of Italy. Moreover, the 'Ibers' mixed with the 'Celts' in central and north-western Spain and their wide ranging sea travels, necessitated by their colonization of Ireland, Wales and Scotland, enabled them, to intermingle with Scandinavian voyagers from the Nordic European Regions.

Whatever their origins, the Vikings, who flourished in northern Europe between *circa* 800-1200 AD, were well acquainted with runes, and used them not only to mark crossroads and river crossings, across their vast dominions, but also as sacred symbols and in the oracular tradition .

Other historians have challenged the Indo-European origin of runes. For example, the Spaniard, Jorge Alonso Garcia, of the *Fundación de Estudios Genéticos Lingüísticos*, in Madrid, believes that the written language of the ancient inhabitants of the Iberian peninsula (Ibers and Tartessians), which ancient Greek historians described as 'one of the most advanced civilizations' some three thousand years BC, and the language of the Etruscans, who dominated Italy before the Romans, actually came from

Africa some time around the New or Later Stone Age. Garcia, who used to work for the American Navy staff at their Spanish military base in Rota in South-West Spain, near Cadiz, is the author of books on the mysterious city of 'Tartessus'.

Alonso even claims that the remnants of these ancient pre-historic languages are to be found in modern Basque, in north-western Spain and across the Pyrenees in south-west France. The Basque language is non-Indo-European and is called *Euskera*.

It is of no small interest, in the present examination, that among the symbols found carved on the walls of the Castle and on the steps of the Winding Staircase there are those with runic correspondences, some of which are given here:

1. The Symbol 'M' or *Ehwaz*: Forgiveness.

It is not part of our good nature to 'withhold forgiveness', but at the same time it is part of our genetic and evolutionary history to have 'vindictive sentiments'. Therefore, as a consequence, most human beings experience an inner emotional conflict. Should I forgive, or be forgiven, or should I wage a vendetta? Of all Christian values, forgiveness is probably the most specific. It is not the 'Golden Rule of Ethics', present in other doctrines and also to be found in the Old Testament. As Jesus reminds us:

> 'Therefore all things whatsoever ye would that men should do to you, do ye even so to them: for this is the law and the prophets.'

To forgive, even an enemy, however, was something entirely new in Judaism. In the Old Testament we find '… an eye for an eye …', but in the New Testament do we not find 'Forgiveness'? The engraved 'M' is to be found on step twenty-four.

2. The 'Arrow' Symbol or *Teiwaz*: Courage.

Drawing this rune in the oracular tradition indicates that you are being asked to recognize and honour the courage and strength of your own spirit. Everyone who has suffered because of illness, bad luck or abuse by others, knows how hard it can be not to fall into despair and depression. But these are transforming experiences which give us hope and teach us that the reward of courage is wisdom. Never react to Evil with panic or denial. Pray for courage, and ask for help from those who love you, from yourself and from God. The 'Arrow' symbol in horizontal aspect, can be found on steps eighteen and twenty-eight. They are also to be found engraved in their vertical aspect, in other places in the Castle.

3. The Double Square Symbol or *Sowelu*: Compassion

Here the two squares are found joined together like a chair, or the number four. Have compassion for yourself, and have compassion for others:

> 'For with what judgment ye judge, ye shall be judged: and with what measure ye mete, it shall be measured to you again.'

Fear, passing through the prism of Compassion, is transformed into the energy of Love. These symbols are frequently repeated, and may be found on steps nineteen and twenty-one to twenty-three.

Other steps and original marks include (*see* Figures 9 to 12, *above*): the 'Cross of Saint Andrew' within a square (step 30); the 'Golgotha' cross on the top of the triangular hill (step 31); an open pair of Compasses resting on a straight line (step 33), which might be considered as an open book or the Volume of the Sacred Law.

In modern Freemasonry, the provenance of the so-called 'Ancient and Accepted Rite', at least in England and Wales, is believed to date from around the early 1760s, when a list of twenty-five degrees was drawn up, although these were probably of earlier origin. By *circa* 1765 a 'Rite of Perfection' of twenty-five degrees was being practised both in Continental Europe and the Americas, and towards the end of the century the Rite was increased to thirty-three degrees.

In 1801 a Supreme Council was formed in Charleston, South Carolina, and in 1819 a patent was granted to the Duke of Sussex to form a Supreme Council in England, however the conservative attitude of this MW Grand Master, which basically excluded all degrees relating to Chivalry, prevented the formation of the Supreme Council of England and Wales until 1845.

Upstairs in the open air, within the cloister of the castle of Mora, one can still find some of the original carved stone columns. On the capital of one of these columns, clearly visible but partly damaged, there is a Pelican, now headless, and a Brazen Serpent. This is, unfortunately, the only column left which has at least part of its original ornamentation remaining.

The exact meaning of the sequence of marks on the winding staircase is, as yet, unknown, but if it were part of an Initiation ritual, that sequence would have been an important sentence written in symbols, full of meaning for a chosen few. The first questions I asked myself on viewing the sequence were:

1. Had this been a sequence of Initiation?
2. Might it have signified a secret prayer?
3. Would the possession of its secret meaning have conferred knowledge or power?

Further evidence for the historical connection between the Templars and the Mora de Rubielos enclave can be found in the nearby Church of St Mary. The Church lies just across the road from the Castle building and the visitor can still find Mary Magdalene and the Dragons there, just as the Knights Templar left them for us. For once, the Inquisition either completely failed to see them, or was unable to remove them, which left them with the option of disguising them as much as possible. The Church, later known as the *Colegiata de Santa Maria*, was built, or rebuilt, in the early fourteenth century (*see* Figures 3 and 13), and is full of the same stone marks which are found in abundance, in the Castle.

The Church is a fine example of 'Gothic Aragonese Style', and consists of multiple arched vaulting over a single nave. Here we find the most extraordinary depiction of Christ crucified, right at the top of the Gothic arch over the Altar. Jesus is carved in stone, and the cross is made out the same wall stones as the Arch itself (*see* Figure 13). Thus instead of hanging from a cross carved from the stone, Jesus is crucified on the very stone of the wall itself – nailed, as it were, to the building!

Figure 13
Interior of the Church of St Mary looking at the Altar. Jesus on the cross, between his mother Mary and his wife, or beloved disciple Mary Magdalene, are almost invisible like chameleon like sculptures.

To the right of Jesus on the Cross, one can see his mother, the Virgin Mary, to whom the Church and Colegiata are dedicated. But to his left, one can see a beautiful young lady, saddened by the tragedy of the crucifixion. This 'young lady' can be none other than Mary Magdalene (*see* Figure 14), according to the Templar tradition the lover, or possibly the wife of Jesus, the rabbi of Nazareth. Traditionally the clergy at Mora de Rubielos have insisted that this statue is not that of the Magdalene, but of St. John the Evangelist, the favourite disciple of Jesus. Hence, as in the famous Fresco by Leonardo da Vinci, The Last Supper, in Milan, there is a seemingly deliberate confusion, or ambiguity, between Mary Magdalene and St. John the Evangelist ('the disciple whom Jesus loved').

Figure 14
Mary Magdalene to the left of Jesus on the cross.
(Picture courtesy of Peter Hamilton Currie).

'And, behold, a woman in the city, which was a sinner, when she knew that Jesus sat at meat in the Pharisee's house, brought an alabaster box of ointment, and stood at his feet behind him weeping, and began to wash his feet with tears, and did wipe them with the hairs of her head, and kissed his feet, and anointed them with the ointment.'

In spite of the hypocritical comments by the Pharisee, for he held this woman to be a prostitute, Jesus said: 'Her sins, which are many, are forgiven, for she loved much'. In the following chapter we read:

'And certain women, which had been healed of evil spirits and infirmities, Mary called Magdalene, out of whom went seven devils …'

Among the books of the Apocrypha, and therefore considered of doubtful authorship, a certain 'Gospel According to Mariam, that some called Mary Magdalene', poses extremely complex questions regarding the essence of material life, and the real meaning of sin. These books form part of the Gnostic tradition, but in this instance, more than half of the original text is now missing, or has been destroyed.

Figure 15
Polychromatic Dragon on one of the roof vaults of the Church of St Mary.
The Dragons, like the Serpents, have been the symbol ov Evil, of Satan and the
***Causa Prima* of Human Suffering. (Picture courtesy of Peter Hamilton Currie)**

'... Michael and his angels fought against the dragon; and the dragon fought and his angels, and prevailed not; neither was their place found any more in heaven. And the great dragon was cast out, that old serpent, called the Devil, and Satan, which deceiveth the whole world: he was cast out into the earth, and his angels were cast out with him.'

The dragons on one of the roof arches of the Church of St Mary were another surprising finding, and more evidence for a link with local esoteric practice in the twelfth to fourteenth centuries. The resident priest claimed not to have seen them, and appeared to be as surprised as I was.

The Dragon of St George, the banner of England, was probably a twelfth century addition to the early Christian legend, to make of him a knight of Christian chivalry. But in the Far East, China and Japan, the dragon is said to represent the 'Yang' force of the Cosmos, in their tradition of 'Yin and Yang'. As such, the Chinese dragons are not evil. They are present in Chinese Temples to frighten and scare away demons, and can bring good luck, fertility and even rain. The Chinese Emperor of the Han Dynasty (206-220 AD), for example, started dressing with nine dragons on his robes. Thus the same symbols can mean different things to different cultures.

For Orientals, and above all in the mystical and contemplative traditions of Hinduism and Buddhism, 'Evil' as such does not exist; all that exists is the Karma law of cause and effect and the destructive forms of the divinity.

One of the Hindu myths narrates the episode in which the god Krishna and the evil genius Kaliya meet. 'Krishna, the intrepid seven-year-old boy, reached the dangerous lake in which the evil genius Kaliya lurks and, full of curiosity, looked into the depths. The child rolled up his tunic, climbed a tree, and plunged into the depths. Kaliya awoke and unleashed hundreds of red warrior serpents who surrounded Krishna, inflicted poisonous wounds on him and twisted themselves around his arms and legs. A group of shepherds, who saw the unconscious boy being dragged along by the serpents took fright, ran home and called Balaransa. Balaransa said to Krishna: Divine Lord of the Gods, why do you show such human weakness? Are you not aware of your divine essence? Reveal now your infinite power, rise up and overcome the mighty doer of evil. These words sang in the ears of Krishna, reminding him of his true essence. Krishna began a frenzied dance, his movements throwing off the serpents until the great king of the serpents, Kaliya, spat blood and became stiff as a tree trunk. The exhausted God of Evil, with trembling voice implored his victor: "I have merely acted according to my nature. You Divine Lord of the Gods, created me with strength and granted me venom, and thus have I behaved, for had I behaved any other way, I would have transgressed the laws established by you for every creature, according to its nature; I would have altered the order of the Universe and deserved punishment".'

Selected Bibliography

1.   Monzon Royo J., *Historia de Mora de Rubielos. Segunda Edición*. Teruel, Ayuntamiento de Mora de Rubielos, 1992

2.   Antonio Almagro Gorbea A. *El Castillo de Mora de Rubielos*: *Solar de los Fernández de Herédia*. Doctoral Thesis (First Edition) , 1974.

3.   Próspero de Bofarull y Mascaró. *Los Condes de Barcelona* (Two Volumes, originally printed in 1836, re-edited by *Fundación Conde de Barcelona*, *La Vanguardia*, Barcelona 1988).

4.   Ralph W. V. Elliott, *Runes: An Introduction.* (Manchester University Press, 1959); also New York: Philosophical Library, 1959 (revd 1989).

5.   Ralph Blum. *The Book of Runes* (Tenth Anniversary Edition, St. Martin's Press, New York, 1993).

6.   Alonso García, Jorge, *Tartesos, Fundación de Estudios Genéticos Lingüísticos* (fourth edition, Madrid, 2005).

7.   Alonso García, Jorge, *Desciframiento de la lengua ibérica-tartésica (Fundación Tartesos*, Barcelona, 1996.

8.   Alonso García J. & Arnaíz Villena A, *El origen de los vascos y otros pueblos mediterráneos* (Editorial Complutense, Madrid 1998).

9.   Arribas A., *Los íberos* (Ayma S.A., *Editora*, Barcelona, 1965).

10.   Sánchez Albornoz C., *Estudios polémicos* (Espasa-Calpe, Madrid, 1979).

11.   Schulten A. *Fontes hispanies antiguas* (*Universidad de Barcelona*, Barcelona, 1922).

12.   *Museu Arqueologic de Catalunya-Ullastret* (*Oppidum*, *Baix Emporda*, Girona, Spain), illustrated in the book *Catars i Trobadors, Occitània i Catalunya* (*Museu d'Historia de Catalunya*, Barcelona, 2003).

13.   Mitchell D., *The Mark Degree* (Lewis Masonic, 2003).

14.   Biedermann H. *Knaurs Lexikon der Symbole* (Droemer Knaur, Munich, 1989).

Chapter Two

The cruel and chaotic end of the Knights Templar in the Kingdom of Aragon

One thousand years ago, Europe was certainly very different from today. Vast parts of Spain , for example, were still under Islam. Although the most glorious days of Spanish Islam were probably over, the large provinces of Valencia, Andalusia (*El Andalus*) and Mallorca were still under Muslim rule.

Muhammad, the Prophet, preached a religion, in the name of Allah, impregnated by Judaism and with many Christian ideas. With an emphasis on a single god, the last judgment, the efficacy of prayer and a number of precise and numerous duties of Muslims, he changed history by promoting a massive expansion of Arab rule, religious self-confidence and a new autocratic model of state and empire. With him, there was no dichotomy between religious and temporal power, nor, indeed, between civilian and military power. Church, State and Army were one.

A century after Muhammad's death, the Muslims were the dominating military power in the Mediterranean, and the Middle-East, gradually extending as far as modern Indonesia and Central Asia. The intellectual and commercial superiority of the Arab world was also evident in the ninth and tenth centuries, which were the golden age of Islam. This was true particularly in Spain, where mathematics, chemistry, geometry, early universities, poetry, literature, medicine and craftsmanship flourished under the Arab domination, without stifling Christian churches or Jewish synagogues, but making sure that the Arabs were the ruling class.

True, that the fatalism which predestination gives to Arab thought and actions, was in part a denial of the right of individuals to seek their own destiny, and the lack of freedoms and private initiatives was probably to be largely blamed for their eventual decline, decrease in military power, and cultural decadence, which led to their loss of land dominion in western Europe in the fifteenth century.

Almost one thousand years ago, Pope Urban II, who had kept his plan for a holy crusade secret, startled everyone at the second Council of Clermont, in Notre Dame du Port, Auvergne, by emerging from the basilica and making an energetic appeal to Christians on 27 November 1095 to rescue the Holy Land from Islamic infidels. Even the Pope was surprised by the enthusiastic popular reaction in favour of such an extraordinary plan. Peter the Hermit, a preacher who believed that by killing the infidels and liberating earthly Jerusalem, all crusaders would be present and triumphant at the Day of Judgement, placed himself at the head of a popular mass, the 'People's Crusade'.

Their long march to Constantinople (capital of the Byzantine Empire) was characterised by the massacre of innocent Jews in the Rhineland, and thieving and destruction in Hungary and Greece. Some sort of 'collective madness' drove Western Europe towards Jerusalem. Alexius, the Byzantine Emperor, was the true heir of the ancient Roman Empire, ever since the emperor Constantine converted the Empire officially to Christianity at the Council of Nicaea in 325 AD, and created the city of Constantinople, now modern Istanbul. It is not hard to imagine the concern of emperor Alexius when he saw the great numbers of poor and ignorant (mainly French and German) peasants reaching his quiet and civilized city of Constantinople. The encounter engendered a profound mistrust and dislike between the Western Christians (known as Franks) and the Eastern Christians (the Byzantines). The architectural beauty of the city of Constantinople, the flourishing arts and sciences, the libraries, the standards of hygiene and the knowledge of geography and history, were unthinkable in the West, except perhaps in *El Andalus* where Islamic Spain had founded its capital in the city of Cordoba.

In just three years the Crusaders crossed modern Turkey and Syria, reaching Jerusalem in 1099. On 10 July 1099 they attacked and five days later took the city. For two days the Crusaders did nothing but kill and pillage. Jews and Muslims alike fell beneath their swords or were burnt. Most of the few surviving Jews were sold into slavery. When Saladin took back the city for Islam on 2 October 1187, he agreed not to avenge the Franks for the massacre of 1099. Of the Christians left alive in the city, eight thousand were freed after paying a ransom, ten thousand were set free without payment, and ten to fifteen thousand were sold as slaves.

The Crusades were also a big blow to Jewish-Christian relations. Suddenly, the Jews were held to be guilty of 'deicide' and therefore easy scapegoats for all kinds of misfortune, including diseases and natural disasters. In some Jewish circles, probably as an angry response to their unjust persecution, an old and strange story about the history of Jesus came back from early Christian days. It is a rather uncomplimentary and critical version of the life of Jesus known as *Toledoth Yeshu*. Various parts of this work can be found in the so-called *Genizath* Texts, and a number of distinguished modern academics have taken an active interest in this rather obscure and controversial subject – among them, Dr

William Horbury, Dean of *Corpus Christi* College in Cambridge, who took the topic as his doctoral dissertation as far back as 1971. Other investigators include Riccardo Di Segni in Rome, Ernst Bammel (also in Cambridge), Ze'ev Falk in Jerusalem and Daniel Boyarin in Beersheba.

In this highly polemical account, the New Testament versions of a virgin birth, the working of miracles, the refutation of the Pharisees and the crucifixion were presented as illegitimacy, sorcery, heresy and shameful death. Not only was Jesus (*Yesu*) a false messiah, he was a '... bastard and the son of a menstruant woman ...' however, strangely enough, this poisonous and morally insulting text admits that *Yesu*, born of *Miriam* in the days of Caesar Tiberius and Herod II Antipas, was very bright and talented: '... he learned in a single day what another man could not learn in a whole year'.

The text also acknowledges that *Yesu* defended himself from blasphemous accusations: '... They say about me that I am a son of a bastard; I am the son of God and they call me the son of a menstruant, and I am the son of the Holy One, blessed be He'. The anonymous Jewish text claims that Jesus was a 'sorcerer' and had supernatural powers endowed upon him by the cabalistic knowledge of the 'Awesome Name of God': 'He entered the Temple of Jerusalem – so the story goes – and there was the stone upon which our father Jacob poured the anointing oil, meant for making the King and the Messiah, and upon it was engraved the awesome name of God, and all who knew its secret could do all he desired' .

This would explain why, according to *Toledoth Yeshu*, Jesus did indeed perform miracles, including 'reviving the dead through the illicit pronunciation of the Tetragrammaton'.

In the Jewish *Shem ha-Meforash* the distinctive name YHVH, commonly pronounced 'Yahweh', was considered so sacred that the privilege of learning its true and correct pronunciation became reserved to a small number of esoteric men chosen by heaven.

During the twelfth and thirteenth centuries, several Hebrew books appeared in Europe with anti-Christian arguments to be used by Jews in religious disputations with Christians. Often and increasingly these disputations were used to humiliate the Jewish participants, and ceased to be free discussions. One such textbook is the so called *Ni-zahôn Vetus*, or 'The Old Polemic', of the late thirteenth and early fourteenth centuries, which is an anthology of all the arguments a Jew would need in order to hold his own in a discussion with a Christian.

One thousand years ago, the two and separate Christian Kingdoms of Castile and Aragon were determined to re-conquer Spanish land from the Arab domination. This *Reconquista* lasted for several centuries, but back in 1151, the kings Alfonso VII of Castile and Alfonso II of Aragon signed an agreement , in the little city of Tudillen, distributing among themselves the lands to be freed and re-conquered from Islam: the South of Spain (*El Andalus*) would be for the Kingdom of Castile, and the East (or Levant) would be for the Kingdom of Aragon (which included Catalonia).

Christians, however, had to wait until 1492, when Isabel of Castile and Fernando of Aragon, the so-called 'Catholic Kings', freed Granada from the last Moorish ruler, to finally realise their dream of a reunified Christian Spain fulfilled.

During this period of time, the frontiers (*Fronteras*) between Islam and Christianity were not fixed and moved as a function of military actions or local political pacts. One of the key frontiers for the Kingdom of Aragon, in the North-East part of Spain was in fact the land that separated the Arab Kingdoms of Valencia from the Kingdom of Aragon.

A key strategic area was called *El Maestrazgo*, (*Maestrat* in Catalan), which means 'The Office of Grand Master', but also 'The Land of the Masters'. This rather poor and almost inhospitable bit of land, lies between the south of Tarragona (in Catalonia) and the provinces of Castellón in Valencia and Teruel in Aragon.

El Maestrazgo was named after the Military Religious Orders that were created by the Pope to help the Crusaders, and also helped the Kings of Aragon to re-conquer it from Islam. Their power in the Kingdom of Aragon was such that at least seven Aragonese kings were educated very much under the influence, of both the Templars and the Hospitallers. Alfonso I of Aragon, for example, even named the Hospitallers, the Templars and the smaller Order of the Holy Sepulchre, direct heirs to his kingdom.

The Hospitallers were also known as the Knights of St John of Jerusalem, afterwards known as the Knights of Rhodes and finally called the Knights of Malta. This society was organized as a military order about the year 1048, for the protection of pilgrims who visited Jerusalem. They became eminent for their devotion, their boundless charity, and their noble hospitality. Like the Templars, they rapidly increased in numbers and in wealth. When they were finally driven from Palestine, they took possession of Cyprus, which they soon lost again, thereafter establishing themselves in 1309 on the island of Rhodes, at which time they took the name of the Knights of Rhodes. Eventually they were driven from thence by the Turks and in 1530 were given refuge by the Spanish and German Emperor Charles V in the tiny island of Malta.

Some historians pay tribute to the Hospitallers as the forefathers of the concept of modern Hospitals, in the same way as they credit the Templars as being the likely founders of modern banking and financing transactions.

In 1118, the Templars were granted a place of habitation within the sacred Mount Moriah by Baldwin II, King of Jerusalem and in 1128 they received rules and regulations for their governance from the Pope, written for them by St. Bernard.

The Knights of the Temple, as they were also known, became so powerful in the Kingdom of Aragon, that they were the tutors and educators, at the castle of Monzon, of King Jaume I (*El Conqueridor*), left orphan following his father's death (Pedro II of Aragon, Pere I of Catalonia, also called *Pere el Catòlic*).

The Kingdom of Aragon had supported the Cathars (or Albigensians), during the fights between the French (and Papal troops) in the South of France, at the time of the Crusade against the so called 'Cathar Heresy'. But unexpectedly, King *Pere el Catòlic* of Aragon was defeated by the combined French and Papal armies (the first Crusade against other Christians on European soil) at the battle of Muret in 1213.

Tragically, the last Cathars (who spoke *provençal*, the *langue d'oc*, a romance language rather similar to Catalan), were defeated at the siege of the spectacular Castle of Montsegur in Southern France. On 16 March 1244, some 225 Cathars who had surrendered were burnt alive by the French, to ensure the eradication of this supposed heresy.

At Montségur the heretics prepared their resistance. Raymond of Toulouse, who had previously protected the Cathars, pressed by the Church and by the French King, was forced to disown his own subjects, and led the final attack on the Castle of Montsegur, the city of refuge of the Cathars. His friend and ally Raymond Trencavel, Viscount of Béziers, was defeated near Carcassone and fled south towards Catalonia and Aragon, followed by many Albigiensians seeking political refuge and protection under the King of Aragon, and the Knights Templar.

Men and women alike took part in the defence of the Castle, together with the most respected of all Cathar bishops but, according to the splendid account by Sir Steven Runciman:

'When the end seemed near, the greater part of the defenders received the *Consolamentum*, the final rite of their church, although by dying and so becoming *Perfecti* they condemned themselves to the fires of the Inquisitors. Then, one dark March night, four of the *Perfecti* crept from the castle with the holiest books and the treasure of the Cathars, to carry them through to the Cathar communities in the high Pyrenees.

Next day the fortress of Montségur surrendered to the Court of Toulouse and the Pope. The fortress was destroyed. The *Perfecti*, to the number of about two hundred, were burnt without trial.'

The Knights Templar had a broad view of the world, and were strong believers in Syncretism: all good theories and religious beliefs are not necessarily incompatible, and tolerance can often put them under the same umbrella. This syncretism coupled with a profound knowledge of Arab culture and language, led them to respect the Arab world while simultaneously fighting against it in order to maintain constant protection of the Jews in the Middle-East and Spain. Their rules preached austerity, chastity and giving aid to all true Christians. As a result, Spain, both in the ancient Kingdom of Aragon and in the Kingdom of Castile, is still full of Templar fortresses and ruins.

One of their mottoes, still used by Masonic Knights Templar today, was *In Hoc Signo Vinces*, referring to the sign (of the Cross) and the inscription that the Roman Emperor Constantine 'saw in the sky' just before his decisive victory at the Milvian bridge, over his rival Maxentius – its meaning: 'By this sign you will conquer'.

It has been also pointed out, that in the thirteenth century, when it was clear that it was going to prove extremely hard, if not impossible, to maintain the Holy Land (essentially including Israel, Palestine, Syria and parts of Egypt and Jordania) under the rule of the Crusaders, the Knights Templar were looking for a 'land' of their own, following the example of the Germanic Teutonic Knights who started their own Crusade against the pagan peoples of Northern and Eastern Europe and created their own independent *Ordenstaat* or *Ordensland*.

According to Mazières, the chosen land of the Knights Templar was no other than the *Langue d'Oc*, including a great part of the dominions of the Kingdom of Aragon at the time, called *Septimania*, *Occitania*, the *Rousillon* and *Provence* – the very lands in which the Cathar heresy had flourished, and, as a result, many Albigiensians, whether Cathar or not, entered the Order of the Knights of the Temple.

Very much more speculatively, Michael Baigent, Richard Leigh and Henry Lincoln suggest in their best-selling book *The Holy Blood and the Holy Grail*, that more or less in these same lands, in *Septimania* (south-east France), a few centuries before, probably around the year 768 AD, a 'Jewish Kingdom' had been created and was ruled by Thierry (or *Teodorico*) and by his son *Guillem de Gellone*, who was also count of Barcelona, a title held by all of the kings of Aragon in later years. Arthur Zuckerman, from Columbia University in New

York, has proposed that these Jewish Monarchs were probably related to the 'Genealogy of King David' of Israel. Inevitably, these historical characters, about whom we know relatively little, have been assumed to be members of the Merovingian dynasty, and form part of the legend in which Mary Magdalene escaped to southern France (near Marseille), pregnant with a child fathered by Jesus, and therefore carrying with her a 'Holy Grail'.

The 'Holy Grail' in literature, was usually held to be the chalice used for the first communion by Jesus at the Last Supper. Thus, it is said that in the eighth century AD, a 'Jewish Kingdom' transiently flourished in the south-east of France, later to be made famous in the writings of Wolfram von Eschenbach.

Von Eschenbach was a German medieval poet and troubadour born in Bavaria in the late twelfth or early thirteenth century. He flourished under Hermann of Thuringia and died in 1217. He wrote several works, most of them unfinished, the exception being *Parsifal*. Many 'romantic' novels have been written around this myth which actually predates Wolfram's version. A French version attributed to Chretien de Troyes is probably the first full account of it, written in 1188 (*Le Roman de Perceval* or *Le conte del Graal*), in precisely the same year as the tragic fall of Jerusalem back into Islamic hands.

Even Maximilian I, crucial figure in the Hapsburg empire, who was crowned Emperor of the Romans in 1507, spent the last twenty years of his life writing Arthurian romances, based on such myths as King Arthur and the Knights of the Round Table. In his novel *Weisskunig*, Maximilian is a chivalrous hero in a world where knights calling themselves the 'King of Troy' and the 'King of Europe' perform deeds of great courage. These romances such as those concerning Tristan and Parsifal later came to be immortalized in the music of Wagner. It was he who introduced the idea that the Holy Grail had been taken to a secret place called Montsarat. Because of its magic properties, and peerless healing powers, some of the most esoteric Nazis became firm believers in the existence of the Holy Grail, and even Heinrich Himmler – engineer of the 'Final Solution' resulting in what is now known as 'The Holocaust', actually travelled to Montserrat, a Catalan Abbey of Benedictine Monks near Barcelona, on 23 October 1940. I, myself have visited the ancient Library of the Abbey of Montserrat and have established a friendly and warm relationship with the monks, but there is no trace whatsoever of what Himmler was looking for.

Whatever the early Knights Templar found buried beneath the Temple Mount in Jerusalem, whether it might have been the Holy Grail, the Ark of the Covenant or the secret knowledge of *Shem ha-Meforash*, it is not to be found in Montserrat. It is however, hard to believe that whatever the Romans found when Titus destroyed Jerusalem and the Temple in 70 AD, had been lost for ever. According to one legend, those ancient treasures were taken by the Gothic King Alaricus I after the sacking of Rome in 410 AD, and while some of those treasures ended up in Toulouse, in southeast France, some went from thence to Spain when his successor, Alaricus II, moved his court across the Pyrenees.

The Ark of the Covenant was probably no longer in Jerusalem in 70 AD as there is no sign of its depiction on the Titus Column in Rome, although the Holy Candelabrum (*Menorah*) stolen by the Romans from the Temple *is* to be found amidst the beautiful marble work.

The *Menorah* is one of the oldest symbols of the Jewish faith. It is a seven branched candelabrum in the Temple, lit by the *kohanim* in the sanctuary every evening and cleaned out every morning, replacing the wicks and putting fresh olive oil into the cups. It has become a symbol of the nation of Israel, and its mission to be, according to the prophet Isaiah, one of the most revered by the Knights of the Temple, 'a light unto the nations' (Isaiah 49: v6).

The sages of Judaism stress that light is not a violent force. Israel is to accomplish its mission by setting an example, not by using force. Another biblical prophet, Zechariah, saw a *menorah* and God explained to him: 'Not by might, nor by power, but by My spirit ...' (Zechariah 4: v6).

Sir Steven Runciman was highly critical of the aims and objectives of the Crusades, as made clear in the three volume opus *A History of the Crusades* (Cambridge, 1951-54). To The Scottish philosopher David Hume, the Crusades were '... the most signal and most durable monument of human folly that has yet appeared in any age or nation'. In this he agreed with the French revolutionary Diderot, who had written in his *Encyclopaedia* that '... the Holy Sepulchre was a piece of rock not worth a single drop of human blood'.

Leaving aside romantic and religious considerations, or even *the irrational component of chivalry* (my italics), it cannot be denied that one thousand years ago the efforts made by Crusaders at least helped to expose the ancient Classic and Eastern Cultures to the western world, including the religion of Islam together with such esoteric practices as alchemy, and the knowledge of both geometry and architecture.

In the *Reconquista* of the Kingdom of Aragon in the thirteenth century, Jaume I (*El Conqueridor*), as a young adult, went on to conquer Valencia (1238) and the Balearic Isles (Mallorca), and is still remembered as the most glorious of all historical Catalan and Aragonese leaders. His ties to the Knights Templar were so close that even his closest financial and legal advisors were prestigious members of the Order. The final attack of the troops of *El Conqueridor* against Valencia, one of the wealthiest and most advanced cities in Europe at the time and under Islamic rule for over five centuries, started from Teruel, and more specifically from close to Mora de Rubielos between 1236-38.

Almost two decades later, when the fertile lands of Valencia, full of orange and lemon trees, had already been colonized by Christian dwellers, *El Conqueridor* returned to Mora de Rubielos to celebrate St. Michael's day, patron of the Knights Templar, on 29 September 1259. This seemingly nostalgic visit to the Castle and Church of Mora de Rubielos is well documented in the Archives of the *Corona de Aragón* (1250 AD) and lasted from 23 September to 26 October 1259. It is known that on 9 October he was still in Mora de Rubielos with his faithful knights, from where he wrote a terse letter to his son-in-law, the equally famous King Alfonso X of Castile (*El Sabio*, 'the wise') complaining and questioning why Alfonso, who had married one of his daughters, had declared himself *Hispaniae Imperator* (Emperor of Spain), as described in *Memorial Histórico Español* (Reg. II, *folium* 218).

At the height of the Order's fortunes, there were almost a thousand Templar houses in Europe and in the East, and around 7,000 members. The number of auxiliaries and dependants (including stone-masons) is estimated to have been seven or eight times that number.

As late as summer 1311, most of the reports reaching the Pope from Christian Kingdoms concerning the Knights Templar held little conviction as to the supposed guilt of the Order. Only those from France contained 'credible' confessions, and those had been extracted under torture. Those from outside France, in particular from Aragon, England and Cyprus, could only come up with 'hearsay evidence' from non-Templars which gave scant substance to the accusations.

Today historians can be fairly certain that there was no institutionalised sodomy among the Templars, while insisting that the infamous accusations of heresy, blasphemy, and idolatry remain unproven.

The Templars' prestige and that of their brethren the Knights of St. John, was at its highest in the twelfth and thirteenth centuries. They were the main instrument, 'Moral and Military', of the 'Catholic' or 'Universal' Church. They answered only to the Pope – according to Catholics, the only heir of St. Peter on earth and St. Peter had been designated by Jesus to be the keeper of the keys to the Kingdom of Heaven.

Thus, the Military and Religious Orders served two 'bosses': the Pope, their only direct 'Chief' and the various Kings of European Nations, who were to be considered 'subsidiary' to the Pope. In addition, the rise in the building of Monasteries whose orders of monks, fired with illuminating energy to spread the Gospel and educate the people, had established special links with the Knights.

A good example is that of the Franciscans, who not only promoted *Ora et labora* (meaning 'pray and work') but also a universal love for all creatures, particularly animals, who were also considered to have souls.

Fratello Sole, Sorella Luna (Brother Sun, Sister Moon) – starts one of the first poems written in ancient Italian by St. Francis, who was born rich but decided to give all his material possessions to the poor and to dedicate his life to helping others. He travelled widely and, for example, walked along the *Camino de Santiago*, the Pilgrimage Route that starts at the Pyrenees, in south-west France, and reaches Santiago de Compostela, in the north-west part of Spain, close to *Finisterrae*, the coastal village on the most western part of Spain to which ancient tribes had already travelled for centuries to see the sun setting, and sinking into the Atlantic Ocean. They believed that this most western point was truly the 'End of the Earth' – hence the name *Finis Terrae*.

St Francis's preaching proved fruitful, and he soon had many followers. Some of whom travelled to Spain to spread the Gospel among the infidels. A beautiful fourteenth century Aragonese Gothic Style Convent still to be found in Teruel, is called *Convento de los Franciscanos*, and may well have been one of the first in Spain. The convent was meant to honour two young Franciscan Monks, who were sent to Teruel to enter Valencia and spread the Christian Gospel. As can still be seen on the modern fresco in one of the side-chapels of the Convent, these missionaries were caught and decapitated in Valencia, using much the same brutal technique as is used by today's Al-Qaeda kidnappers and killers.

St Francis of Assisi had fairly close ties with the Crusaders, and the Knights of St. John in particular. He tried, for example, to persuade Sultan al Kamil, Saladin's brother, to seek peace with the Christian forces at the siege of Damietta in 1219. Although he failed to do so, he set an example which his mendicant friars were to follow.

I have found more data on the two young Franciscan Monks who were slaughtered in Valencia in the thirteenth century, and to whom the Convent in Teruel is dedicated. Their real names were: *Giovanni di Perugia* (Juan de Perusa) and *Pietro di Sassoferrato* (Pedro de Saxoferrato). They were both Italian, and are thought to have first arrived in Teruel around 1220. As St. Francis founded his Monastic Order in 1209 (not 1205 as initially believed), their martyrdom is clearly early in the history of the Order. Following their failed mission, preaching Christianity in Islamic Valencia, the two future saints, and Patrons of Teruel, were buried in the Franciscan Convent, built by none other than the Grand Master of St John, don Juan Fernández de Heredia, in 1370.

The historical and intellectual links between the Templars (and the other large Religious Military Order, the Hospitallers) and Modern Freemasonry are still hypothetical but this hypothesis seems to be becoming again more popular, and gaining in credibility.

Take, for example, Christopher Knight and Robert Lomas, whose (relatively) recent best-sellers – *The Hiram Key* and *The Second Messiah*, concerning the controversial, but certainly fascinating possible origins of Freemasonry before the official establishment of the Grand Lodge of England in 1717, conclude that perhaps the purpose of Freemasonry has been subsumed in these latter days by its own bureaucracy. This 'virtual and complex reality' of Lodges, Grand Lodges, rituals, degrees and various honours and distinctions, should not preclude us from attempting to know the true origins of Freemasonry, and to fully understand its principles and main objectives.

Unfortunately, despite extensive research, it is difficult not to share the sceptical opinion that the true meanings and exact nature of the so called 'Higher Degrees' perhaps will never be really known to us. Might not these degrees have been an invention by the Jacobite Chevalier Andrew Michael Ramsay who, in his celebrated 'Oration' in Paris in 1740 (supposedly given earlier on 26 December 1736), proposed that freemasons were a society of knights who had devoted themselves to the purpose of rebuilding the sacred temples destroyed by the Saracens? There are still considerable disputes among freemasons and historians of this ancient Craft regarding the exact meaning and purpose of the 'Oration'. In it, Ramsay stated, but gave no proof whatsoever, that the 'Crusader ancestors of our Order eventually formed an intimate union with the Knights of St John'.

The next exposure, the secret *Le Sceau Rompu* (in 1745), takes this legend a little further in terms of ritual content and sets the context firmly in the camp of the exiled Jacobites. It describes how the Crusaders, who wanted to rebuild King Solomon's Temple in Jerusalem in the eleventh and twelfth centuries, took the name of the 'Knights Free Masons', and subsequently these Knights joined forces with the Knights of St John of Jerusalem.

Was Andrew Michael Ramsay, the presumed 'father' of the so called 'Scottish Degrees', just another quixotic dreamer? Even worse, might he have been a traitor and conspirator who, like the Duke of Wharton, tried to bring the Stewarts back to the throne of England and, failing that, turned himself to the Catholic religion? Wharton, Grand Master and a key figure of the very early days of the premier Grand Lodge of England, had exiled himself to Spain.

Under the Grand Mastership of the Duke of Wharton, Freemasonry began increasingly to come before the public eye. Freemasons walked in public processions clothed in 'masonic apparel' with leathern apron and symbolic badges, to Stationer's Hall in London. It became a tradition for freemasons to attend the laying of the foundation stones of churches and other public buildings, and the Sword of State of the Grand Lodge, and the *Book of Constitutions* were carried by prestigious freemasons in procession, in a most solemn manner.

It is believed that Wharton withdrew from English Freemasonry having been thwarted, *in absentia*, in his wish to remain as Grand Master for a second term, Dr Desaguliers (Wharton's Deputy) having cast the deciding vote in favour of the Earl of Dalkieth (*later* 2nd Duke of Buccleuch), as his successor.

Wharton left England, became a Catholic in 1728, organized a small army of mercenaries to take Gibraltar back from the English, following 1730, founded the first Speculative Lodge in Continental Europe, in Madrid and was buried in 1731 at the Monastery of Poblet, near Barcelona, which now belongs to the Order of the Cistercians and is, curiously, the burial site of most of the Kings of Aragon, including Pedro IV *El Ceremonioso*, who was mentor and personal friend of don Juan Fernández de Heredia, Grand Master of the Order of St. John, in the second half of the fourteenth century.

In the *Dictionary of Freemasonry* by the American Robert Macoy (1815-95), he lists as the first Landmark of Freemasonry the 'modes of recognition'. These he says are, of all the landmarks, the most legitimate and unquestioned. They admit of no variation. Similarly, he lists as Landmark twenty-three 'Secrecy', concerning these modes of recognition. If Freemasonry were to be divested of its secret character, it would lose its identity and cease to exist. Macoy also suggests that signs and tokens are the most secret, for they cannot be as easily transmitted as words.

Secret societies have their origins in the deepest and most pressing wants and needs of humanity. The 'Mysteries' of India, Egypt, Greece and others, were secret Orders, great educational institutions for the advancement of men in wisdom and virtue. In a supposed letter, probably false, written by King Henry VI, he asks: 'What do the masons conceal and hide?' The answers are '... the art of finding new arts, and the art of keeping secrets ...' Should we have no secrets at all? – asks the celebrated metaphysician John Locke (1696) '... even that must be a secret, which if discovered, might expose us to the highest ridicule.

In *The History of English Freemasonry*, John Hamill reminds us of the dangers of divulging our passwords, and in 1730, one Samuel Prichard, describing himself as a 'late member of a Constituted Lodge', published a pamphlet entitled *Masonry Dissected* which eventually led the Grand Lodge to take the drastic step of actually altering the recognition words in the first two degrees, to prevent impostors gaining entry into the lodges.

We cannot be entirely sure if our 'secrets' (signs, tokens, words and symbols) truly derive from medieval stone-workers, but they may well do because, as pointed out in a letter by Bro. Derek Stuckey in *Ars Quatuor Coronatorum* Vol. 113, p. 58, '... stone masons were and still are different. They bring rude matter into due form ...', with the help, I would add, of Prudence, Temperance, Fortitude, and Justice. In the Middle Ages, these stone-workers travelled from country to country to build splendid temples and cathedrals, with their knowledge and craft in their minds, and in their hands. They did not use official University Degrees or Professional Documents in those days. And they probably recognised each other, and their respective professional degrees, by secret and universal modes of recognition (signs, tokens, words and symbols). In the same way that modern Masonic rituals state, in the days of King Solomon, the Junior and Senior Wardens checked the status of Entered Apprentice (EA) and Fellow Craft (FC) to grant them the pay due for their labours. Those secrets, according to these rituals, eventually cost the life of the master builder Hiram Abif, credited for the architectural splendour of King Solomon's Temple.

It is likely that the history of stone masons is as old as civilization itself, which would mean at least ten thousand years. As those who have had the privilege of travelling to Egypt, and feeling the magic of the ancient temples know, the power of their stones, ashlars and pillars, remains alive almost five thousand years after they were built . There is even a hypothesis popularised by G. Oliver in his book *Antiquities of Freemasonry* (1823), that Moses himself was a Grand Master of the Order! Moses, like many historical and at the same time legendary characters, is an enigma. Nobody knows exactly where he was born, nor where he is buried. All we know is that he was initiated into the arts, sciences and esoteric knowledge of the Egyptians by the High Priests. He had very close ties with the Pharaoh himself, who regarded him as his 'Brother', and probably surrounded himself with the brightests minds of those Jews exiled in ancient Egypt. According to the Old Testament only Moses heard the real, ineffable and mysterious name of God before the burning bush in Mount Horeb. A bush that burned but was not consumed by flames. '... And God said unto Moses, 'I AM THAT I AM' (Exodus 3: v.14).

Such ancient skills, symbols and the esoteric and philosophical messages contained in them, may well have been transmitted verbally from Master to Fellow-craft to Entered Apprentice throughout the centuries of Operative Freemasonry.

The Templars may have been familiar with these practices and rituals while in the Holy Land during the Crusades and up until the fall of Jerusalem to Saladin in 1187. Thereafter they may have spread them throughout Europe, in their role as protectors of the various Gilds of Masons and Stone Workers.

One such place in Europe is to be found in Scotland: Rosslyn Chapel. One small but fantastic piece of evidence to be seen there is the carving of two men, side by side, showing a blindfolded man in medieval garb, kneeling and holding a book with a cross on the cover, in his right hand (presumably the Volume of the Sacred Law). Around this man's neck is a running noose, the end of which is held by the second man who is wearing the robe of a Templar. When this little carving, now thought to be the work of Scottish architect and freemason David Bryce (*circa* 1860), was found by Knight and Lomas, they were in the company of brother Edgar Harborne, an officer of the United Grand Lodge of England, and Worshipful Master of the 'Caius' Lodge who installed me in the chair of King Solomon in Cambridge, England, in 2002.

In the appendix to this book, 'Is Don Juan Fernandez de Heredia (1306-96) the "missing link" between the Templars, the Knights of St John and medieval freemasons?' I provide an alternative and innovative 'Templar/Masonic hypothesis' to that of Rosslyn, which may fit the historical facts and dates better, without in any way questioning the sheer beauty and strong symbolical and mystical energies of Rosslyn. It is, for example, well documented that a later Sinclair – an eighteenth century descendant of founder William St Clair (and his namesake), who built Rosslyn Chapel in the fifteenth century – became the first appointed Grand Master of the (Masonic) Grand Lodge of Scotland. Needless to say, this hypothesis requires further research and has no intention of questioning Scotland's long term Alliance with both the (historical) Knights Templar and Freemasonry. It places the ancient Kingdom of Aragon squarely on the map at the time of the medieval *Reconquista* from Islam and before modern Spain was created.

Our trip to Mora de Rubielos invites enquiry into a key issue: exactly when did these Masonic rituals and practices start to become speculative, rather than remaining purely operative? Our findings inevitably suggest that some speculative rituals and ceremonies were probably already in use at the time the Templars first (twelfth-thirteenth centuries), and later the Hospitallers (fourteenth-fifteenth centuries) dominated the Castle of Mora de Rubielos. To quote Keith Jackson: '... it is not unreasonable to estimate that commencing with the Entered Apprentice a zealous brother, possessing the requisite time, finance and ready acceptance, could conceivably advance through more than 110 degrees ... in England alone.' Freemasonry is, in its essence, a ceremonial method of approach to truth, and it is beyond dispute that most degrees have a distinct lesson to impart, with an inner meaning. It is in this context, and no other, that one must understand the modern Chivalric degrees in Freemasonry, including the degrees of Knight Templar, Knight of St Paul or Mediterranean Pass, and finally Knight of St John of Jerusalem, Palestine, Rhodes and Malta.

Another interesting link between Freemasonry and operative stonemasons is, without any shadow of doubt, the so-called 'Mark Degree'. Many learned and influential freemasons believe earnestly that 'Choosing his Mark' was, in addition to being important as a part of the Fellowcrafts' Degree in England, an integral part of the qualifications for the degree of Mark Master Mason. The symbolism of this degree is based on the marks on the stone, on the meaning of ancient Hebrew characters with allegorical reference to the building of King Solomon's Temple, as well as on the beautiful Cedars of Lebanon, and the responsibility of another master builder – Adoniram. The lesson of this degree is that 'The stone which the builders refused is become the headstone of the corner'.

In the Kingdom of Aragon, as in England, Scotland, Portugal and elsewhere, the Knights Templar were not found guilty on all the charges brought against them by the Pope and the King of France. The 'National Archives of Catalonia' are within walking distance from my home. They are in a modern fully equipped building by St. Cugat, near Barcelona. But the ancient 'Archives of the Crown of Aragon' are still in Barcelona. They used to be next to the ancient Cathedral of Barcelona, in the 'Gothic Quarter', or *Barrio Gòtico* of this beautiful Mediterranean city. Possibly, some of the documents will return to the Gothic Quarter once their premises have been redecorated. They contain some of the most complete documents regarding both the Knights of the Temple and the Knights of St. John of Jerusalem, but unfortunately these documents consist almost entirely of administrative and accounting information. There is virtually nothing, as one might expect following centuries of the Inquisition, on their secret practices or esoteric knowledge.

These unique ancient archives were first researched in depth by Joaquim Miret I Sans (Barcelona, 1858-1919), and later by many Catalan and foreign scholars, among whom I cite two that I have met personally: Jesús Mestre i Godes, and Josep Maria Sans i Travé.

Jews, who played a very important part in the day to day life of the Kingdom of Aragon in the twelfth to fifteenth centuries, until their expulsion by the Catholic sovereigns Fernando of Aragon and Isabel of Castile, kept their own records, either by oral tradition or in Hebrew script. So that although it seems likely that there were contacts between Jews and both the Knights Templar and the Hospitallers, documentary evidence is hard to find.

The story is long and complex, but it turns out that, as might have been predicted, the end of the Knights of the Temple in the Kingdom of Aragon was not as tragic as in France where many knights were tortured and burnt alive, but it was 'chaotic' to say the least. Demoralised by unfair betrayal by the Catholic Church, the Pope (Clement V), and also unexpectedly betrayed, by the King of Aragon, Jaume II, despite the ties of honour and mutual trust created over two hundred years between the Order and his Crown, the Templars felt abandoned, betrayed and totally devoid of their *raison d'être*. The ten years period between 1 December 1307 and the same day in 1317 could be described as their decade of chaos. A number of reliable documents testify to their immense disappointment, confusion and even depression, which led many down the wrong path, resorting to wine, women and violent rebellious behaviour.

It has been calculated that at least 20,000 Templars died in the Holy Land defending their faith, and six out of twenty-three Templar Grand Masters died in battle or in captivity. Recent research shows that the Crusader often sold or mortgaged all his worldly possessions in the hope and dream of spiritual reward as well as social prestige and recognition.

Pope Clement V, under pressure from the French King Philip IV, *Philip le Bel*, finally convened a commission on 22 November 1309 in the episcopal hall of the Bishop of Paris. In spite of later legends, the role of the last Grand Master of the Order of the Templars, Jacques de Molay, in this tragic affair came across as rather 'pathetic'. When de Molay appeared before the commission on Friday 28 November he repeated that he felt unable to mount a defence of his Order because 'he was a knight, unlettered and poor'. According to Piers Paul Read and other historians, it was not just that de Molay was 'illiterate', as he had attested at the time of his arrest, but that under his rule, the Temple had failed to adapt to the political changes in Europe, and the increasing legalism of the period. The Templars were simply caught unprepared for the challenge. Saving the obvious differences, his defence was as 'pathetic' as that of Rudolf Hess during the interrogations that followed his arrest in Scotland in 1941 or at the Nuremburg Trials, at the end of the Second World War.

Jacques de Molay, perhaps expecting to be able to persuade the Pope personally, told the Commission in Paris in 1309 only three things: that the liturgy in the Templar churches was more beautiful than in any churches other than cathedrals, that the Order had been very generous in its charitable donations, and that no Order 'had shed its blood so readily in defence of the Christian faith'. He insisted that he did believe 'in one God and in a Trinity of Persons, and in other tenets of the Catholic faith, '… and when the soul was separated from the body, then it would be apparent who was good and who was bad, and each of us would know the truth of these things which were being done at present'.

Almost four years later, on 18 March 1314, three Cardinals and a Council of Doctors of Theology and Canon Law met again in Paris to read their final judgement on the four leaders of the Temple: Jacques de Molay, Hugh de Pairaud, Geoffrey de Gonneville and Geoffrey de Charnay. The judgement was:

'Since these four men, without any exception, had publicly and openly confessed the crimes which had been imputed to them – they, of course, omitted "under torture"– they were to be thrust into harsh and perpetual imprisonment'.

This was too much even for the Grand Master Jacques de Molay and here he showed his final freedom of choice and innate heroism. The Pope had betrayed him. All he could hope for now was justice from God. Both Jacques de Molay and Geoffrey de Charnay stood up and publicly retracted their 'confessions', proclaiming their innocence. The French Cardinals and Doctors did not know what to do, as they were clearly not expecting this last exercise of dignity.

However, following orders from King Philip IV, that very same night the two old men were taken to a small island in the River Seine called the Ile-des-Javiaux, to be burned at the stake.

Figure 16
Gargoyle overlooking the river Seine in Paris from the Cathedral of Notre Dâme. Not far from this, on the Ile-des-Javiaux, Jacques de Molay, the last Grand Master of the Knight Templars, and Geoffrey de Charney were burned to death in public. (*see also* Figure 29).

In the Kingdom of Aragon, King Jaume II, in spite of the traditional good relationship between his Crown and the Orders, tried for ten years to persuade two consecutive Popes of the need to give all of the Templar properties to the Crown, and not to the Hospitallers or the Knights of St. John. He insisted that the security of his Kingdom depended upon the royal possession of the Templar holdings. Both the Templars of Miravet, in Catalonia, and the Templars of Monzón, in Aragon, had resisted his troops in 1308-09, for they too had proclaimed their innocence.

Even before the execution of Jacques de Molay, the 'Concilium of Tarragona' had declared the Templars innocent on 4 November 1312, and it was agreed that following the dissolution of the Order by the Pope, all of the Knights, Priests and others (including Masons) belonging to the Order would be paid economic allowances, like modern pensions, according to their status and needs, until they died. This financial reward had already been ordered by a Papal Bull dated 6 May 1312, perhaps to appease hostilities and revolt. As in England (Yorkshire, for example), and elsewhere, the former Templars found it difficult to accept that their former Order no longer existed. Most of them were still alive, and they were a Fraternity, with considerable individual skills and knowledge.

Some ex-Templars turned into military mercenaries, and took wives. Others, like the former Commander of Monzón, Berenguer de Bellvís, indulged in material pleasure and kept a mistress, or two. The same King Jaume II was forced to write on 26 October 1314 to the Archbishop of Tarragona to ask for his intercession concerning this embarrassing case. The old Archives of the Crown of Aragon contain even more scandalous situations. For example, one Fra Martí de Frigola is recorded as having been sent to prison accused of kidnap and rape.

It is difficult to know exactly what happened, because a certain 'Black Legend' implicating both Orders (the Temple and St. John) was being deliberately spread as a rumour. In August 1317, the Head of the Knights of St. John in the Kingdom of Aragon, also known as the 'Castellán de Amposta', was Fra Martí Pérez de Oros and, to placate the King and score 'good points' with the Pope, agreed with the Archbishop of Tarragona to ask the former Templars to behave and once more embrace their proper conduct and morals.

Many of them, but never more than two per Convent, in case they became too powerful again, joined their Brethren, the Knights of St. John. But many others, no doubt, went astray and there can be little doubt that they continued with their secret rituals, and perhaps even with the Installation of new Knights, albeit in a clandestine fashion.

Things did not improve, in fact they got worse after Pope John XXII who succeeded the wretched Clement V, made public his final agreement with King Jaume II to hand to the Order of St. John, or Hospitallers, all of the properties of the Temple in Aragon, other than in Valencia, where a new military Order was created based on 'Montesa'.

Not even the penalty of reduced pensions imposed upon the former Knights Templar stopped their independent and proud behaviour. Few of them were beset by financial hardship, even if some led a frustrating existence. As their numbers dwindled so probably did the Church's concern with them. They were left to end their days with little interference .

In some cases, however, pensions were reduced between 1319 and 1330 to half their initial amount. Until 1350, there were a few Knights Templar left here and there in the Kingdom, as testified to in a document regarding one Fra Berenguer Dezcoll. It was during this chaotic period of time that don Juan Fernández de Heredia, future Grand Master of St. John, was born, somewhere in the Kingdom.

Selected Bibliography

15. Georges Tate. The Crusades and the Holy Land. Thames and Hudson 2002
16. Steven Runciman, A History of the Crusades. Volumes 1 to 3. Cambridge 1951-54.
17. William Hutchinson, *The Spirit of Masonry* (Wilkin & Goldsmith, 1st Edn, 1775), Grand Lodge Library, London.
18. Cohen M.R., *Under crescent and cross. The Jews in the Middle Ages* (Princeton University Press, Princeton, N.J., 1994).
19. Stow K.R., *Alienated minority. The Jews of Medieval Latin Europe* (Harvard University Press, Cambridge, Mass., 1992).
20. Abulafia A.S., *Christians and Jews in dispute: disputational literature and the rise of anti-judaism in the West (c.1000-1150)* (Ashgate Variorum, Aldershot, UK, 1994).
21. Horbury, W.A., Critical examination of *Toledoth Jeshu*, Ph.D. dissertation,Cambridge, 1971.
22. Horbury, W.A., 'The trial of Jesus in Jewish tradition', *The Trial of Jesus*, (ed. E. Bammel , London, 1970, pp. 103-121).
23. Berger, D., *The Jewish-Christian debate in the High Middle Ages. A critical edition of the Nizzahon Vetus* (Philadelphia, 1979).
24. Read Piers Paul, (The Templars, Phoenix Paperback, 2004,9th impression).
25. Josep Maria Sans I Travé, *El procés dels Templers Catalans* (Pagès Editors. Lleida, 1991).
26. *Jesús Mestre i Godes. Els Templers: Alba I crepuscle dels cavallers (Edicions* 62, Barcelona 1996).
27. Alan Forey, The Templars in the Corona de Aragon (Oxford, 1973).
28. Alan Forey, The Military Orders: from the Twelfth to the Early Fourteenth Centuries, London 1992.
29. Zambon F., *El legado secreto de los cátaros (Ediciones Siruela*, Madrid 1997).
30. Runciman, S., *The Medieval Manichee. A study of the Christian Dualist Heresy*

(Cambridge University Press, 1947).

31.   Atienza, J.G., *Los enclaves templarios: Guía Mágica de la Orden en España* (*Ediciones* Martinez Roca, Barcelona 2003).

32.   Barahona, P., *Los Templarios: Una Historia muy Presente* (*Libsa Editorial*, Madrid 2003).

33.   Mazières, Abbé M.R. '*La Venue et le séjour des Templiers du Roussillon à la fin du XIIIème siècle et au début du XIVème dans la vallée du Bézu* (*Aude*). In : *Mémoires de la société des arts et des sciences de Carcassone*, 4, Vol. 3 (Carcassone 1957-59).

34.   Michael Baigent, Richard Leigh, Henry Lincoln, *The Holy Blood and the Holy Grail* (Jonathan Cape Ltd, London, 1982).

35.   Zuckerman, A. L., *A Jewish Princedom in Feudal France* (New York, 1972).

36.   Miret I Sans J., *Itinerari de Jaume I El Conqueridor* (*Edició Facsímil*, ed Maria Teresa Ferrer i Mallol, *Institut d'Estudis Catalans*, Barcelona 2004).

37.   Knight, C., & Lomas, R., *The Hiram Key* (Century, 1996).

38.   Knight, C., & Lomas, R., *The Second Messiah* (Arrow Books Ltd, 1998).

39.   Macoy, R., *A Dictionary of Freemasonry* (Gramercy Books, New York, 1989).

40.   Hamill, J., *The History of English Freemasonry* (Lewis Masonic, 1994).

41.   Derek Stuckey, 'Stonemasons and Freemasons' (Letter) in *AQC* 113, 2000.

42.   Michael Baigent, 'Seeking the Heart of Egypt', *Freemasonry Today* (issue 25, 2003: pp. 22-24).

43.   Keith Jackson, *Beyond the Craft* (Lewis Masonic, 1980).

44.   Frederick Smyth, *Brethren in Chivalry 1791-1991. A Celebration of the Two Hundred Years of the Great Priory of the United Religious, Military and Masonic Orders of the Temple and of St John of Jerusalem, Palestine, Rhodes and Malta of England and Wales and Provinces Overseas* (Lewis Masonic, London, 1991).

45.   Anthony Luttrell, 'Hospitaller life in Aragon: 1319-1370'. *God and Man in Medieval Spain*. Essays in Honour of J.R.L. Highfield. Ed. De Derek W. Lomax and David Mackenzie, Warminster, Aris and Phillips, 1989.

46.   Batlle Carme, '*L'Expansió Baixmedieval* (*segles XIII-XV*)'. In: *Historia de Catalunya* Ed. Pierre Vilar (co-ordinator Joseph Termes), Vol III, *Edicions* 62 (Publishers), Barcelona 1988.

47.   Josep Vives, *Juan Fernández de Heredia, Gran Maestre de Rodas. Vida, obras, formas dialectales* (*Analecta Sacra Tarraconensia*, 3, Tarragona 1927).

48.   Miquel Batllori, *El Gran Maestre don Juan Fernández de Heredia y los orígenes del Humanismo aragonés* (*Estudios del Departamento de Historia Moderna*, Zaragoza, 1973).

Chapter Three

The occult roots and great achievements of the Grand Master of the Order of St John, Juan Fernández de Heredia (1310-96 AD)

Following the Templars dissolution in 1312, and the execution of Jacques de Molay, the property of my 'Secret Castle' at Mora de Rubielos was under dispute, and it is not altogether clear who owned it, nor who inhabited it, until it was bought, together with the ancient Church of Saint Mary, and the whole village of Mora de Rubielos, by the historical figure of Juan Fernández de Heredia (1310-96).

Juan Fernández de Heredia was one of the most fascinating and cosmopolitan personalities of the fourteenth century, and is well remembered in Mora de Rubielos because of his ties with the military-religious order of the Hospital, and his own extended family that ruled over Mora for some 250 years. He is being given increasing recognition (better late than never), by the Scholastic community and in particular at the Universities in Zaragoza, Barcelona, Oxford , Uppsala and Madison (Wisconsin, USA).

He was a man of enormous charm and energy, vast culture and expertise, who became chief advisor to several Popes at a critical time for the Avignon papacy in France, and several Kings, including the powerful Pedro IV *El Ceremonioso*. In 1377 he became Grand Master of the Order of St. John of Jerusalem and Rhodes (*later* the Order of Malta) by decision of Pope Gregory XI.

In brief, don Juan Fernández de Heredia was a soldier, a diplomat, a sailor, a humanist, a builder/architect, and a religious Grand Master. In other words, he was an exemplar of Renaissance man. He was Counsellor to the King Pedro IV of Aragon (*El Ceremonioso*), who ruled for almost fifty years (1337-87), and who recovered Mallorca and Menorca, as well as the French Rousillon, which his ancestor Jaume I (*El Conquistador*) had recaptured from Islam although, for reasons unclear, he had bequeathed these to a different son, unlike the rest of his Kingdom. This re-unification of the Kingdom of Aragon was paid for with many lives and the loss of the French City of Montpellier (where Jaume I was born, of a French mother and an Aragonese father, on 1 February 1208).

He was a master of sorting out and surviving political intrigues as shown by the fact that he became, first as *Castellán de Amposta* and later Grand Master of the Order of St. John', key advisor to three real Popes and two Pseudo-Popes (or Anti-Popes). I cannot think of any other historical or figurative personage who can claim anything remotely similar. To be more precise, he was elected Governor of the French city of Avignon in 1361, by Pope Innocent VI, where the Papacy and the Catholic Church had established their headquarters following several barbarian rebel attacks on Rome. He was also consulted by Pope Urban V (between 1362 and 1370) in connection with several political crises, despite not being his favourite, and he had other kinds of problems during this period of time, such as the premature death of his only son, born illegitimate, don Juan Fernández de Heredia II and to whom he had intended donating the Castle of Mora de Rubielos which clearly meant something very special to him. Fortunately for the succession, when Juan Fernández de Heredia II died at an early age, his wife was pregnant with Juan Fernández de Heredia III and so the Castle of Mora de Rubielos passed on to Juan Fernández de Heredia's first grand-son.

Perhaps the best relics of don Juan Fernández de Heredia under Pope Urban V are the splendid images left of them both in the Church of Santa Maria Novella, in Florence (*see* Figures 17a and 17 b).

The Pope, adorned with all of his Jewels and Attributes, sits in the middle, and is flanked to his left by the German Emperor Charles IV. This fresco, painted by Andrea Bonaiuti between 1366 and 1368 in the Dominican Church of *Santa Maria Novella* in Florence, and more specifically for the so-called 'Chapel of the Spaniards', is a real *Who's Who?* of European Political Power of the time.

The dogs at the bottom represent Dominican Friars (*Domini Canes* or Dogs of God), who look after the sheep (representing Christianity), guarding them from the heretics. Among the prelates, priests, friars, princes, soldiers, pilgrims, knights, heretics and saints who crowd this amazing fresco (also known as 'The Way to Salvation'), is an intriguing middle-age, clean-shaven man, in a reddish gown, who confronts the spectator 'face to face' with a large closed book. Several authors, like Henri Hauvette or Edward Hutton, have identified this book-bearing man as Boccaccio, the great Florentine poet who wrote the famous *Decameron*.

Boccaccio, who was born in Paris of Florentine parents, is often credited, together with his friend and master Petrach, to be the real founders of the 'Renaissance' concept. They investigated several monastic libraries in search for classic documents and works, not only in Latin but also in Greek, and translated them to the new and 'vulgar' language of Italian, already mastered by their temporal precursor, Dante Alighieri. In this respect, Juan Fernández

Figure 17a
'The Church Triumphant'. Fresco in Santa Maria Novella, Florence. (Only the part of the fresco to the right of the Pope is reproduced in figure 17a; the characters to the left of the Pope are visible in figure 17b).

47

Figure 17b
'The Church Triumphant'. Fresco in Santa Maria Novella,
Florence. The Pope is the first character on the left.

de Heredia, who had direct access to the Library of the Popes, the Library of the Knights of St John (now in Malta), as well as to likely literary and esoteric sources used by the Knights Templar (unfortunately lost for ever), accomplished a personal education in the most renaissance style.

More recent authors, like Paul F. Watson or the aforementioned Luttrell, have argued that the only place reserved for poets in this Florentine fresco must be the garden set above, where they dwell with luxurious noblemen and beautiful amorous ladies. The inquisitorial Dominicans believed that 'The songs of poets are the food of devils'. The man with the closed book, behind the pilgrims, must have represented the *Podestá*, Florentine civil authority, seriously displaying the Statutes Book of the City of Florence. The Pope, sits in the middle, and is flanked to his left by the German Emperor Charles IV, of the Hapsburg dynasty, elected in Nuremburg, the 'secret capital' of

Figure 17c
Detail of the same fresco, showing a pilgrim of the 'Camino de Santiago', with the
classic shell of St Jacques on his hat, and, at the top, the 'Veronica' or image of Christ.
This pilgrimage route became a holy and esoteric path in medieval Europe and starting
at the Pyrenees in France crossed the north-west of Spain to the city of Santiago.

of Franconia, who was crowned Emperor of the 'Sacro-Roman Empire',
also known by the Nazis as the 'First Reich', in August 1368. To the left
of the German Emperor, there are several Crusaders, among them Pierre
de Lusignan, the fanatic who destroyed Alexandria in 1365, and the more
civilized Amedeus of Savoy, who had bought the Shroud of Turin from
mysterious sources, and who reconquered 'Gallipoli' from the Turks in
1366. King Pierre of Cyprus is next to them.

The characters visible in Figure 17a are all pictured at the right of the
Pope, and represent the Church. One can see the Spanish Cardinal Gil de
Albornoz, also born in Aragon, as well as the Grand Master of St. John, who
was at that time the Frenchman Raymond Berenguer, predecessor of don
Juan Fernández de Heredia. Among them one can clearly see two Knights of
St. John, with their characteristic Cross of Malta. The elder of the two, with

the forked beard and grey hair, is don Juan Fernández de Heredia himself.

It should be remembered that in 1362, Fernández de Heredia was guardian of the Conclave which elected Urban V as Pope. In about 1367 his portrait appeared in the church of Santa Maria Novella at Florence in this fresco by Andrea Bonaiuti. It is interesting this apparent connection with the Savoy family and the Hapsburgs, as these two families have been part of the History of Europe for the past millennium, and are mysteriously related to a number of esoteric events and objects.

For example, the 'Shroud of Turin', which Christopher Knight and Robert Lomas suggest, but do not prove, that it is an extraordinary 'photographic image' of Jacques de Molay , following his tortures in Paris, had been bought by the Savoy family (whose city of residence has traditionally been Turin, in northern Italy), when Leonardo da Vinci was only one year old, thereby making it impossible to be a 'work of art' by Leonardo , as it has also been suggested by others.

Pope Gregory XI, who succeeded Urban V on 30 December 1370, asked don Juan Fernández de Heredia, and his masons, to rebuild the city walls of Avignon, in the South of France. This beautiful city, that still displays with pride the ancient Palace of the Popes and a good part of the old City Walls, had grown considerably , from five thousand to over thirty thousand inhabitants, under the establishment and guidance of the Popes.

Don Juan took very active part in the recruitment and supervision of the masons's work, and some 4.5 kilometres of robust city walls were built in just about a decade. He was very familiar with their knowledge and traditions, and employed them also to build war-machines, useful to take by siege Castles and Fortresses.

Following this achievement, don Juan was again appointed Governor of the City, and remained in charge of its defence for a number of years, until 13 September 1376 when Pope Gregory XI finally decided to leave Avignon and return to the eternal city of Rome. The complex political background of the time merits a little explanation, so that the great political abilities of our character, don Juan Fernández de Heredia, can be properly understood.

This period of the Papacy in Avignon was called by Petrarch 'the Babylonian Captivity' of the popes, a term coined by the Italian poet who obviously lamented the absence of the papacy from his native land. The fourteenth century Avignon papacy has been depicted as being totally dependent on the French kings, and treacherous to its spiritual role and heritage in Rome. Prosperity of the church at this time was accompanied by shameful corruption and a profound compromise of the Papacy's spiritual integrity, especially in the alleged subordination of the powers of the Church to the ambitions of the French kings. Coincidentally, the 'captivity' of the popes at Avignon lasted for about the same length of time as the exile of the Jews in Babylon, making the analogy even more potent.

The beginning of the fourteenth century, which would later be characterized by the beginnings of the Renaissance was also marred by calamities such as the Black Death, or bubonic plague, probably brought into Western Europe by ships sailing from the Crimean peninsula under the flag of Genoa. It was to see a Papacy apparently at the height of its power. Pope Boniface VIII (1294-1303), born Benedict Caetani, was an experienced politician, sometimes described as difficult and arrogant, and a strong proponent of the Universal Sovereignty of the Papacy over all Christendom. The concrete issue that sparked conflict with the King of France was the question whether secular lords were allowed to tax the clergy. In his bull *Clericis Laicos*, Boniface VIII prohibited any taxation on church property or the payment of such taxes except by the Papacy. Under great pressure, only a year later he granted the King of France the right to raise taxes on the clergy in cases of emergency. The great success of the Jubilee Year 1300 (it is reported that up to 2 million pilgrims visited Rome) considerably strengthened the prestige of the Papacy, brought funds to Rome and led the Pope to grossly overestimate his temporal powers. After the arrest of the Bishop of Pamiers by Philippe IV, the Pope issued the bull *Salvator Mundi*, retracting all privileges granted to the French king by previous popes, and a few weeks later issued another provocative Bull, *Ausculta fili*, with charges against the French king, summoning him before a council to Rome. In a bold assertion of Papal sovereignty, Boniface declared that 'God has placed us over the Kings and Kingdoms'. In response, Philippe wrote 'Your venerable stupidity may know, that we are nobody's vassal in temporal matters', and called for a meeting of the Council of the Lords of France, who supported his position. The King of France, in revenge, issued charges of sodomy, simony (a corruption offence of accepting or offering money for a position in the Church), sorcery and heresy against the same pope and summoned him before the French Royal Council. The pope's response was the strongest affirmation to date of papal sovereignty. On 18 November 1302, he decreed that '... it is necessary to salvation that every human creature be subject to the Roman pontiff'. He was preparing a bull that would excommunicate the King of France and place an interdict on France and to depose her entire clergy. In September of 1303, William Nogaret, the strongest critic of the Papacy in the French inner circle, led a delegation to Rome, with intentionally vague orders from the king to bring the pope, if necessary by force, before a council to rule on the charges brought against him. Nogaret coordinated with the cardinals of the Colonna family, long standing rivals to pope Boniface VIII, against whom the pope had even preached a crusade earlier in his Papacy. In 1303 French and Italian troops attacked the pope in his home town of Anagni, arresting the pontiff himself. He was freed three days later by the population of the same Anagni. However, Boniface VIII, then eighty-six years of age, was deeply shattered by this attack on his own person and died a few weeks later.

After the very short conciliatory Papacy of Benedict XI (1303-04), the infamous Clement V (1305-1314) became the next Pope. He was born in southern France in Gascony but was not directly connected to the French court. He certainly owed his election to the French clerics who were under the influence of the French king. He deliberately decided against moving to Rome and established his court in Avignon, and initiating the 'Babylonian Captivity', one of the most critical moments for the Catholic Church that eventually saw the unexpected antagonism of don Juan Fernández de Heredia, a 'foreigner' from the Kingdom of Aragon, who nevertheless became Counselor to several Popes, and eventually Grand Master of the powerful Order of the Knights of St John, now the most powerful Order, as a consequence of the abolition of the Knights Templar.

In those days, the Popes were temporal rulers over The Pontifical States (today limited to the small Vatican City, but then encompassing a great portion of central Italy), and their possessions included land around Avignon (*Comtat Venaissin*), and a small enclave to the east. They remained part of the Pontifical States up until the French Revolution, when they became part of France (in 1791).

In this situation of direct dependency on the powerful neighbours in France, three principles characterised the politics of pope Clement V: the complete suppression of heretical movements (such as the Cathars in southern France); the reorganisation of the internal administration of the church; and the preservation of an untainted image of the church as the sole instrument of God's will on earth. The latter was directly challenged by Philippe IV when he pushed for a trial against his former adversary, Pope Boniface VIII, for alleged heresy. Exerting strong influence on the cardinals of the *collegium* could mean a severe blow to the church's authority and Clement's politics were designed to avoid such a blow, which he finally achieved. However, the price was that he had to make concessions on various fronts to the King of France and so, despite strong personal doubts, in the end he pushed for proceedings against the Templars, when he personally ruled, with the aim of suppressing the order.

With this Pope, the Pontificate in Avignon commenced in 1305 and lasted until 1378 when Gregory XI moved the Pontificate back to Rome, sailing with don Juan Fernández de Heredia as the Admiral of his fleet.

The Avignon Papacy consisted of seven Popes, all of them French, who although preserving apparent independence from the French Kings, were nevertheless always under scrutiny and direct pressure from them. The Popes were: Pope Clement V (1305-14), Pope John XXII (1316-34), Pope Benedict XII (1334-42), Pope Clement VI (1342-52), Pope Innocent VI (1352-62), Pope Urban V (1362-70) and Pope Gregory XI (1370-78).

In 1378, Gregory XI moved the papal residence back to Rome and died there in that same year. Due to a dispute over the subsequent election, a faction of cardinals set up an 'antipope' back in Avignon. This was the beginning of the period of difficulty from 1378 to 1414, which Catholic scholars refer to as the 'Western Schism', when parties within the Catholic church were divided in their allegiances between the various claimants to the office of pope. Finally, the Council of Constance in 1414 resolved the controversy, dismantling the last vestiges of the Avignon papacy although disputes continued until at least 1417.

Pope Clement VI had been Archbishop of Rouen, and advisor to Philippe IV previously, so his links to the French court were much stronger than those of his predecessors. At some point he even financed French war efforts out of his own pocket. He reportedly enjoyed a luxurious wardrobe and under his rule the extravagant life style in Avignon had reached new heights. He was pope during the Black Death epidemic that swept through Europe between 1347 and 1350, killing millions of people, perhaps more than a third of the population (considerably more than any war before or after). In some European towns, the blame for this calamity was placed on the local Jewish population, and several massacres of innocent victims followed.

Clement VI's successor, Pope Innocent VI himself did his best to achieve peace between England and France during the 'so called' 100 years war, and wrote to the Duke of Lancaster: 'Although we were born in France and although for that and other reasons we hold the realm of France in special affection, yet in working for peace we have put aside our private prejudices and tried to serve the interests of everyone'.

Urban V himself, under the influence of don Juan Fernández de Heredia, is described as the most austere of the Avignon popes after Benedict XII and probably the most spiritual of them all. However, he was no strategist and made substantial concessions to the French crown especially in matters of finance, a crucial issue during the war with England.

The most influential decision of the reign of Pope Gregory XI (1370-78), also very much under the influence of don Juan Fernández de Heredia, was the return to Rome in 1378, but he was to die in that same year. In his decision to return, the Pope was also heavily influenced by Catherine of Siena, later canonised, who had preached for that very return.

Although Pope Gregory XI was also French born, and still strongly influenced by the French King, the increasing conflict between factions both friendly and hostile to the Pope posed a threat to the Papal lands and to the allegiance of Rome itself. When the Papacy established an embargo against grain exports during a food scarcity in 1374/75, Florence organised several cities into a league against the Papacy: Milan, Bologna, Perugia, Pisa, Lucca and Genoa. The papal legate, Robert de Geneva, a relative to the House of Savoy, against the advice of don Juan Fernández de Heredia, pursued a particularly ruthless policy against the league to re-establish control over these cities. He persuaded Pope Gregory to hire Breton mercenaries. To quell an uprising of the inhabitants of the Italian city of Cesena he hired the Englishman John Hawkwood, who had the majority of the people in the city massacred (between 2500 and 3500 people were reported dead). Following such events opposition against the Papacy obviously strengthened. Florence came out openly against the Pope in a conflict called 'the war of the eight saints' in reference to the eight city-states in Italy involved. The entire city of Florence was excommunicated and in reply, the export of clerical taxes was stopped. Trade was seriously hampered and both sides had to find a solution.

Don Juan Fernández de Heredia was the Admiral of the Pope's Fleet when they returned to Rome, but the voyage was a rather 'stormy' one, and , perhaps as an omen of things to come, it took three months to reach Italy from southern France so that they entered Rome on 17 January 1377. Don Juan Fernández de Heredia was Pope Gregory XI's Standard Bearer when they entered the Gate of St. Paul in the imperial city. On 24 September 1377, Pope Gregory XI made him Grand Master of the Order of the Knights of St. John of Jerusalem and Rhodes, notwithstanding the fact that he had only visited Rhodes for a few months, prior to his nomination as Grand Master.

Figure 18
Miniature of Juan Fernández de Heredia, Knight of the Order of St. John of Jerusalem, characteristically within the first letter of the text, portrayed as a Soldier. His sword is clearly visible, and so is his characteristic *barba bifurcata*, or forked beard (picture taken from *Grant Corónica de los Conquiridores* II, by Juan Fernández de Heredia. (*Biblioteca Nacional de Madrid*, MS. 10134 bis)

One of his first tasks from Rome was to stop the Turks advancing from the east. In eastern Europe, as early as 1335, the Turkish Sultan Murad I, had become the master of at least six key Balkan cities, and commanded four-fifths of the former Roman highway from Constantinople to Belgrade.

Within a generation Murad I had raised the Ottoman state of his fathers into an empire destined to endure as a powerful force in the world until the First World War. He became concerned that life in the conquered Christian territories should continue under Islam with as little social and economic disruption as possible. The Orthodox Church Patriarch himself testified in a letter to the Pope written in 1385 that the Sultan had allowed his Church considerable liberty of action earning Murad I the soubriquet – the 'Tolerant Sultan'.

Nevertheless, the Turkish threat was real and was getting worse. The Grand Master of St. John was among the first to realize just how serious this Turkish threat was to Western Powers and the Church. So don Juan Fernández de Heredia, left Naples with a small fleet and some allies from Florence, but in the meantime Pope Gregory XI had died in Rome, and the new elected Pope Urban VI was slower than don Juan expected in sending more troops and galleys, probably from Venice. Don Juan and his Florentine allies fell into a trap, and were taken prisoner by the terrible Ghin Boua Spata in Albania, with the complicity of the mercenary leader from Serbia Preljubovich. The plan to re-conquer the region of Morea had failed. The Grand Master of St. John spent some time in jail, one year according to some but up to three years according to others, and the experience must have been rather unpleasant. There is more than circumstantial evidence that he was sodomized. In his writings years later, ne wrote: 'to sodomize your captives is a local custom of the infidels'.

That was his biggest military fiasco, and was an omen of worse things to come for Christendom in that part of the world. In fact, on Murad I's assassination in the famous battlefield of Kossovo, his elder son, Bayezid I, was instantly proclaimed his successor. His first act as Sultan, over his father's dead body, was to order the death by strangulation with a bowstring of his own younger brother. This cruel and abominable practice of 'imperial fratricide' was to establish itself permanently in the history of the Ottoman dynasty.

Bayezid I, 'The Thunderbolt', arrogantly declared that he would ride to Rome and would feed his horse with oats on the altar of St Peter's. He challenged King Sigismund of Hungary, who, with the help and support of the 'intermittently mad' King Charles VI of France, declared a new Crusade against the Ottomans. The western knights, who might be considered the last

Crusaders, enjoyed a few minor victories and camped near the city of Nicopolis, without any sign of an invading Turkish army. With no enemy to fight, they relaxed, enjoying the women and the wine. Suddenly Bayezid's troops appeared. It was 1396, the year don Juan Fernández de Heredia died in Avignon.

At the battle of Nicopolis, the Christian Knights, the English under the banner of St George and the French under the banner of 'Our Lady', were heavily defeated. At least ten thousand men died on the Christian side. Next day Bayezid, inspecting the battlefield, ordered a general massacre of prisoners.

The French Knight, the Comte de Nevers, was forced to stand beside the Sultan to watch his keeling companions at arms roped together and beheaded one by one.

Don Juan Fernández de Heredia probably never forgave Pope Urban VI for not sending them help earlier and he joined a number of Cardinals of the Conclave when they refused to recognise the validity of the election of the new Pope. They claimed that the Italian Cardinals *en masse* had cheated when electing Urban VI, and therefore proceeded to elect another Pope – Clement VII. This caused a Schism in the Catholic Church which was not solved by the premature death of Clement VII, back in Avignon with don Juan Fernández de Heredia. A new Pope, later styled the 'Anti-Pope', was chosen named Benedict XIII and nicknamed *Papa Luna*.

Benedict XIII, last of the schismatic anti-popes of Avignon was also born in Aragon but there is no evidence that his election was in any way due to don Juan Fernández de Heredia. With the gradual collapse of support for his papacy, in 1415 he walled himself up until his death in 1423, in the Castle of Peñiscola, near Castellón (north of Valencia), a beautiful fourteenth century castle, well worth a visit.

There are still many unanswered questions about don Juan Fernández de Heredia, but in my view the two most important ones are:

1.) how did he ever become a Knight of St. John if, as most scholars believe, he was probably the illegitimate son of a nobleman?
2.) why did he buy the Castle of Mora de Rubielos for his only, albeit illegitimate, son?

His origins are probably rather humble. According to some, he was born somewhere in *Bajo Aragon* near Albarracin, Teruel or, according to others, near Calatayud (in the village of Muniebraga). He was probably the second son of don Lorenzo Fernández de Heredia, whose ancestors had fought and died with King Pedro II (*El Católico*) in the Albigiensian Crusade in the south east of France.

Nobody has yet found out who don Juan's mother was, nor his precise date of birth. Neither has anyone yet found or reported any legal document to legitimise his noble birth. I have searched through as many documents as I can find, comparing the legal signatures of the time, and I have failed to find any evidence for a legally authentic legitimacy of don Juan's noble origins. Thus, while everybody seems to agree that he was of noble descent, no-one has a proven explanation as to how he joined the Order of St. John when to do so, it was mandatory to be of noble or aristocratic origin.

Perhaps unlikely although not improbable, is the possibility that, in the midst of the chaotic situation in which the Temple now found itself, some rebel Templar Knights had continued their more esoteric and ritualistic conclaves in some 'Secret Castle' where they could give vent to their frustrations for the most serious and outrageous injustice they had suffered.

It is possible that a number of them still hoped that the set-back was only temporary, and that a future Pope might return to them both their dignity and worldly possessions. *Mientras hay Vida hay Esperanza*, or 'As long as there is Life there is Hope', says the Spanish Proverb.

If such 'Secret Castle' ever existed, it was probably in just such a place as Mora de Rubielos. Up in the Aragonese *Meseta*, on the way to the inhospitable Sierras of Teruel, it was out of reach for most people. It is therefore tempting to speculate that a tough, shrewd young man, born the illegitimate son of a nobleman, may have been protected and educated by sympathetic Templars who, having communicated to him their signs, secrets and tokens, facilitated his subsequent entrance into the fraternal Order of St. John.

At this time the Castle having lost all of its strategic importance, was probably not regularly inhabited because the war with Islam in the region was over. It re-established some strategic importance during the war between the Kingdom of Castile, ruled by King Pedro I of Castile (ruled 1350-69), and the Kingdom of Aragon, ruled by Pedro IV. This was, not surprisingly called *La Guerra de los Pedros* – the War between the Peters, which lasted, in various phases, between 1356 and 1375. Pedro I of Castile was not a nice enemy. He was known as 'The Cruel', murdered several people with his own hands, locked up his wife Blanca in the Fortress of Siguenza (now converted into a beautiful *Parador Nacional*, or National Hostel near Guadalajara), and ended up being assassinated in the city of Montiel by his half-brother Enrique.

The first serious attempt to bring both of the great kingdoms of Spain, together with Navarra, under the same crown was achieved, about one hundred years later by the marriage between Queen Isabel of Castile and

Fernando of Aragon. In 1363, the Castilian troops succeeded in penetrating far into Aragonese territory and took Mora de Rubielos, and its castle, by siege, with no significant military resistance. However, one year later, on 11 April 11 1364, while don Juan Fernández de Heredia was already in Avignon with the Pope, the Castle and the city were taken back from Castile by troops led by Captain Juan de las Montañas de Prades in the name of King Pedro IV of Aragon. The document of surrender by the troops of Castile, and the Charter of Privileges given by Pedro IV to the citizens of Mora de Rubielos on that day, make it clear that the people of Mora de Rubielos felt 'Aragonese', rather than 'Castilian'; that the witnesses of the agreement were a certain Knight called don Pedro Fernández de Arenoso and the squire Gonzalvo Pérez de Resa. The Charter was sealed in the Name of God and the Cross, and the 'Four Holy Gospels'.

It is therefore possible that the young don Juan Fernández de Heredia, unable to enter directly the 'safer' Order of St. John because of his illegitimate birth, was initiated by some 'rebel' Knights Templar in either 1327 or 1328, when he was just seventeen or eighteen, according to some accounts, or already twenty-one according to others. His actual date of birth is reputed to be a few years earlier than the 'official' 1310. According to the historian Josep Vives, who has made great study of de Heredia, he was made a Knight of St John in 1328 but the only documents available today indicate that he started his 'official' life in the Order of St. John much later, in 1333, when he joined the *Comendador* of Alfambra, and later that of Villel. It is of interest to us that both the Commanderies of Alfambra and Villel had in fact been part of the Temple, before they were given to St. John.

In contemporary Freemasonry, a Master Mason is exhorted to 'complete his Third Degree' by being Exalted into Royal Arch Masonry, a 'degree' suffused with Judaic concepts and frequently referred to as the 'essence of Freemasonry'.

The content of this degree, based on the allegorical story of three Master Masons from Babylon who, having heard that the Jews were about to rebuild the first Temple at Jerusalem, to the honour and glory of the Most High, which had been destroyed by the Babylonians of Nebuzaradan under Nebuchadnezzar, decided to assist in that great and glorious undertaking. In doing so, they accidentally dug into a vault of the ancient Temple. They discovered a pair of pillars of exquisite design and workmanship, and further on another six pairs of pillars of equal symmetry and beauty, which, from their position, appeared to have supported the roof of a subterranean passage leading to where the Most Holy Place in the Temple formerly stood.

Also by accident – according to the *Aldersgate Ritual* – that which at first appeared to be solid rock proved to be a compact piece of masonry wrought in the form of a dome. Aware of who had been the Architect of the former Temple and that no part thereof had been constructed in vain, the three Master Masons determined to examine it further, for which purpose they wrenched forth two of the Arch stones, when a Vault of considerable magnitude appeared to view.

While reading this ritual, I recalled the vault that I had found at the bottom of the South-West Tower of the Castle of Mora de Rubielos, which had an Equilateral Triangle on depicted on its eastern stone wall (*see* Figure 4, Ch 1). The 'All Seeing Eye' within the Equilateral Triangle is also reproduced on the, One Dollar bill of the U.S.A. (*see* Figure 19), presumed by some to be of Masonic origin.

Figure 19
One dollar U.S. bill, the most famous banknote in the world,
with the All-Seeing Eye symbol at the top of a pyramid.

Two of the three Master Masons – the ancient ritual explains – tied a strong cord or lifeline round the body of the third Master Mason and he was duly lowered into the vault.

On arriving at the bottom he felt something like the base or pedestal of a column, with certain characters engraven thereon, but for the want of light he was unable to decipher the meaning. He then found with his left hand an ancient scroll of vellum or parchment, containing the first words promulgated by Moses at the foot of Mount Horeb in the Wilderness of Sinai. The possession of this precious treasure stimulated them to enlarge the aperture of the Vault by removing the 'keystone', and the Master Mason descended as before.

The sun by this time darted its rays with meridian splendour into the vault, and this time he saw in the centre of the Vault a block of white marble, wrought in the form of the altar of incense, a double cube, on the top of which was a plate of gold – white being an emblem of innocence, and gold of purity. When these findings by the three Master Masons were communicated to the Three Principals of the Royal Arch Lodge, the First Principal, the Most Excellent Zerubbabel, explained:

> 'At the building of King Solomon's Temple – completed around 957 BC – vast numbers of masons were employed, and their names or marks were found engraven on some part or other of the building, but the names of the three Grand Masters who presided over the building were nowhere to be found, until they were discovered accidentally by the three Master Masons engraved on the front of the altar. There was likewise the 'Triple Tau' on the altar. The Tau is that sacred mark or sign spoken of by the angel, whom the prophet Ezekiel saw in the spirit when it was said: "Go through the midst of Jerusalem, and set a mark on the foreheads of the men that sigh and that cry for all the abominations that be done in the midst thereof", by which mark they were saved from amongst those who were slain for their idolatry by the wrathful displeasure of the Most High.'

In ancient times this mark was placed upon those who were acquitted by their judges in proof of their innocence, and military commanders caused it to be set on the foreheads of the men who returned unhurt from the field of battle, denoting that they were in perfect life. For this reason it has ever been considered a mark or sign of life. The First Principal of a Royal Arch Chapter continues thus:

> 'On this plate of gold are a Triangle and a Circle. These mathematical figures have ever been selected as referring to the Deity, or some Divine attribute. The Equilateral Triangle has long been considered a Sacred symbol. The Circle is an emblem of Eternity, for as it has neither beginning nor end, it may justly be deemed emblematic of God, who is without beginning of days or end of years. Finally, on the plate of gold is that great, awful, tremendous and incomprehensible Name of the Most High...'

We cannot know for sure whether something resembling this ancient ritual was used in the fourteenth century as part of admission to the Royal Arch, and therefore achieve eligiblity for installation as a Knight of the Temple.

It is curious however that the same (or similar) symbols, and in particular the triangle and circle were adopted as powerful symbols in alchemy and gold was the material object of the 'Philosopher's Stone', the result of alchemical transformation (*see* Figure 20). In the Spanish Middle Ages, during the rule of Islam, Alchemy was widely practised and taught in esoteric circles from Cordova to Teruel.

Figure 20
The Equilateral Triangle within the Circle in ALCHEMY. The smaller triangles have different meanings. Those pointing down (inferior vertex) were symbols of 'WATER', and those pointing up (superior vertex) were symbols of 'FIRE'. (I found this drawing in a pottery shop in Teruel, decorating a typical vase painted in green and white colours)

As already explained in chapter 2, the Castle of Mora de Rubielos, is not only full of Stone Marks, some of them runic and others alchemic, but has a South-East Tower, that goes back to the twelfth or early thirteenth centuries, that has no windows and goes down by a mysterious 'winding staircase' into a bottom 'Temple', presided over by a large Equilateral Triangle on the East. Another, more direct but more dangerous way to descend to this bottom Temple, was through a hole in the Vault.

This could only be done with the help of a rope, strong cord or lifeline round the body of the candidate for initiation, as explained in modern rituals. Presumably, the Candidate was lowered blindfold vertically from the Chapel, at ground-level, down three floors to the Temple Hall, to add to the mystery and drama of the ritual, prior to being given the privilege of Light or Initiation. The square hole on the Chapel's floor through which he was descended is still visible.

When King Solomon's Temple was destroyed in Jerusalem around 587 BC, it has been estimated that the total number of Israelites deported to Babylon was extremely large, between 500 thousand and one million. In 539 BC , the Persian King Cyrus released the Jews from their captivity, but according to the Roman historian Josephus only some fifty thousand returned under the leadership of Zerubbabel to their native land to rebuild the temple in Jerusalem.

This Second Temple was utterly destroyed again by Antiochus Epiphanes, brother of the King of Syria, in 169 BC Herod the Great, the father of Herod Antipas under whom Jesus was crucified, refurbished what remained of the Second Temple and built what was known as the Third Temple. Again, this was destroyed by the Romans under Titus in AD 70, as Jesus had predicted, following the Jewish Rebellion of 66 AD. The Romans could not be appeased, and relentlessly fought the Jews until their total expulsion from Israel.

It is not too hard to imagine a young and brave don Juan Fernández de Heredia being exalted as a Companion of the Royal Arch, by whatever ritual was employed in those days, to be later installed as a 'Knight Templar'. Again we are totally ignorant of the exact rituals in those days, but modern 'Knight Templar' rituals, as used in Freemasonry today, were deeply researched as far back as the eighteenth century. As far as I know, the first positive evidence of a 'Scottish' Templar degree being worked in modern times is that of 1769, and not in Scotland but in a lodge at Boston, Massachusetts (USA). The ritual was probably introduced into the USA from France or the Netherlands. Fuller accounts of the birth, life and death (around the 1790s) of the Rite of the Strict Observance by Baron Karl Gotthelf von Hund, who had become a Freemason about 1742 in Paris, are to be found in the six volumes of R.F. Gould's *History of Freemasonry*.

What matters to us is that this 'Initiation in to Chivalry', or Installation as Knight Templar, is calculated to impress the mind of the candidate deeply. If properly conducted, and in the appropriate environment, these rituals can truly change the person, and his life by inculcating the basic principles of chivalry and in this case the essence of the mystery of Jesus, the Holy Trinity and our own death.

In modern rituals, the Eminent Preceptor, or Past Preceptor, of a Preceptory, or Lodge of Knights Templar, explains to the Novice that he was first, as a trial of his faith and humility, asked to perform a symbolic pilgrimage for seven years, to represent the pilgrimage of life, through which we are all passing, for we are all weary pilgrims.

The Novice is then asked, as a trial of his courage and constancy, to perform seven more years of warfare. This represents the constant warfare with the lying vanities and deceits of this world, in which it is necessary for us to be engaged. Then, the Novice is asked for one year of penance, as a further trial of his faith and humility.

> 'Let the emblem of life (the light of a candle) and death (a skull) which lie before you, in the darkness of this Holy Temple – proclaims the Eminent Preceptor surrounded by the Knights Templar of the Preceptory and their Chaplain – remind you of the uncertainty of our earthly existence and teach you to be prepared for the closing hour of your mortal life; and rest assured that a firm faith in the truths revealed to us will afford you consolation in the gloomy hours of dissolution, and ensure your ineffable and eternal happiness in the world to come'.

Later on the Eminent Preceptor asks the Novice to repeat the following words with him:

> 'May the spirit which once inhabited this skull rise up and testify against me, if ever I wilfully violate my obligation as a Knight Templar; and may my light be extinguished among men as was of Judas Iscariot for betraying his Lord and Master and as I now extinguish this light'.

The impact of these words, symbols and allegorical ritual, is and should be life-long, and it would be a good reason for don Juan Fernández de Heredia to buy the 'Secret Castle' in 1370 for his only son, the illegitimate Juan Fernández de Heredia II. This secret bond with the Castle of Mora de Rubielos would give us the answer to our second question.

It was probably not just his lifelong love and passion for his native land of Aragon that led him in 1367 to engineer a complex financial operation, that lasted some three years, for the purchase of Mora de Rubielos in favour of his half-brother Don Blasco Fernández de Heredia, who paid for the village and the small village the very considerable sum of 260,000 pounds of the time (*libras barcelonesas*).

It was mainly because the 'Secret Castle' meant a lot to him, emotionally and spiritually, that don Juan Fernández de Heredia engineered such a complex financial transaction, through his half-brother, with the complicity also of the Viscount of Cardona and of the King Pedro IV himself. In this way, he would not be blamed for breaking two 'mundane rules' to which he was theoretically obliged by the Order: Chastity and Poverty.

Why he paid such a high sum is not known for sure but it is tempting to speculate that he already knew, because of the Templar connection, and his knowledge of the Masonic secrets of the Castle and *Colegiata* at Mora de Rubielos, as well as his deep knowledge of the rituals and ceremonies, the fact that after their final demise all of the properties belonging to the former Knights Templar, together with their Archives, would be confiscated, destroyed or sold.

Being Grand Master of the Order of St. John, he was unable to own any property in his own name (everything he owned belonged to the Order, rather than to himself), so he helped his extended family, and set one singular condition for the inheritance of Mora de Rubielos uponn future generations: all of his offspring with a claim to such a bountiful gift, were required to change their first name to Juan. A little condescending vanity, perhaps. But don Juan Fernández de Heredia was a remarkable man, though no saint. He had several mistresses during his life, and as a soldier killed more than once.

On one occasion, while rescuing a Venetian Knight in the Greek city of Patrás, he beheaded the Turkish leader of the fortress with a single and swift blow of his sword. Perhaps to expiate all of his mortal sins, he also left a lot of money to the Monastic Order of St. Francis of Assisi, which he really admired, with the agreement that whenever his dynasty was in future unable to keep the Castle, then the control of the same would fall to the Franciscans Monks.

Juan Fernández de Heredia also left vast amounts of money to his family to repair and virtually rebuild the Castle in the late fourteenth century so that it soon lost its former role as a fortress. Since the victory over Islam it began to assume its present image and status as a Castle-Palace of the Gothic-Spanish Renaissance style.

We also know that he was devoted to the cults of both the Virgin Mary and St. Michael. Curiously, it turns out that St. Michael was, and still is, the Patron Saint of Mora. St Michael, the Sacred Hermes of the Templars, is often depicted fighting the evil Satan, or weighing the souls of Jews, Muslims and Christians with the metaphysical scales of good and evil.

Tragically, all of the personal archives of don Juan Fernández de Heredia and his family at Mora de Rubielos, were burnt in the year 1700, when the castle/palace was already inhabited and controlled by Franciscan monks.

His life is full of anecdotes. One rather charming one is that he fought bravely at the battle of Crecy in 1346, and, after being wounded at least four times, gave his own horse to the King of France, Philippe VI de Valois so that he might escape from the English. They were so upset that they captured and imprisoned the badly wounded Juan Fernández de Heredia. He, however, being of such high lineage and held in great regard, King Edward III of England gave the order to set him free, with full honours.

He was also a prolific writer, and although many of his works have been lost, some (for example, *Cartulario magno de la Orden de San Juan de Jerusalén*, in six beautiful fourteenth century volumes) may still be found in public libraries such as the *Archivo Histórico Nacional* in Madrid.

Other written works (or at least 'supervised' by him) included the first *Marco Polo* in Europe, the *Book of the Emperors* (*Libro de los Emperadores*), *Thucydides*, *La Crónica de Morea*, *Flor de las ystorias de Orient* (translated from the original French work written by Haytón de Gorigos in 1307), where the author posits an interesting military alliance between the Christian and the Mongols (Tartars) to fight Islam and re-conquer Jerusalem.

One of most impressive literary achievements of the Grand Master of St. John was the re-discovery for western culture of the Roman classical writer and historian Plutarch, who lived *circa* 100 AD. One of the historical characters that Plutarch described in depth was Alexander the Great, who had lived almost 250 years before. Alexander died at the young age of thirty-three having conquered most of what was the then civilized world. Among the many anecdotes explained by Plutarch regarding this military genius are the following:

Representatives of the Greeks assembled at Corinth and named the young Alexander as leader in a war against Persia. While he was at Corinth, politicians and philosophers came to congratulate him, but he noticed that the famous Corinthian philosopher Diogenes, was distinguished by his absence. Alexander went to visit Diogenes at his home and found him lying down, sun-bathing. Diogenes raised himself up a little when he heard the crowd approaching, and Alexander asked the philosopher very courteously if there was any favour a king could do for him. Diogenes only said: 'Yes, please take your shadow off me'.

Alexander's companions, on the way back, were making fun of the simple-minded old man, but Alexander told them: 'Laugh if you must, but if I were not Alexander I would choose to be Diogenes'.

Between 30,000 and 43,000 infantry and between 3,000 and 4,000 horsemen followed Alexander into Asia Minor in 334 BC. He had only seventy talents for their pay, and no more than thirty days' provisions. He was also 200 talents in debt, having spent everything he had in making sure that his best men were able to provide for their families. When one of his generals asked what he had kept for himself, Alexander answered: 'My hope', whereupon the general promptly refused the pension that Alexander offered him, saying: 'Your soldiers will be your partners in that'.

Armed with such desire and determination, Alexander and his army crossed the Hellespont into Asia and came at length to Troy. At the tomb of Achilles, who was his ancestor on his mother's side, Alexander anointed the gravestone with oil and then ran around it naked with his companions, according to ancient custom.

Achilles, he said, was a lucky man to have had a good friend while he was alive and a good poet (Homer) to preserve his memory after he was dead.

Figure 21
Miniature of Juan Fernández de Heredia, as Grand Master of the Order of the Knights of St. John of Jerusalem and Rhodes. (Picture from *Grant crónica de Espanya*, I, *Biblioteca Nacional de Madrid*, MS 10133, *folium* 1)

The above portrait portrays de Heredia (characteristically within the first letter (E) of the text), as a 'Wizard'. This is probably why his Maltese Cross is no longer visible – probably erased by the Inquisitors. Here he is again distinguished by his penetrating gaze, his characteristic *barba bifurcata*, and his fingers pointing solemnly upwards.

For many years Plutarch served as one of the two priests at the temple of Apollo at Delphi (the site of the famous Oracle), twenty miles from his home. By his writings and lectures Plutarch had become a celebrity in the Roman empire, despite which he continued to reside where he was born, and actively participated in local affairs, even serving as mayor.

At his country estate, guests from all over the empire congregated to engage in serious conversation, presided over by Plutarch in his marble chair. Many of these dialogues were recorded and published, and the seventy-eight essays and other works which have survived are now known collectively as the *Moralia*.

In the *Moralia*, Plutarch expresses a belief in reincarnation, unusual for a Roman of his day and age. His letter of consolation to his wife, after the death of their two-year-old daughter, gives us a glimpse of his philosophy:

> 'The soul, being eternal, after death is like a caged bird that has been released. If it has been a long time in the body, and has become tame by many affairs and long habit, the soul will immediately take another body and once again become involved in the troubles of the world. The worst thing about old age is that the soul's memory of the other world grows dim, while at the same time its attachment to things of this world becomes so strong that the soul tends to retain the form that it had in the body. But that soul which remains only a short time within a body, until liberated by the higher powers, quickly recovers its fire and goes on to higher things.'

I practised 'Pediatric Oncology' while training in London at the Royal Marsden Cancer Hospital, from 1984-86, and to witness a two year old baby dying from cancer, after months of chemotherapy or radiotherapy treatments and in front of its own parents, engenders an emotion that memory cannot erase. It requires words like those of Plutarch to overcome the pain and frustration.

Once Plutarch's judgment had been seasoned by old age, and his writing skill by long practice on his essays, he commenced the composition of his immortal *Parallel Lives*.

The Grand Master of St John, don Juan Fernández de Heredia, displayed a great thirst for knowledge, and used Plutarch's masterpiece as a pattern in both his own *Crónica de los Conquiridores*, and *La grant crónica de Espanya*. His personal collection of books and *Scriptorium* in his Avignon Palace was famous throughout Europe.

Well over the age of seventy, he was nevertheless still approached by kings and princes for copies of his precious manuscripts, it being remembered that these were the days before the invention of the printing press.

Although other Renaissance sources are often credited with the re-discovery of Plutarch, who was both mystic and historian, many reliable experts suggest that it was indubitably don Juan Fernández de Heredia who, between 1370-86 supervised the translation and copying of several of his works, including the famous *Parallel Lives* have since been found in the collections of either Simon Atumanos, son of an Ottoman and an Orthodox Christian lady, or to Dimitri Calodiqui (sometime between 1379-82).

Figure 22
Miniature of Juan Fernández de Heredia, Knight of the Order of St. John of Jerusalem. Again characteristically within the first letter of the text, portrayed as a Scholar. His Cross of Malta is this time clearly visible, and so is his characteristic *barba bifurcata*, and an Open Book. (Picture taken from *Grant crónica de Españya* III, *Biblioteca Nacional de Madrid*, MS. 10134)

According to Lutrell (Oxford University) it was actually a certain Nicolau, Archbishop of Drenopolis, who eventually translated, under don Juan Fernández de Heredia, Plutarch from the Greek into colloquial 'Aragonese' around 1380.

It is difficult to classify the *Parallel Lives* as history, biography, or philosophy.

These timeless studies of humanity are truly in a class by themselves. Plutarch's Greek heroes (including 'Alexander the Great') had been dead for at least 250 years by the time he wrote their lives (*c*.100 AD). Plutarch therefore had to rely on old manuscripts, most of which are no longer available today.

Plutarch's spiritual beliefs are also difficult to classify. They were original and ahead of his Roman times. He believed in one unitary god, with different names for its different aspects. In between god and mortal men, Plutarch believed that there was an infinite hierarchy of other beings, who were subject to death and rebirth but on longer cycles. Inasmuch as they had not completely purged all of their passions, these spiritual beings had weaknesses such as anger. Men could be promoted into angels, and angels could be demoted into men, according to how they had lived their previous lives.

At the beginning of the Renaissance, it was likely the rediscovery of Plutarch's *Lives* that stimulated popular interest in the classics. 'Epitomes', which hit the highlights of the best stories and were written in Tuscan (the most ancient Italian language) and other local dialects, circulated as popular literature.

Military men and rich merchants took time to read the popularized Plutarch for its practical wisdom, and thus the *Lives* not only survived, but became a huge hit all over Europe during the Renaissance. The first French edition, however, had to wait until 1559 when Sir Thomas North prepared the first full English edition of Plutarch's *Lives* as late as1579.

There are many examples of the great influence of Plutarch on Shakespeare: Coriolanus, Julius Caesar , Anthony and Cleopatra, and Timon of Athens, are good examples. Characters having Plutarchean names are also found in 'A Midsummer Night's Dream', 'Pericles' , and The Winter's Tale by this greatest of all English writers.

Many artists have found comfort in Plutarch's wisdom. Beethoven, for example, growing deaf, wrote in 1801: 'I have often cursed my Creator and my existence. Plutarch has shown me the path of resignation . If it is at all possible, I will bid defiance to my fate, though I feel that as long as I live there will be moments when I shall be God's most unhappy creature ... Resignation, what a wretched resource! Yet it is all that is left to me.'

He was also a favourite author in the Military Academia. Facing death in Khartoum, the famous British Commander General Gordon took time to note: 'Certainly I would make Plutarch's *Lives* a handbook for our young officers'.

By the twentieth century, however, Plutarch's popularity began to fade. Professional classicists produced no revitalizing new edition of the Lives in modern English, and by the 1990s, classical studies had so declined in popularity that a riot at Stanford University in California, featured thousands of the top students in the United States proclaiming the end of western culture, and chanting the battle cry of the new 'creed' :

'Hey Hey, Ho Ho, Western Culture's Got To Go.'

Plutarch's heroes had apparently no place in this 'brave new world' of 'fast food' and even 'faster words', of grey equality populated by Hollywood stars, rock or pop music groups, famous sportsmen and other 'puppets of money'.

A modern new world, strangely resentful of elitism and eminence, while indulgent in sexual customs and the abuse of drugs and alcohol. Moreover, as will be discussed again in Chapter 10, all discrimination between good and evil was actively suppressed among the twentieth century intellectuals. For there was no good or evil, there was neither Heaven nor Hell, there was no longer any chance of a 'Last Judgement'.

In the oft quoted words by Simone Weil:

'The essential characteristic of the first half of the twentieth century is the growing weakness, and almost the disappearance, of the idea of Value'.

But, I would add, that the second half of the twentieth century was even worse.

While writing this book, I have done my very best always to remember the wise advice of Plutarch regarding 'History':

'My intention is not to write histories, but lives. Sometimes small incidents, rather than glorious exploits, give us the best evidence of character. So, as portrait painters are more exact in doing the face (where the character is revealed) than the rest of the body, I must be allowed to give my more particular attention to the marks of the souls of men. By these, rather than the historical events they participated in, I try to portray their lives. I leave the task of a more complete historical chronicle to others'.

Don Juan Fernández de Heredia, who was rather long-lived for his times, died at the very respectable age of eighty-six, and must have been as highly regarded by friends and foes alike. For example, he is said to have been a true polyglot with a sure mastery of seven different languages, including Hebrew, Arab, Latin and Greek, as well as being an expert in ancient History and Philosophy.

He died peacefully in his own bed, and was laid to rest in a grandiose carved tomb in the beautiful *Colegiata* he had created for the Order of St. John in the small town of Caspe in Aragon, now almost abandoned. Nobody knows exactly why he chose Caspe as his burial site.

One hypothesis is that it was in Caspe that he entered the Order of St. John. Whether he did so by initiation as a novice, or whether he became incorporated into the Hospitallers from a secret lodge of Knights Templar, during the chaotic period in the Kingdom of Aragon, between *circa* 1310 and 1335, prior to their natural physical extinction, as I personally believe, remains hypothetical.

My visit to Caspe, not far from Zaragoza, to visit whatever remains of his burial ground was a great disappointment. This small city has lost most of its ancient splendour and is, from the architectural and historical points of view, a rather sad and uninspiring place. The remains of the Grand Masters's skeleton are said to be buried outside the Church of St. Mary, under a second century AD Roman Arch that was taken deliberately from several miles away but which is of very doubtful relevance.

A modern, and rather ugly, statue of don Juan standing up with a book in his hands is virtually all there is to see.

Figure 23
Modern statue of Don Juan Fernández de Heredia (holding a book) just outside the fourteenth century Colegiata de Santa María la Mayor in Caspe (Teruel).

Selected Bibliography

49. Anthony Luttrell. Juan Fernández de Heredia at Avignon 1351-1367. *Studia Albornotiana*, XI, Bologna (*Real Colegio de España en Bolonia*), 1962.

50. Regina af Geijerstam, *J. Fernández de Heredia. La Grant Cronica de Espanya, Libros I-II, edición según el manuscrito 10133 de la Biblioteca Nacional de Madrid*, Uppsala 1964.

51. Juan Manuel Cacho Blecua, *El Gran Maestre Juan Fernández de Heredia, Caja de Ahorros de la Inmaculada de Aragón, Colección 'Mariano de Pano y Ruata* (Zaragoza, 1997).

52. Aurora Egido & José Maria Enguita (eds), *Juan Fernández de Heredia y su Época, Insitución 'Fernando el Católico'* (Zaragoza 1996).

53. Jean Gilkinson Mackenzie, *A Lexicon of the 14th century Aragonese Manuscripts of Juan Fernández de Heredia* (Madison, Hispanic Seminary of Medieval Studies, 1984).

54. Lord Kinross, *The Ottoman Centuries: The Rise and Fall of the Turkish Empire* (Morrow Quill Paperbacks, New York 1977).

55. Canellas A., *'Algunos signos regios, eclesiásticos, notariales y privados medievales aragoneses'* In: *Graphische Symbole in mittelalterlichen Urkunden* (*Beitrage zur diplomatischen Semiotik*), *Herausgegeben von Meter Rück*(Jan Thorbecke Verlag Sigmaringen, 1996).

56. Gould, R.F., *History of Freemasonry* (six volumes, Poole's 1951 edition, London).

57. Richard Weiss, *Lo studio di Plutarco nel Trecento. La parola del passato* (Milano 1953).

58. Giovanni Di Stefano, *'La d'ecouverte de Plutarque en Occident: aspects de la vie intellectuelle en Avignon au XIVe siècle'* In: *Memoria dell'Accademia delle scienze di Torino*, 4, Vol. 18, 1968.

Chapter four

Teruel Exists

'Teruel exists!', says a recent slogan recently in vogue in Spain, to point out to all Spanish citizens that this little province, far to the south of Aragon between Valencia and Zaragoza, does exist, though it seems to have been forgotten by the rest of Spain, and the Modern World.

Part one

The multicultural historical background of Teruel

The little town of Teruel takes its name from the arab *Tirwal* which meant 'Castle' and which was re-conquered by Christian forces in 1171 by Alfonso II, King of Aragon, aided by his troops and the Military and Religious Orders of the Temple and St. John of Jerusalem. As crusaders they required no long journey to the Middle East to fight the infidels. Islam was in Spain, and in some parts of Spain it remained for nearly nine centuries.

When the *reconquista* of Teruel took place, the king decided to attract as many Christian dwellers as possible. This colonisation of the territories was not easy because of the poverty of the land, harsh and infertile conditions, scarcity of water for irrigation and extreme weather. It is therefore unsurprising that many of the inhabitants had escaped from far worse places. A classic example was that of the Albigiensians, who came down from the *Langue d'Oc* in South Eastern France during the so-called 'Albigiensian Crusade' against the Cathar Heresy, which started in 1208.

The town of Teruel occupies an isolated plateau, on a *Meseta*, or 'table shaped' plateau, characteristic of Spain. It is part of its geographical and geological characteristics that the land, especially in the centre and along its eastern coast, rises from sea level to a plateau, or *Meseta*, around 1000 metres above sea level. The landscape is fairly dry and similar all over, and it is reminiscent of the not too distant *Meseta* of *La Mancha*, made universally famous by the figure of *Don Quixote*, created in the sixteenth century by the greatest of Spanish writers, don Miguel de Cervantes.

> 'In a village of *La Mancha* – starts the story of *Don Quixote* – the name of which I have no desire to call to mind, there lived not long since one of those gentlemen that keep a lance in the lance-rack, an old buckler, a lean hack, and a greyhound for coursing. An *olla* of rather more beef than mutton, a salad on most nights, scraps on Saturdays, lentils on Fridays, and a pigeon or so extra on Sundays, made away with three-quarters of his income. The rest of it went in a doublet of fine cloth and velvet breeches and shoes to match for holidays, while on week-days he made a brave figure in his best homespun…'

It is not difficult to imagine how in this type of rough and lonely land, isolated from the rest of the world, with clean air, blue skies, red and yellow hills, with steep slopes, *Sierras, Barrancos y Cañones*, with dry and warm summers but cold winters, with seas of yellow grain for harvesting in June or July, but barren and icy fields from October until March, the tendency for a cultivated mind, like that of *Don Quixote*, is to read and think about 'Good and Evil'.

> And that is exactly what happened to him:

> '… You must know, then, that the above-named gentleman whenever he was at leisure (which was mostly all the year round) gave himself up to reading books of chivalry with such ardour and avidity that he almost entirely neglected the pursuit of his field-sports, and even the management of his property; and to such a pitch did his eagerness and infatuation go that he sold many an acre of land to buy books of chivalry to read, and brought home as many of them as he could get.'

> 'But – continues the story;

> '... of all there were none he liked so well as those of the famous Feliciano de Silva's composition, for their lucidity of style and complicated conceits were as pearls in his sight, particularly when in his reading he came upon courtships and cartels, where he often found passages like "the reason of the unreason with which my reason is afflicted so weakens my reason that with reason I murmur at your beauty"; or again, "the high heavens, that of your divinity divinely fortify you with the stars, render you deserving of the desert your greatness deserves.'

Over conceits of this sort the poor gentleman lost his wits, and used to lie awake striving to understand them and worm the meaning out of them; what Aristotle himself could not have made out or extracted had he come to life again for that special purpose. Chivalry is part of the history of the land and, inevitably, so is 'Romantic Love'. In fact, the real Romeo and Juliet actually lived in Teruel.

In the early years of the thirteenth century, around 1217, the young Juan Diego Martinez de Marcilla and the beautiful Isabel de Segura lived in the town of Teruel, and their friendship soon turned into love. Refused by her family, because Juan Diego was not rich enough to marry her, the young man bravely decided to join the crusaders in Palestine and disappears for some five years. His promise to Isabel was that five years were long enough for him to become rich and famous and that was the length of time he asked her to wait. Having gone to war in the Middle-East, he returns to Teruel just a little bit too late. Isabel is in the process of getting married to the brother of the *Señor* of Albarracin – Juan Diego. Destroyed and despairing, Diego asks Isabel for just one kiss, but Isabel is now a married woman. She refuses.

Young Diego is found dead and the next day his funeral rites take place in the church of San Pedro. During the funeral, Isabel approaches the corpse to give him the last kiss she denied him in life. At that very moment, probably because she used the same poison as he, she also fell dead in front of everybody. The story is real. The remains of the unhappy pair lie in a side chapel in San Pedro Church close by the ancient Jewish Quarter. They rest in a splendid alabaster mausoleum, by the artist Juan de Avalos (*see* Figure 24).

Figure 24
The Lovers of Teruel, Juan Diego de Marcilla and Isabel de Segura.

Teruel was also famous during the late Middle Ages and Spanish Renaissance, for the cultural integration of Christianised Muslims, who created the *Mudejar* Style (*see* Figure 25), now in the World Heritage list of UNESCO, and by the commercial and cultural activities of Jews.

Spanish Jews, present in the Iberian peninsula ever since the destruction of the first Temple and their exile to Babylon, largely escaped the continent-wide persecution of their race which marked the first Christian Millenium, and the beginning of the First Crusade and which led to the expulsion of Jews from England in 1292, pogroms in Naples, Germany and other parts of Europe.

Under the Muslims, surprisingly, whom they were thought to have assisted in their conquest of Spain, the condition of the Jews was much better than under the Visigoths, or Germanic tribes who had invaded Spain and subsequently became fervent Christians. Most historians agree that in those days, many eminent Jews flourished under Islam, as merchants, physicians and philosophers. Their official language was Arabic, even if written in Hebrew characters. Until their expulsion in 1492, the Jews of Spain were the true middle class of Aragon and Castile. They were tax gatherers as well as tax payers. They were also advisers and physicians to many Monarchs and founded several schools of Jewish Mysticism or Kabbalah, especially in Catalonia (Barcelona and Girona), Castile (Leon and Toledo), and Aragon (Teruel). Their secret rites employed magic (*see* Figure 26) as well as religious and ritualistic content.

The real troubles for the Jews in Europe began in the eleventh century for a number of complex reasons, comprehensively reviewed by authors such as Gavin Langmuir, Kenneth Stow, Mark Cohen and Anna Sapir Abulafia, among others.

Foremost amongst these were Christian religious fervour, outright fanaticism and the idea that the Jews were guilty of Jesus's crucifixion, together with charges of usury engendered by the great fortunes amassed by a number of rich Jewish merchants – the whole leavened with a new species of intellectual rivalry between the literate Jews and the new European administrators, also called *literati* or *clerici*. Another cause of trouble in 1096, at the very start of the first (and only victorious) Crusade, was the direct responsibility of the Franks for the massive killing of Jews in the Rhineland (now the German cities of Ellen, Speyer and Worms), on their way to Byzantium, via Turkey and Syria to reach the promised land of Israel. These criminal activities were of course done '... in name of the Christian faith'. The linking of Jews to the Devil, Hell, the Last Judgement and Anti-Christ was particularly prevalent.

Over many centuries the percentage of Jews who were literate was significantly higher to the equivalent in Christian society. Judaism is not just a religion. It is also a way of life built around a book, the *Torah* or Bible. With the advent of medieval monasteries, books became an essential part of Christian intellectual life. Langmuir takes these ideas further by contrasting the religious ideology of three most prominent twelfth century churchmen: Peter the Venerable, Bernard of Clairvaux and Peter Abelard. Peter the Venerable hated Jews and wrote violent diatribes against them. The mystical ascetic Bernard, in many ways the ideological father of the Knights Templar, had no such attitude and protected the Jews from persecution during the run-up to the Second Crusade. Abelard had no qualms about confronting faith with reason and displayed sympathy for the Jews.

In the twelfth and thirteenth centuries a number of public challenges or 'Christian-Jewish Disputations' took place. Two of the most famous are the disputation of Ceuta (in Spanish Morocco), and the disputation of Barcelona.

In his book *Barcelona and beyond*, Chazan explains what happened at the public disputation of Barcelona in 1263, under the auspices, protection and patronage of King Jaume I of Aragon, and its aftermath. The representative of the Jewish community of Girona (north of Barcelona) was Ramban (also known as Nachmanides or Bonastruch Saporta). Just as in modern television debates or challenges, the public was attracted to these sorts of controversial event.

Ramban was a brilliant cabalistic scholar from the prestigious school of Girona, where one may still visit the remains of his school and the synagogues in the vicinity of the Cathedral. His opponent and challenger was a certain Dominican monk, called Pau or Fray Pul, who was a convert from Judaism. Dominicans were of course the instruments of the Inquisition. Their goal at the time was that they might convert Jews in Europe to Christianity by reason alone. Ramban's defence rested on the concept that the Messiah could not be a 'man', but must be 'the spirit of God'.

On another controversial point, Fray Pul asked the Jewish thinker and rabbi 'What is the Trinity?' Jews believing in but One God, have no room in their faith for a 'Trinity'. Fray Pul argued that Christians also believed in only One God, but that the Trinity was ' Wisdom, Will and Power'. At this point, the King offered an analogy which he had been taught, perhaps by his mentors at the Castle of Monzon (where he spent his tough infancy and early youth under the protection of the Knights Templar, following the death of his own father in the Albigensian Crusade). The King observed that there are three things found in wine – colour, taste and smell – and yet they are but one thing. Ramban disagreed with the argument, and Fray Pul then arose and declared that he believed in the real unity but that nevertheless it was threefold. He said further that it was a very profound matter which even the angels do not understand.

Ramban courageously, but perhaps unwisely, stood up and said: 'It is clear that man does not believe what he does not know. If so, the angels too cannot believe in the Trinity'. Fray Pul's friends prevented him from answering further, for they had already achieved what they wanted. Knights Templar, even in their contemporary obedience had to declare by oath their belief in the Holy Trinity even if the concept cannot be comprehended by human reason.

The King, who was the real 'moderator' of the debate, then stood and descended from the pulpit, and his party left the synagogue of Barcelona. On the following day, Ramban stood before the King, who deeply admired him. The King said to him: 'Return to your city (Girona), to life, and to peace' and then gave him three hundred *dinarim*. The respect was no doubt mutual, as Ramban never spoke against the King who defended him from subsequent actions taken against him by the Dominicans. Unfortunately, the debate was used against the Jews in Girona, and even Ramban (Nachmanides) was forced into exile, first in the south-east of France (*La Provence*), and then in Israel, where he died.

Figure 25
Mudejar Teruel, a rich and unique architectutal style invented and developed by Christianised Muslims, following the *Reconquista* of Aragon.

By the fifteenth century, the public had begun to dislike the Jews' high rates of usury while the Church looked on the rich synagogues and merchants' houses as valuable booty. Furthermore, the peasantry in Spain resented the 'Superiority Complex' displayed by the Jews in regarding themselves as God's Chosen People' while at the same time they were responsible for 'condemning his Son to die on the Cross'. Ferdinand, King of Aragon in the fifteenth century, and probably of Jewish blood himself, defended their rights more than did his wife Queen Isabel of Castile. In 1481, for example, when there had already been several minor pogroms in Spain, Ferdinand (*el Catòlic*) reproved the Prior of the Archbishop of Saragossa for his persecution of the Jews, saying openly that he regarded the Jews as 'our treasure chests'.

In 1492 a decree of expulsion was signed by the Catholic Kings, Ferdinand and Isabel. It was not a 'Final Solution', as later imagined by Hitler and executed by Himmler, but almost half a million Jews who lived and were born in Spain (*Sephardi*, according to their ancient tradition), were given the choice of abandoning Judaism, and becoming Christians, or leaving the country with whatever they could carry with them. There are, of course, neither official, nor for that matter, credible figures, but it is generally accepted that considerably more than half, preferred to remain in Spain, and became Christians, or at least simulated their new faith, giving rise to considerable underhand investigation by the Spanish Inquisition to say nothing of innumerable *Autos da Fè*. The families of the Christian mystic Saint Teresa and the previously mentioned Miguel de Cervantes, had Jewish blood. Others, more religious or wealthier, left for Amsterdam, Italy or the Ottoman Empire, where Byzantium had just fallen to Muslim rule (1453).

Jews, having been expelled from England in1292 were not however allowed back until the seventeenth century when Oliver Cromwell allowed them to return immediately after the English Civil War.

Figure 26

ABRACADABRA

the Magic Word best known by children around the world, had cabalistic origins. In the Middle Ages it was used as a charm having power to guard off ague when written in a triangular form (ABRAXAS stones were Cabbalistic symbols of the 365 Spirits of Basilides). I found this peculiar charm on a modern baked and glazed fine white clay adorned with the star of King David in a Teruel traditional pottery shop.

```
ABRACADABRA
ABRACADABR
ABRACADAB
ABRACADA
ABRACAD
ABRACA
ABRAC
ABRA
ABR
AB
A
```

Chapter four

Part two

The Cathar Heresy and why Satanael rules this world

It is just not possible to find any traces of 'Cathar Heresy' in Teruel. There are probably several reasons for this. It is clear that a certain number of Albigiensians took refuge (political asylum) in Teruel and nearby lands in the twelfth and thirteenth centuries, under the auspices of several Kings of Aragon, and, in particular, of Alfonso II , who conquered Teruel in 1171, *Pere el Catòlic* (Pedro II de Aragon), who died at the battle of Muret in 1213 precisely during the Albigiensian Crusade, his son Jaime I *El Conquistador* (1208-1276), who ruled for several decades and conquered Islamic Valencia from Teruel, and Pedro III of Aragón , who ruled for nine years (1276-1285) and was excommunicated by the Pope for daring to conquer Sicily.

But King Jaime I, left orphan after the battle of Muret and educated and raised by the Knights Templar in Monzón, was forced to accept the Inquisition, led by the fanatic Dominican monks, and by the monk Domingo de Guzmán, in particular.

Besides, it seems more than likely that the military efforts of the kings of Aragon, and Counts of Barcelona, across the Pyrenees in South East France, or Langue d'Oc and Provence, were not due to any special sympathy for the Cathar Heresy, but more due to their military ambition to retain a considerable proportion of what is today French Territory, under the banner of their Kingdom of Aragon, which included territories in Montpellier, Perpignan, Carcassone and important allies in Toulouse and the city of Albí.

Nevertheless, there are in Teruel several surnames of French origin that are likely to derive from the Albigienses. Bronchud, my maternal grandfather's surname, is one of them.

The third time I got to see the Castle at Mora de Rubielos, was in 1972, with the soccer team of Sarrión, the nearest village in Teruel's direction. I never played soccer, as my sport was basketball. I can pride myself on having been a more than average young basketball player: with Italian Awards (best player of my age, at the national basketball championship in 'Benevento',

Naples 1970), Spanish Awards (Champion of the Junior League in 1976), and University of Cambridge Awards ('Half Blue'). But my soccer skills were dreadful. However, during my summer holidays in 1972, several key soccer players of my age in Sarrión were injured or away from the pueblo. And the nearby rival pueblo of Mora de Rubielos had challenged us. Even if I was not a good player, the local priest, don Dionisio, who was also the coach of the soccer team, decided to ask me to play for them. I just could not say NO. I came from a family of 'vanquished', or *Rojos* as they called us contemptuously and scornfully because of the association between the Red Army and the Republican Forces, but this time they were really desperate, and I had the chance to proclaim 'my patriotism' for the pueblo by playing soccer with them against the rival pueblo of Mora de Rubielos.

Before the match, in Mora de Rubielos, the priest don Dionisio showed some sympathy for me, among other reasons because he knew that I lived and studied in Italy at the time, and he could practise his Italian learnt while visiting Rome as a seminarist. He took us to see the castle, that was no longer the Headquarters of the Guardia Civil, but was closed to visitors and in a state of pitiful ruin. I saw for the first time a part of the interior and the Cloister, through one of the multiple holes in the wall.

Following the match, that surprisingly we won 11 goals to 3, on the way back to Sarrión, don Dionisio sat next to me on the old and noisy *Pegaso* minibus, and started talking in his mixed Italian-Spanish.

He asked me whether I knew that my grandfather had been in that Castle as a prisoner of war, to which I replied that I did know. Then he asked me a totally unexpected question: 'Is Bronchud a Spanish surname?' – to which I answered that I honestly did not know, for the only Bronchuds I knew were very few close, and some not so close, relatives in Sarrión or Valencia. He said, with all the authority of the *Cura de Sarrión*, or Priest of our Church, that my surname came from France.

My father, driven by curiosity, had also investigated my mother's surname. In spite of his hypothesis that it must have come from Napoleon's troops who had fought near Zaragoza in the 1808-10 War of Independence, when Wellington's troops had suddenly become very popular among patriotic Spaniards, resentful of the French Invasion, my father could not find any solid evidence for this Napoleonic origin of the surname Bronchud, or 'Bronchoud' as it was often spelt. But don Dionisio said that the origins of this surname were much much older than Napoleon.

Don Dionisio thought the name came from the time of the Albigiensian

Crusade, back in the thirteenth century. Similar surnames, *Bronchard* or *Bronchat*, and others starting with *Bron* (or *Bon*) are also not uncommon in that region of south-east France. In a smile he added ironically, but happy for his 'discovery', that I was not only the grand-son of a *Rojo*, meaning a Republican, but perhaps also the descendant of some Medieval Heretics called the Cathars. He said it with some tenderness, and friendly words.

I was so intrigued by what don Dionisio said that day, by the way he said it, and by the Castle at Mora de Rubielos, that it became my 'Secret Castle'. One of my 'missions in life', my subconscious mind decided, was to find out the secrets of this Secret Castle. I started reading, at that time in Italian, about the 'Cathar Heresy' and the 'Albigiensian Crusade'.

Many years later, when I had already become a member of my Cambridge College Lodge of Freemasons, Caius Lodge, No. 3355 of the United Grand Lodge of England, named Caius (but pronounced like 'keys') after one of the founders of the College, Dr Caius, Physician to Queen Elizabeth I of England, and when I had been regularly initiated, passed and raised at Great Queen Street in London, and finally installed as Master of 'Caius' Lodge in Cambridge, I came across an astonishing poster at the entrance hall of the Castle of Mora de Rubielos (*see* Figure 27): a picture commemorating the death of Sir Steven Runciman, one of the world experts on the Cathars and Christian Dualistic Heresies, as well as an authority on the Crusaders as well as the Military and Religious Orders.

Sir Steven Runciman was certainly not an ordinary fellow, and we shall come back to his personal biography in one of the next chapters. It is well known that during the Second World War he lived and studied in Istanbul inTurkey but that his main function there was probably to help the British Intelligence Services. Runciman signed the Foreword to the first edition of his famous book *The Medieval Manichee* in Athens in 1946. From Istanbul he had been able to study the Christian Dualist traditions and heresies that he argued originated in the East, and it was from the East that they reached and kept alive the 'Cathar Heresy'.

TERCERAS JORNADAS INTERNACIONALES
Medio siglo de estudios sobre las Cruzadas y las Órdenes Militares, 1951-2001

THIRD INTERNATIONAL CONFERENCE
Half a Century of Studies on Crusades and Military Orders, 1951-2001

Teruel, Mora de Rubielos, Rubielos de Mora, La Iglesuela del Cid, Cantavieja
19-25 de julio de 2001 • 19th-25th of July 2001

Un homenaje a Sir Steven Runciman,
1903-2000
A Tribute to Sir Steven Runciman,
1903-2000

Organización: Facultad de Huesca, Facultad de Humanidades y Ciencias Sociales de Teruel,
Escuela Universitaria del Profesorado de E.G.B. de Teruel (Universidad de Zaragoza)

Organized by the Faculty of Huesca, the Faculty of Humanities and Social Sciences of Teruel
and the Teacher Training College of Teruel (University of Zaragoza)

UNIVERSIDAD DE ZARAGOZA

TERCERAS JORNADAS
INTERNACIONALES
Medio siglo de estudios sobre
las Cruzadas y las Órdenes Militares,
1951-2001

Figure 27
A poster commemorating the death of Sir Steven Runciman, 1903-2000,
one of the world experts on the Cathars and Christian Dualist Heresies.

In his preface (1946) , Sir Steven Runciman acknowledges:

> 'The recent circumstances of the world [meaning the Second World War] and certain "personal handicaps" have prevented me from having access to certain material that I should have liked to consult and from handling more fully one or two points on which I have touched. I must ask for indulgence for such omissions. I do not, however, believe that they affect the main argument'

Runciman's main argument, still widely but not universally accepted today, is that the Dualist (Good and Evil) heretic traditions in Christianity from their Gnostic origins, came from Armenia, Byzantium and the Balkans (Bulgaria, in particular), before moving west to Italy and Southern France.

These 'heretic traditions' are still under active investigation, for it is now absolutely clear that in its origins, Christianity was not a uniform religious movement at all, but that , in spite of the multiple 'dogmas' that the various Christian Churches have gradually developed over the past two thousand years, early Christianity was a 'vivid kaleidoscopic character of the lives and beliefs of its different adherents'.

According to the Reverend William H.C. Frend, sometime also Fellow of Gonville and Caius College (Cambridge):

> 'Apart from the intrinsic value of the discoveries, the churches, catacombs, manuscripts, frescos, and the multitude of small objects which tell us about the life of early Christians, the historical significance of Christian archaeology falls under two main headings. First, the discoveries have helped to throw light on the major transitions in the history of the early Church, from paganism to Christianity in the late-third century, from Late Antiquity to Byzantinism in the second half of the fifth century, and from Byzantium to Islam during the seventh century. Secondly, major finds have enabled the non orthodox traditions to speak for themselves'.

For example, the accidental and unexpected discoveries from Nag-Hamadi and Qumran had suffered from massive hindrances to research and publication. Today publication of the so-called Dead Sea Scrolls is still unfinished fifty years after their fortuitous discovery. It was in March 1947 that an Arab shepherd, Mohammed ed Di'b, was looking for a goat that had wandered up among the rocky cliffs that rise above the marl terrace bordering the western shores of the Dead Sea, just south of the modern Jericho. It was getting hot and Mohammed sat down in the shade of a hollow in the rock. To amuse himself he threw a stone into a cleft in the cliff face in front of him. Instead of driving out his missing goat, he heard the clink of something breaking inside. He looked in, saw potsherds. He retired in haste but returned next day with his cousin. They saw six complete pots with their lids still on. Five were empty – or so we are told – but the sixth contained three rolls of leather parchment wrapped in linen. One of these, the largest, was later to be identified as the Isaiah Scroll. Isaiah is one of the most powerful and mysterious prophets of the Old Testament, and will be discussed again in the final chapter of this book.

The writing was not Arabic, so they were not Koranic, and the boy's uncle decided to take them into Bethlehem to a local Syrian antiquities dealer... As several very good books have been published on this subject, I shall not pursue the details of this fascinating story further.

Suffice it to say, that according to experts such as William Frend, the primary value to scholars of the documents published so far is to Old Testament and inter-testamentary scholarship. For early Christianity their significance lies mainly as illustrating and witnessing the background of 'the prophetic, apocalyptic and messianic expectations' against which Jesus preached and healed some two thousand years ago. This 'greatest manuscript find of all times' has not given up all its secrets. The Jewish sect of the Essenes emerged forcefully as a strong influence in these years of conflict. John the Baptist, revered by the Knights Templar, and the writer of the 'Fourth Gospel', John the Evangelist, or Mary Magdalene, remain an enigma.

Since then, the history of the Christian Church is no longer a history of orthodoxy and heresy. A whole new world of divergent beliefs and teaching has been opened up. We now know a great deal more, but not enough, about Montanism, Donatism, Manicheism and Monophysitism, than ever before. In Islam the tendency to heresy and division is smaller; for the revelation of Islam is a simpler thing, contained in the word of Mahomet. Even so, the political differences between the Shi-ites and Sunnis are well known and still active in Iraq and other Islamic countries.

Mani began his preaching at Ctesiphon in Mesopotamia in 242 AD. In 276 AD he was martyred at Gundeshapur in south-west Persia. Within a century of his death there were Manichean churches established from Turkestan to Carthage, and it seemed that these churches might dominate the Christian world. According to Mani, Apostle of Jesus Christ as he always called himself:

'From all eternity the two realms of Light and Darkness existed side by side. In the former dwelt the Eternal God, the Lord of Greatness with His light, His power and his Wisdom, in His five dwellings of Sense, Reason, Thought, Imagination and Intention. In the latter dwelt the Lord of the Dark with his disorderly anarchical restless brood. Evil began when the denizens of the Dark, impelled by curiosity of some vague unregulated desire, began to invade the realm of Light. The realm of Light had no natural defences, so the Lord of Greatness evoked the Mother of All who evoked the Primal Man to ward off the attack. The Primal Man set out for the fight clothed in the Five Bright Elements, Light, Wind, Fire and Water, and a fifth called variously the Breeze, Aether, Air or Hyle.

But in the battle this Primal Man was defeated and left unconscious on the field, and the Five Bright Elements were swallowed by the princes of Darkness, the Archons. Primal Man on his recovery begged God for further help. God therefore evoked more beings of Light, the Friend of the Luminaries, the Great Ban and the Living Spirit. These, by methods, never clearly explained, succeeded in defeating and capturing the Archons of Darkness but they had unfortunately already 'digested' the Five Pure Elements, and the Realm of Light was thereby the poorer. A wall had to be built to prevent the Darkness spreading farther; then these mixed elements had to be localized. To do so, the Universe was created, held in place by five spirits evoked by the Living Spirit, of which Atlas, who bears the Universe on his shoulders, is the most familiar...'

Mani was born within the realm of the Zoroastrian King of Persia, and he declared that Hermes and Plato, or Jesus, Buddha and Zoroaster (later to be elevated to the highest prophetic level by Nietzsche, in his famous book *Thus spake Zarathustra*), were Messengers sent by God. It is interesting that Hitler, who did not receive a higher education or training, took advantage of his imprisonment in Stadelheim prison and later his enforced confinement at Landsberg, to educate himself and Nietzsche was one of his favourite authors. Nietzsche despised weakness and human pain. Like the German philosopher, Hitler in those days was 'passion incarnate', but entirely without measure or sense of proportion.

Hitler incarnated the Evil forces of Satanael. As Hitler the 'drummer' and German patriot, who suffered the surrender of Germany in the First World War while he lay gassed in the trenches, became Hitler the *Führer*, he evidently lost touch with the suffering of others. He lost one of the most important human values: **Compassion**. Only on two occasions, during his period in power, 1933-45, is Hitler known to have felt real pain:

'We all have our graves – he told Frau Bruckmann on the death of her husband in 1941– and we all grow more and more lonely, but we have to overcome and go on living, my dear gracious lady! I, too, am now deprived of the only two human beings among all those around me to whom I have been truly and inwardly attached: Dr. Todt, the builder of Westwall and Autobahn, is dead, and Rudolf Hess has flown away from me!'

Frau Bruckmann is reported to have replied:

'That is what you say now to me – but what does your official press say about Rudolf Hess? That he is insane! Year after year we all go to Bayreuth, and are deeply moved by Wagner's music, but who understands the real meaning? When our unhappy age at last produces a man, like Rudolf Hess, who, like the Valkyrie, fulfils the deeper meaning of Wotan's command – as we shall see, Wotan was the principal god in the pagan Germanic pantheon, and inspired the Gnostic religion of the Teutons, and centuries later the Nazis – then you, our *Führer*, makes him described as "insane"!'

Surprisingly, according to Frau Bruckmann's witness report, Hitler was moved:

'Is it not enough, what I have said to you – and to you alone – about my real feelings? Is that not enough for you?'

Causing pain, to themselves or to others, was something the Manichaeans were forbidden to do by their religion but this , taken to the extreme, became anti-social. According to Runciman, the authorities in those days (and it must be stressed that all this happened long before the appearance of Islam), with civilization on the defensive against the barbarian invader, could not approve of a faith wherein all killing, even of animals, was forbidden.

Increasing numbers of 'heretic' believers started wandering about, refusing to work (*Ora* but not *Labora*), refusing to notice secular regulations, living exclusively on the charity of others, and exercising a great influence on the whole community. Manicheans inevitably met with persecution, and their church was too passive to survive. In the end it was stamped out.

Sir Steven Runciman, who later questioned in no uncertain terms the goodness of the Christian Crusaders from the first Crusade, at the turn of the first Christian Millenium until the Fall of Constantinople (Byzantium) in 1453, starts Chapter I of his book 'The Medieval Manichee' with the following self-explanatory paragraph:

'**Tolerance** is a social rather than a religious virtue. A broad-minded view of the private belief of others undoubtedly makes for the happiness of society; but it is an attitude impossible for those whose personal religion is strong.'

Towards the end of the first Christian Millenium, a new, but ideologically related Christian heresy, started to appear and rapidly grew in the Balkans. By the year 950 AD the priest Cosmas, who belonged to the Orthodox Christian Church, stated:

'In the days of the Orthodox Tsar Peter there lived in the land of Bulgaria a priest called Bogomil ('loved of God') who in reality was not loved of God (*Bogu ne mil*)'.

According to Cosmas, the Bogomils were simply Dualists. They believed the Devil created our world, thereby rejecting the Old Testament which assigns to God the role of Creator. Christian Sacraments were all rejected as useless, for they dealt with material things. Icons were equally debarred, feast days were pointless, and the Cross should be detested, not worshipped, because it was a material object and the instrument of Christ's murder. The Lord's Prayer (*Pater Noster*) was the only prayer that they permitted, and they repeated it four times daily and four times nightly. They drank no wine and ate no meat, they taught their people not to obey masters, to denounce the wealthy, loathe the Tsar and the Orthodox Church. They behaved like sheep and detested anything to do with the material world, because it was dirty, and made by the Devil. They welcomed a new born baby as prison inmates would welcome a new prisoner, and gave the baby love and protection only to survive to see the other World, that created by God: the Kingdom of Heaven.

A couple of hundred years later, Zigabenus wrote at the request of the Emperor of Byzantium (the real historical Capital of the Roman Empire, as Rome was the Capital of the Catholic Church but not of the Roman Empire), that the Bogomils of Constantinople (Byzantium) in the early twelfth century were Monarchian rather than true Dualists. Satan had not always been the Prince of Evil. God alone had reigned at first over a spiritual universe. The Trinity existed in Him; the Son and Holy Ghost were emanations that took a separate form. The Father begat the Son, in this sense of emission, the Son the Holy Ghost; and the Holy Ghost begat the twelve apostles, including Judas.

Satan was also the Son of the Father; he was in fact the elder son, and called *Satanael*, the suffix 'el' indicated divinity as in 'Angel' or 'Michael' or 'Gabriel'.

But out of pride, Satanael revolted against the Father, and many angels joined him – in some kind of coup or *Pronunciamiento* – believing that under his rule there would be less work for them to do. The rebellion failed and Satan with the rebel angels was cast froth from Heaven. In order to have a realm where he might be God, Satan (who lost the *el*) created the Earth and a second Heaven (or Hell). To people his dominion, Satan made Adam out of earth and water, but he asked his Father God to give life to Adam, to share him between them. God breathed a little life into Adam, and the process was repeated later for Eve.

Thus, according to this belief, Satanael created man, but his force and powers were not enough to give life to his creature. This also means that Satanael, the elder Son of God, cannot be the wicked and ugly beast, with red or green fur and horns and hooves, as depicted in medieval and later drawings and paintings (*see* Figure 28), such as those by Andrea Buonaiuti in Florence.

Figure 28
Devils as portrayed by Andrea Buonaiuti in the fourteenth
century Chapel of Santa Maria Novella, in Florence.

Satanael is said to be the most beautiful of all Archangels, supernatural and king of this our Universe, but part of his Father, the Almighty and the Most High. Our seemingly endless universe is the Empire of Satanael, but also part of something bigger and eternal. Satanael cannot be defeated in his own home, but it was God's desire that Adam, and every future man or woman, can freely choose between good and evil, between light and darkness. I look Satanael 'in the face' every day, when I see in my clinical practice a patient with cancer. Because I see the malignant side of nature, and human suffering, I also see Satanael in Hitler and Franco and Stalin. I see Satanael in the history of the twentieth century, and of every century. He is here and everywhere but as long as we understand that he is part of God, and so are we, we should never fear him, even if he cannot be totally defeated and erradicated in this his own house.

The most interesting part of the story of the Bogomils, according to Zigabenus, is what follows:

> 'After 5,500 years, God sent the Son, the Word, who is the same as the Archangel Michael and the Counsellor of the prophet Isaiah, to go down to the world as 'Jesus', to cure all ills, and as 'Christ', the Anointed by the Flesh, to appear to die, without actually dying, to be able to descend to Hell, and bind 'Satan' for ever. Then He returned to the Father.'

As with the Gnostics, so with the Bogomils the heroes of the Old Testament tended to become villains. Moses, for example, was the 'dupe' of Satan, and the Flood was sent by Satan to wipe out the race of giants born of the fallen angels and the daughters of men described in Genesis.

The Bogomils too were eventually destroyed by the Orthodox Church, and the same fate was suffered in the thirteenth century by the Dualist Cathars in the Albigiensian Crusade, sent against them by the French Monarchy and the Catholic Pope. In some ways their Religion was bound to lead them to extinction on account of their passive behaviour, and their loathing for this material world was really incompatible with survival (*see* Figure 29). Those who could and wanted to escape moved to Italy, across the Alps, or to the kingdom of Aragon, across the Pyrenees.

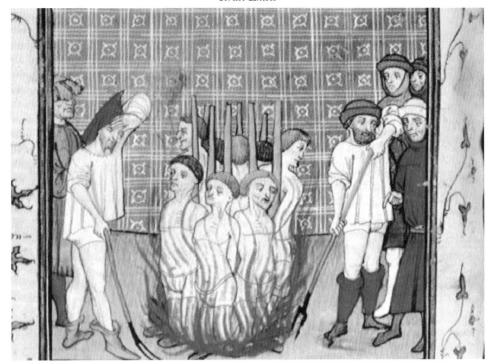

Figure 29
The burning of the Templars. A fourteenth century illustration from the 'Chronicle of France or of St Denis', British Museum/Bridgeman Art Library. The Templars, who had shown tolerance for the Cathar Heresy, shared the same fate in France as the 'Dualists'.

Selected Bibliography

84. Teruel, *Albarracín y Montes Universales* (*Susaeta Ediciones*, Madrid 1993).

85. Steven Runciman. *The Medieval Manichee, A study of the Christian Dualist Heresy* (Cambridge University Press, 1947).

86. Chazan R. *Barcelona and beyond. The disputation of 1263 and its aftermath.* (University of California Press, Berkeley, 1992).

87. Ramban (Nachmanides). *The Disputation of Barcelona.* Ed. Rabbi Dr Charles B. Chavel (Shilo Publishing House, New York, 1983).

88. Ramban (Nachmanides), *The Book of Redemption.* Ed. Rabbi Dr Charles B. Chavel (Shilo Publishing House, New York, 19780.

89. Frend, W.H.C., *The Archeology of Early Christianity: a history* (Geoffrey Chapman Publishers, London 1996).

90. Montserrat Torrents J., *La sinagoga cristiana. El gran conflicto religioso del siglo* (I. Muchnik Editores, 1989).

Part II

What happened to our grandparents?

Preamble

In this Second Part of the book, I explain the main results of my research on what exactly happened to my grand-parents in the first half of the twentieth century. In so doing, I based the work on the following considerations:

a) What happened to my grand-parents is relevant to the parents or grand-parents of most, if not all, present readers of this book. Because they were all part (as protagonists a few, as victims too many, as mere witnesses to) the majority of the political, economical, and military convulsions of the time.

b) The first half of the twentieth century was marked by the predominance of the Western World, but a switch from a premier power role of several European states (such as Great Britain, Germany or France) to the premier power role of the United States of America.

c) This period can be seen as an example of 'Chaotic History', with unexpected revolutions, terrible wars (such as the First World War, the Spanish Civil War and the Second World War), and the rise and fall of extreme totalitarian political systems: fascism – which in Spain lasted until 1975 under the form of *Franquismo*; Nazism, and finally Soviet communism which lasted until 1989. Irrational forces and passions were the real movers of these events. We find again a fascination for ancient symbols (e.g. runes), and fanatical ideas – in this case not related to religions – as was the case in the Middle Ages, but to political ideologies and racism.

Chapter One

Blenheim Palace Revisited: Churchill's birth-place

Yes – my grandparents lost our war: the Spanish Civil War. A lot has been written about this war (1936-39), which was to mark the prelude of World War II. Historians and famous writers have written acclaimed novels on this sad episode in Spanish History, particular examples being American Ernest Hemingway *For whom the bell tolls* and British author George Orwell's *Homage to Catalonia*.

A civil war is probably the worst of all kinds of war. Your enemies can be your brothers, or your next-door neighbours. Among other considerations, this means that after any civil war victors and vanquished are forced to live next to each other, unless the vanquished choose to exile themselves. In ancient Roman times, exile was a punishment tantamount to a death sentence but to wake up in the morning and find your foes, vanquished or victors, next door, at work or in the street, every day of the week represents a constant reminder of hatred. For example, the Germans lost both World Wars (1914-19 and 1939-45), of the twentieth century but, in spite of the forced division of Germany, they were somehow 'united' in their collective defeat, pain and shame. Spanish Democrats, and their children and grand-children, who lost the Spanish Civil War, 1936-39, where constantly reminded at home, by TV or wireless, at work, at school, during Franco's regime which lasted for almost forty years, of their defeat, and of all their sins, presumably committed before and during the war. They were not only regarded as losers, they were 'guilty' and often humiliated.

The pain felt by so many individuals and families, and over such a protracted period of time (almost four decades) is hard to communicate. Why then does war exist? What are the causes and consequences of war?

Winston Churchill, recently chosen in a 2002 nationwide poll in the United Kingdom as the 'Greatest Briton' throughout history, felt an unusual special attraction for War. In 1924, in an article for *Nash's Pall Mall* entitled 'Shall we all commit suicide?', he had written:

'The story of the human race is War. Except for brief and precarious interludes, there has never been peace in the world; and before history began, murderous strife was universal and unending'.

As in most cases, Winston Churchill was right. A world without wars is 'Utopia'. John Lennon sang of this utopian world in his famous song *Imagine*, and ended up killed by a lunatic in New York. Jesus based his teachings on peace, and ended up on the murderous cross. Even before the world was created, according to Jewish, Christian and Islamic beliefs, there was war in God's Kingdom. The rebellion by Satan and other angels required the action of St Michael and his followers. Cain killed his brother Abel, and the Bible, the Homeric poems, and almost every literary work of art related to historical evidence, are all full of terrible wars to the death.

In his book *An unfinished History of the World*, Hugh Thomas states that 'overpopulation' is a rather unlikely cause of most human wars. 'In general, wars have seemed, like crime, more often than not to have been caused by the desire of the audacious to seize the goods of the comfortable.

Historical wars are fought by armies, but it is not always their size and power that determines victory or defeat. Both Greece and Persia, for example, were reduced a few centuries BC, by Alexander's 35,000 men, a force that proved enough to conquer half the world. The Roman army at its zenith in the second century AD included thirty legions each of about 12,500 soldiers or about 375,000 to 400,000 men in total, to preserve the peace (*Pax Romana*) in the Mediterranean and the Western World.

The King of France commanded the largest army in feudal Europe at the battle of Crécy, during the One Hundred Years war, and yet, his life was saved by a young Knight of St. John, don Juan Fernández de Heredia, from the Kingdom of Aragon, who gave the French King his own horse to escape from the English.

In contrast, China had trained several million men under the Sung dynasty, and yet, in spite of being overpopulated, remained at peace.

Most historians take the view that the Roman army, in spite of its cruelty and determination was really an armed institution which undoubtedly preserved life more than it destroyed it. It might have fought to the death the enemy Carthaginians, the Phoenicians competitors in the Mediterranean commerce, even throwing salt on the still burning ruins of Carthage to prevent any rebirth of its city and civilization. *Cartago delenda est* proclaimed Cicero in Rome – Carthage is destroyed. Two thousand years later, in conscious emulation of Cicero, Winston Churchill stated on more than one occasion: 'Hitler must be destroyed'.

Unlike the methods employed by most modern professional historians and philosophers, who are striving to find the underlying reason for **war** in material externalities, I believe that it is the **irrational** (passions, fears, ambitions, religious and politically biased personal decisions by fanatics or leading individuals) that determine the mood and will to fight, kill, destroy and dominate others. These are, in my view, the key elements that shape the world.

Another, by itself also irrational, factor that determines the History of Nations, and our own little individual history, is **luck** or **bad luck**, that some tend to classify under the overpowering effects of **fate** or **destiny**.

Winston Churchill's origins were aristocratic. I used to walk around Blenheim Palace, while an Oxford student, where Sir Winston Churchill was born, prematurely, on 30 November 1874. Ironically his lack of punctuality in adult life eventually became so notorious that having been born prematurely was described by many as one of the few things in life which he did 'ahead of time'. Another of the things which allowed him to 'interpret ahead of others', was his political foresight. He never underestimated Hitler, and there can be little doubt that he understood Hitler better than Hitler ever understood him.

I used to visit Blenheim Palace alone, on my often boring Oxford student weekends, with a book or two to read, and some ten pounds in my pocket, for lunch and a cup of tea. The Palace is the magnificent stately home that Queen Anne had given to Churchill's ancestor, the Duke of Marlborough, to show the nation's gratitude for his epic victory over the French in 1704 at Blenheim, near the Danube river, during the War of the Spanish Succession. This complex war (1702-13) eventually led to the defeat of the pro-Hapsburg Catalans, and other Spanish supporters of the Hapsburg candidate to the Spanish Throne. A defeat that became inevitable following the sudden withdrawal of English forces (a fact that is still considered 'pure treason' by the Catalans) to allow, paradoxically, the establishment of the French Bourbon dynasty on the Spanish throne. In exchange for this 'treason', wicked but intelligent, the English retained possession of Gibraltar and, for some years, the island of Menorca, as a result of the Peace Treaty of Utrecht.

The Hapsburg dynasty is one of the key dynasties of European history. In my view, probably the greatest of them all, although it has practically vanished in the literal sense of the word 'extinction'. Maximilian I, a crucial figure in the Hapsburg empire, was crowned 'King of the Romans', meaning the 'Western Romans', in 1507. The Venetians refused him permission to cross their territory, and he had to be content to declare himself Roman Emperor Elect – only later, with the tacit approval of Pope Julius II (1503-13).

Dynastic marriages amassed the vast territories eventually inherited by Maximilian's grandson Charles V of Germany, also known as Charles I of

Spain, whose huge kingdom lasted almost forty years (1517-56). These 'Holy Roman' emperors, leaders of the First Reich according to the Germans, were 'secretly' elected in Nuremburg, the 'secret capital' of Franconia, later to be incorporated into Bavaria. Maximilian's less public diplomacy involved support for Warbeck as Richard Duke of York. Warbeck was given a place of honour at the funeral of Maximilian's father, Frederick III (1452-93), and was recognised as Richard IV of England. In return, Warbeck made Maximilian his heir, so that he should succeed the Yorkist heritage. Small wonder that Henry VII (1485-1509) was highly suspicious: '... the cautious Tudor distrusted the flighty Hapsburg'.

Queen Isabel of Spain (also known as the 'Catholic') had died in 1504, and her daughter Juana was now married to Philip the Fair, son of Maximilian (who died in 1506). Both of them eventually became 'supporting statues' in the beautiful church, the *Hofkirche*, dedicated to Maximilian's tomb and cenotaph, in the Austrian city of Innsbruck. This church is where Emperor Maximilan and his entourage rest for ever and is an example of Chivalric ideals at their highest, with statues of King Arthur, Godfrey of Bouillon and many other knights. It is so special that it has attracted creative visitors like the great modern English composer Elgar. Following their marriage, Philip the Fair and Juana sailed for Spain on 10 January 1506 but appalling weather drove them unpredictably to England, more precisely to Melcombe Regis in Dorset. Curiously, a somewhat similar 'unexpected accident' happened during the Second World War.

On 16 June 1940, two days after the German army entered Paris, and a little more than a week after the defeated British forces 'miraculously' escaped from Dunkirk, Hitler met General Juan Vigon, Head of the Spanish Army Defence Council and key figure in Fascist Spain at the time.

As will be seen, General Vigon played an important role in the secret Anglo-German peace discussions in 1940-41. Hitler informed General Vigon that the Duke of Windsor, formerly King Edward VIII of Great Britain, would shortly be travelling to Spain on his way to Lisbon and his 'exile' in the island of Bermudas in the Bahamas. Hitler suggested that Nazi Germany would have a substantial interest in the Duke and his wife being delayed long enough in Madrid for secret contacts and peace talks.

The recently married Philip and Juana, back in 1506, were conducted to Windsor Palace with due ceremony and received by king Henry VII. There was an exchange of chivalric courtesies. Prince Henry of Wales was made a Knight of the Golden Fleece, and Philip became a Knight of the Garter.

Unfortunately, the vane of St. Paul's cathedral in London, a brazen eagle and therefore also a Hapsburg symbol, fell during the same storm and smashed the sign of a nearby Inn, also an eagle. This was considered an evil omen for Philip the Fair, who died later that year. The extraordinary grief of his widow, madly in love with Philip, turned her mind, and history knows her as *Juana la Loca* (Juana the Mad).

Only a few people were allowed to see her in her chronic state of mental insanity. One such was their son and future emperor Charles V. Such were the tragic beginnings of the great Hapsburg role in the Spanish Empire. The end was equally tragic.

On 1 November 1700, Charles II of Spain died without any heirs to his coveted throne, and Louis XIV (the 'Sun King of France) immediately supported the candidature of Philip V, Duke of Anjou and Bourbon by dynasty. He took this decision at the Palace of Versailles, a place later connected to the Treaty that ended World War I. The English, always concerned about a single dominating power in Europe, decided to support the Hapsburg candidate, the Archduke Charles of Austria (Charles III of Spain to his supporters) and sent troops under the command of Churchill's ancestor, the Duke of Marlborough. The Catalans were clearly on their side, because the Hapsburgs had always accepted the true multi-national nature of Spain. One has to remember that Spain became a single state earlier than most other European states, when Queen Isabel (the 'Catholic'), queen of Castile, married King Ferdinand of Aragon (and Catalonia). In fact, Spain should probably have been called "The United Kingdoms of Spain".

With the help of the English, the smaller Austrian and Catalan armies, helped by a representative of another intriguing and ancient aristocratic European dynasty (the Savoy, later, in 1870, to become the Kings of Italy), took control of most of Spain including Barcelona, Zaragoza and Madrid. It was with the help of Catalan troops that the English Admiral Rooke landed and conquered Gibraltar, as testified by a beach in the Rock, still named the 'Catalan Beach.

Unpredictably, the Austrian Hapsburg emperor Joseph I died in 1711 and the candidate to the Spanish throne, the Archduke Charles, became Emperor of Austria. That was too much for the English, who decided to cease supporting the Catalans, negotiating the favourable Treaty of Utrecht-Rastadt with the French. That is probably when and where the first British Empire was born. Suddenly the French left the English to their colonies and territories in North America. Spain is still trying to recover Gibraltar! The real losers where the Catalans and Spain. Utrecht was the dagger that killed the concept of the 'United Kingdoms of Spain'. Barcelona heroically resisted the French and Castilian troops, until 11 September 1714. The Catalans have never felt 'comfortable' again in a 'single' Spain dominated by Castile, and ruled according to classic French centralism and bureaucracy.

While it is inconceivable that in the United Kingdom today any serious politician might disregard Scotland as a 'nation', it is still a problem for modern and democratic Spain to regard Catalonia, or the Basque country, as 'nations', even within a United Kingdom of Spain. This is probably why the 'United Kingdom' is also known as 'Great Britain', whereas Spain, in spite of its past grandeur, is not known as 'Great Spain'.

The first thing that Philip V of Spain did following the fateful year of 1714 was to abolish the historical privileges of autonomous government enjoyed by Catalans for centuries. The first Borbón King of Spain issued a decree (entitled *Decreto de Nueva Planta*) stating: '*Habiendo, con la ayuda de Dios y la fuerza de las armas, pacificado mis tropas el Principado de Catalunya, toca a mi soberanía poner gobierno en él*'– meaning 'with the help of God and the force of arms, King Philip V had 'pacified' Catalonia with his troops and now it was entirely up to him to rule there. Some two hundred years later, General Franco used a very similar declaration at the end of the Spanish Civil War in 1939.

I can never forget the grandeur and baroque beauty of Blenheim Palace nor its lakes, the fields that stretched for miles and the famous terraces. Neither can the Catalans forget the 'treason' of the English in 1704, and the revenge of the Castilian forces who continued the war with French support, eventually laying siege to Barcelona, finally conquering it then burning it to the ground, killing thousands of civilians, on 11 September 1714. (A year of infamy indeed!) This sad day is still celebrated as Catalonia's 'National Day' even though it denotes a great defeat rather than a victory.

On my solitary visits to Blenheim Palace, I enjoyed reading about Winston Churchill, and European historical events. I remember reading *The Prince* by the Italian statesman Machiavelli (1469-1527), who clearly and elegantly advocated putting expediency above political morality, and defended the deliberate use of deceit in statecraft. '*Il fine giustifica i mezzi*' (the end justifies the means), showing or having no scruples in gaining what is wanted.

I suspect the young Winston Churchill must have read it too, perhaps in the Library at Blenheim Palace. I also suspect, the young Winston never showed any real interest in chivalry, which he probably regarded as something aesthetically attractive, but essentially stupid.

From the point of view of a democratic Spaniard, Churchill was politically and ethically right when he attacked the 'Politics of Appeasement', which unfortunately dominated British politics in the early 1930s. A swift and tough action against the Fascist coup of General Franco and other military conspirators in 1936, in alliance with the French, might certainly have saved Spanish Democracy, and should have stopped, or at least slowed down, the imperialistic attitudes and dictatorial expansionist policies not only of both Mussolini and Hitler, who became the decisive supporters of General Franco, but also the ambitions and cruelty of Stalin, who became the only real supporter of the democratic Spanish Republican forces. Stalin's involvement was the first major international attempt to expand Soviet influence and domination, giving General Franco that great excuse (the 'Communist Threat') to gain direct or indirect support from Britain, even during the Spanish Civil War and eventually, after the end of World War II, from the United States of America.

From the European point of view however, Churchill's adamant decision to stop by any means, ethical or otherwise, any serious attempts at reaching a peace agreement between Nazi Germany and Britain in the heroic days of 1940-41, I find it more difficult to judge, in the light of present evidence, particularly with regards to the so-called 'Rudolf Hess Case'. I rather suspect that Churchill's decision to take Rudolf Hess as a Prisoner of War in May 1941 was probably still politically correct but ethically wrong.

Unlike Hitler or Stalin, there is no doubt that Churchill was endowed with an admirable sense of humour. Not long after his surprising defeat in the British elections at the end of World War II, in spite of having led the country to victory, when King George VI offered him the Order of the Garter, he remarked: 'I could not accept the Order of the Garter from my sovereign, when I have received the "order of the boot" from the people'… When his wife Clementine said to him that the defeat at the polls 'may well be a blessing in disguise', Churchill replied 'At the moment it seems quite effectively disguised'.

Churchill was always grateful to Harrow School, a magnificent public school near London, for all he learnt in spite of his 'natural resistance'. He was so grateful to the school, that he continued to visit it, particularly around Christmas, in his old age. Robert Anderson, a good friend of mine and god-father to my son, was a student at Harrow, and remembers the old man very clearly, in the late 1940s and early 1950s, visiting the school and listening to the School Choir in the charming little Chapel. It is true that Winston was not a very good student. His mother, American by birth, wrote to him on one occasion 'Your school work is an insult to your intelligence'. It took the young

My Secret Castle

Winston three tries to get accepted into the Royal Military College, Sandhurst.

He did not waste any opportunities to see War close to, and visited Cuba in 1898. Cuban pro-independence guerrillas (obviously a Spanish word), supported by the United States, had mounted a new revolt against their Spanish rulers. Churchill and another young officer obtained permission to visit Cuba to 'observe the fighting', but were themselves forbidden to fight, except in self-defence. The Cuban Spanish-American War (1898) marked the beginning of the 'American Empire', and the sad but inevitable end of the 'Spanish Empire'. As a child I learnt from my paternal grand-mother, Catalina, that her father Pau Onna i Marquès, like many other Catalans, was sent from Spain to Cuba, and came back to Spain deathly ill where he soon died from yellow fever.

The United States of America won that War, and occupied the great former colonies of Spain: Cuba and the Philippines (named after, emperor Philip II of Spain). In Cuba, American troops were welcomed as 'Liberators', but later developments, which led to the Fidel Castro Revolution, ended this short 'love affair' between the USA and the Cuban people. In the Philippines, even poorer and farther away than Cuba, the local natives were allowed to keep their names and religion, so that while the majority of Philipinos still kept Spanish surnames and remained Catholic, the public use and teaching of the Spanish language was forbidden there and a substitute 'American' English became the new official language.

This is probably one of the best examples in recent history of 'cultural imperialism', which I believe would be totally politically unacceptable today, but no doubt comparable to the action of Spanish *Conquistadores* and Catholic Missionaries in much of Latin America. It resulted in the imposition of a foreign language. All of a sudden, local schools and universities in the Philippines, most of them run until then by Spanish Jesuits, were banned from using the Spanish language, and teaching became exclusively in English. With time, of course, most natives ended up speaking and writing their own Philipino native language, or Tagalog.

The American Eagle, like a young, large and strong bird of prey, with keen sight and clear objectives, entered the international arena with immense power, and with an entirely new imperialistic approach based on more modern ideas on public administration and economic growth, but, unavoidably, the poor old Spanish Eagle (no longer the Hapsburg's double-headed much respected eagle) sank into oblivion and extreme poverty.

The following year, with the start of the second Boer War in October 1899, Churchill, now out of the army, was appointed by the *Morning Post* as a special correspondent in South Africa. Although only a journalist, he could not resist real action, and was captured by the Boers along with his friend Captain Haldane. They were kept in prison near Pretoria, but Winston got away by 'climbing out of a public convenience, into world-wide acclaim and notoriety'. The Boers searched for him in vain, offering £25 sterling for his capture, describing him as '... an Englishman who cannot speak a word of Dutch, speaks through his nose, and cannot properly pronounce the letter "s".'

The Boer War was a tough, cruel armed conflict between two colonial European powers, the Dutch and the British, and is distinguished *inter alia* by that example of madness – the 'concentration camp'. When Rudolf Hess, Deputy-Führer of the Nationalist Socialist totalitarian state which led to the Second World War, was accused of the atrocities committed in the Nazi concentration camps, even though by the time they had taken place he was by then already a prisoner of war in Britain, as we shall discuss in detail, he stated that it was not the Nazis who had invented concentration camps, but that they were 'invented' during the Boer War by the British! Apparently even women and children were interned in South African camps.

Churchill later admitted that during his escape, his sole companion '... was a gigantic vulture, who manifested an extravagant interest in his condition and made hideous and ominous gurglings from time to time'. Later, in his flamboyant style, he wrote a short piece to the Secretary of War, of the South African Republic: 'Sir, I have the honour to inform you that as I do not consider that your Government have any right to detain me as a military prisoner, I have decided to escape from your custody'.

While Churchill was on the run, and the English composer Elgar was completing his *Enigma Variations*, one of the finest pieces of music ever written, the Boer cause had enjoyed notable success, as the great doctor and writer Conan Doyle makes it clear: 'The week which extends from 10 December to 17 December 1899, was the blackest one known during our generation, and the most disastrous for British arms during this century. We had in the short space of seven days lost, beyond all extenuation or excuse, three separate military actions …'

Despite his extreme criticisms aimed at the tactics and methods of the British commanders, Conan Doyle's most deadly scorn was reserved for the European powers who apparently rejoiced in every British setback: He could partly excuse the French, the Russians and the Vatican, but not the Germans. The French, he claimed, could be excused 'since our history has been largely a contest with that Power'. The Russians and the Vatican for 'they have a natural antagonism of thought, if not of interests, to the Power (meaning Great Britain) which stands most prominently for individual freedom and liberal institutions', but it was the hostility of Germany which seemed incomprehensible to Doyle: 'What are we to say of the insensate railing of Germany, a country whose ally we have been for centuries? In the days of Marlborough, in the darkest hours of Frederick the Great, in the great world struggle against Napoleon, we have been the 'brothers-in-arms of these people ...'

Conan Doyle the doctor insisted that 'bad water can cost us more than all the bullets of the enemy', and suggested that 'drinking unboiled water should become a military offence'.

Winston Churchill's passion for War, should have suffered a major drawback during the First World War. One of the few politically intelligent things that Spain has done in the past three hundred years, was not to take part in this horrible and most stupid and meaningless of all wars. To put it simply, the bizarre assassination of the Austrian Archduke Francis Ferdinand, by a bunch of youthful murderers in Sarajevo, meant that Austria (the Hapsburg Empire) declared war against Serbia. This meant that Russia, Serbia's ally, declared war on Austria. Prussia, linked to Austria by Germanic ties, declared war on both Serbia and Russia, and France and England declared war on Prussia, Austria and the Ottoman Empire. A real 'bloody mess'.

To add more 'fuel' to the explosive cocktail, as in other dramatic and mysterious circumstances, the whole plot was blamed on Freemasonry. An Englishwoman, Edith Durham, published a book, *The Sarajevo Crime*, containing the absurd story of a secret plan by the Grand Orient of France to murder the Archduke. Strangely, this plan, was written in the Spanish language, because the communications between the Grand Lodge of France and the Balkan States were carried on (for whatever reason) in 'that language'.

The western front of World War I, in France and Belgium, became a cemetery for hundreds of thousands of young soldiers, who died in their trenches. The diaries of Gerald Burgoyne (1874-1936) describe the horrific situation at the start of 1915:

> 'About 50 yards in front of us – in the trenches – are some old French rifle pits full of dead, and I can see the red breeches of one poor fellow; yesterday, when the sun came out for an hour, the men opposite them said they commenced to smell ... We slosh on our way, my men, sullen, patient, spiritless, I cursing, urging, imploring, threatening, exhorting, in every endeavour to get my poor sheep safely and quickly across 300 yards of high, open, shell-pitted, slippery, waterlogged clay plough ...'

In June 1916, at the battle of Verdun, a young and idealistic German patriot, originally born in Alexandria in Egypt, named Rudolf Hess, was hospitalised because of a wound in the left arm and hand caused by shrapnel. In 1917 he was again seriously injured, the bullet travelling through his left lung and exiting through his back. Before joining the German Flying Corps, as he passionately desired, he was given his last assignment as an infantryman: to provide an escort for a unit to the List Regiment back in the Western Front. The expedition was a disaster, and there were only a few survivors. Among them, Rudolf Hess and an unknown corporal born in Austria, and called Adolf Hitler (*see* Figure 30).

Figure 30
Photograph by Harry Schulze-Wilde. Hitler is seen third from the left with his dog Fuchsl. Hitler does not look like the future Führer. He is much thinner, less assertive, a bit like 'a tired stray dog looking for a master', as his Captain, Karl Mayr, later described him.

Churchill and Lloyd George, the Prime Minister who many years later thought Hitler 'a great man', and said privately that he had not shown half the ferocity in the persecution of the Jews that Oliver Cromwell, in the English Civil War, had shown towards the Irish Catholics, both thought that it would be wise for British Forces to open other fronts, as the French army could not break through the German lines of defence, and they looked at the Bosphorus, and the collapsing Ottoman Empire, to make new progress in this wretched war.

As is well known, the Gallipoli expedition ended in disaster. Churchill took full blame for the plan was his although the military mistakes were not. What probably irritated him the most was the futile loss of life among the Australians and New Zealanders. This contingent represented the first army sent to Europe against Germany:

'Anzac is the greatest word in the history of Australasia. Is it for ever to carry to future generations of Australians and New Zealanders memories of forlorn heroism and of sacrifices made in vain?' Churchill asked.

The failure of Gallipoli left an indelible mark on the Australasian consciousness, with a sense of betrayal uppermost. Churchill's vision, never accomplished, was the creation of a political space or union of all English-speaking Nations, and this first international defeat by his beloved Australian and New Zealand forces must have been a very painful experience indeed for him.

At the end of the First World War, Britain was the most industrialized and urbanized country in the world, considerably more so than the USA. Over three-quarters of Britain's population lived in densely populated towns and cities and one third of national wealth was owned by one per cent of the population. The hereditary caste of the great landowning families retained most of the traditional social and political power. Churchill was part of this highly influential circle of privileged people as was his cousin Lord Londonderry.

Lord Londonderry (the 7th Marquess of Londonderry), was a true pillar of the Conservative Party and was on first-name terms with all the major political figures of the day. King George V used to call him 'Charley'! An educated, aristocratic man, who had witnessed the bloodshed of the Great War, he was obviously worried and deeply concerned by the rapid growth of the British Labour Party, which won 4 million votes in 1922 and 5.5 million at home in 1924, to say nothing of the threatening spread of Bolshevism from the East.

The Great War had totally crippled Europe, with the complete collapse of the long established Ottoman and Austro-Hungarian Empires, the separation in 1922 of Northern from Republican Ireland, the extinction of the Russian Monarchy and State (no more Tzars, or Russian Orthodox Church), the generation of new 'unstable' states such as Yugoslavia and Czechoslovakia, the increasing agitation of Mahatma Gandhi's Indian Independence Movement, and not least, the total humiliation of Germany which was blamed for having been the prime cause of the conflict.

The Kaiser of the 'Second Reich' was forced into exile. Country boundaries were redrawn, to the benefit of France and Belgium in the west, and Poland in the east. The German army was reduced to only 100,000 men and the navy to 15,000. No tanks, submarines or aircraft were permitted, the Rhineland was occupied by allied troops for fifteen years, and Germany was condemned to pay such a vast amount of compensation at the infamous Treaty of Versailles, especially to the French, that, had it not been for the Second World War, the outstanding German debt would have lasted until 1973.

The penalties imposed on Germany by the Treaty were, quite simply, too much for the nation to bear. Even before the Treaty was signed, the French, still smouldering with resentment at losing the 1870 Franco-Prussian War, coupled with the huge loss of human life and goods they had now suffered in the First World War, were already asking for more. They demanded permanent occupation of the Rhineland and yet more money from the Germans. Churchill, then Chancellor of the Exchequer, had more political vision. Unwilling to support all of the terms of the Treaty, he simply suggested that 'France should stew in her own juice'.

In 1925, an article in *The Times* commented 'In every chapter of the Treaty of Versailles, almost in every clause, we have the clear distinction between "the victors" and "the vanquished" … This is no Peace; it is merely the perpetuation of War!'

Again in 1938 Churchill reminded the House of Commons that 'the grievances of the vanquished should be redressed before the disarmament of the victors was begun; but exactly the reverse was done …'

For these and other more irrational reasons, such as pro-German partiality, Lord Londonderry, who had been appointed Air Minister of Great Britain in 1931, was partly blamed for the failure of Britain to rearm or put pressure on Hitler to limit rearmament of the new Nazi Germany. Eventually, Londonderry lost his position in the government when it had become clear that the 'new' Germany was again preparing for war. Hitler's much publicised claim in 1935 that Germany already possessed military air parity with Britain stirred great alarm, and prompted Londonderry's dismissal from office as Air Minister.

He later said '... there were really only two things I could do. Build an Air Force, or try to make friends with the Germans. They wouldn't let me do either'. A statement whose pathos was underlined by its truth.

Londonderry visited Germany on a number of occasions, met Hitler several times, enjoyed staying with Göring, whom he liked very much, and with whom he shared a passion for hunting. Göring was head of the German *Luftwaffe* and, like Rudolf Hess, was one of the first true loyal supporters of the Führer. In 1937 – while the Spanish Civil War was already under way – Hermann Göring, who combined brutality and ruthlessness with charm and joviality, entertained Lord Londonderry as his guest at Karinhall, the splendid palatial hunting residence of the *Luftmarschall*.

In *The Second World War*, a work that contributed to his Nobel Prize for Literature, Churchill wrote: 'Back in 1932 I had no national prejudices against Hitler at this time. I knew little of his doctrine and nothing of his character. I admire men who stand up for their own country in defeat, even though I was on the other side'.

In the first days of 1923 a quarrel between the French and British at the Reparations Commission resulted in the withdrawal of the latter's delegation. This gave France the opportunity to 'solve the reparations problem' by force. On 11 January, French and Belgian troops marched into the Ruhr region on the excuse that Germany had failed to fulfil her obligations. This act not only infuriated all Germans, but also gave strength to Hitler's political role, and plunged the value of the German currency (the 'mark') from 6750 to the US dollar to 50,000 within two weeks.

Hitler's hatred of Jews was irrational, and is still beyond comprehension. His obsessive anti-Semitism bordering on the edge of sanity, though expressed in logical terms, far surpassed all boundaries of logic. The people of Germany however, needed to join Hitler's Crusade in order to save their country from ruin. True, anti-Semitism was not new in Germany nor, for that matter, Europe. True also that many others were to blame. For centuries Catholics had been instructed that it was the Jews who had killed Christ. This doctrine was not peculiar to Catholicism as even the first Protestant, the German Martin Luther, had charged that the Jew had not only transformed God into the Devil, but was a 'plague, pestilence and pure misfortune'.

Alfred Rosenberg, the young architect from Estonia, had impressed Hitler in 1920 when he blamed the rise of 'Bolshevism' on the Jews, as a vast global plot to conquer the world. Both Hitler and Rosenberg gave credit to the amateurish forgery known as *The protocols of the Elders of Zion*, purporting to be a verbatim report of twenty-four secret sessions of the 'Elders of Zion' in Basel, Switzerland. It is true that several of the leading thinkers of the Bolshevik revolution were Jews, as was Karl Marx, who died in exile in London but to amalgamate Judaism with Communism, and later, in a totally irrational manner, with Freemasonry as well as Capitalism, was pure demagogic nonsense.

Yet, these 'connections' were part of the political propaganda of Fascism (in Italy), Nazism (in Germany) and, particularly with reference to the 'Communist-Masonic Plot' of Spanish Fascism or *Franquismo* (in Spain).

Italian members of Freemasonry, such as Garibaldi or Mazzini (and, perhaps, even the Prime Minister Cavour) took an active and decisive role in the patriotic reunification of Italy, re-establishing Rome as the Capital of the new Kingdom of Italy, ruled by the Savoy dynasty. But soon after the famous 'Fascist March on Rome' in 1922, Mussolini sent his 'black shirts' (*Camice Nere*) to wreck Masonic lodges in most Italian cities and to attack and physically abuse members of the Fraternity, culminating the passing of an 'Anti-Masonic Bill' in January 1925. Mussolini described his mode of campaign against Freemasonry in the following way: 'First of all I break the bones of the enemy, and then I take him prisoner! My principle is: all that is good for my friends, and all that is bad for my enemies. I shall therefore oppose Freemasonry to the uttermost.'

The fact that several thousands of Italian Freemasons, including several key military men, were at first active members of the Fascist Party, did not placate Mussolini. The Fascist journal *Battaglie Fasciste* published the following:

'The end justifies the means. Purifying fire must follow upon the breaking of windows …'

Mussolini seriously miscalculated the tenacity of the British when in June 1940 he finally declared war on the Allied Forces, officially communicating via the French and British ambassadors in Rome. He openly declared to his closest collaborators that nobody could defeat Hitler, and that total military victory was only a matter of 'two to three months' for the combined Italian and German Forces. The Italian King, a member of the ancient Savoy Dynasty did not share Mussolini's enthusiasm. Neither did Mussolini's foreign minister Count Galeazzo Ciano, as he explained in his Personal Diaries, They were worried, depressed and it would seem, resigned to Italy's fate.

In characteristically vivacious style, while Churchill was visiting Germany in 1932, the half-American – half-German graduate from Harvard, Ernst (Putzi) Hanfstängl, who had become the foremost international Public Relations man for the future Führer, tried to introduce Hitler and Churchill although as far as I can ascertain, they never met. Churchill, staying at a famous Hotel in Munich, told Hanfstängl:

There are a few questions you might like to put to Hitler, which can be the basis of our discussion when we meet. For example: 'What is the sense of being against a man simply because of his birth? How can any man help how he is born? Tell your boss from me that anti-Semitism may be a good starter, but it is a bad sticker'.

Hitler evidenced his total ruthlessness in the famous 'Night of the Long Knives' purge of his own Nazi Party and the SA (*Sturm Abteilung*), in June 1934, by executing his internal political rivals 'Mafia style'. Nazi hatred for Jews exploded in another famous night: *Kristalnacht* (9-10 November 1938), ironically so called because of the broken glass from Jewish shop-windows littering the streets of Berlin and other cities. Close to one hundred Jews were killed and 30,000 male Jews were impressed into concentration camps with their associated horrors. These numbers, although impressive, are as nothing in comparison to the total figure of dead or missing Jews, totalling nearly 6 million by 1946. But worse was to come, and perhaps – as we shall discuss when examining the case of Rudolf Hess – it might perhaps have been avoided. Hitler's Nazi Machine gradually progressed to a point which may truly be regarded as the last and hopefully 'final' violent attempt by any single European Nation to dominate the rest of the European Nations by force and the first systematic and almost 'industrial' approach to making an entire people (the Jews) disappear from the face of the earth.

To be fair to Lord Londonderry, the 'appeasers' in Great Britain were in the 1930s very powerful indeed, and practically controlled most of the Press, large-scale industry, large land-owners and aristocrats, and above all the Royal Family. Hindsight is a perfect science.

The uncrowned King Edward VIII (*later* Duke of Windsor,) who was forced to abdicate because of his marriage to a divorcée, has recently become an easy 'scapegoat' for the movement, and has even been dubbed the 'Traitor King'. It is certainly true that he defended a special 'British-German' relationship, probably because of blood ties with the German people, and with the Hanoverian German Aristocrats, a natural aversion and fear of Communism, an obvious desire to preserve peace, and, almost certainly, a naïve view of what Hitler was really capable of, and wanted to do.

Dr John Charmley, wrote an interesting article in the *Sunday Telegraph*, in December 1996, suitably entitled 'The King of Appeasers', where he says:

'George V, Edward VIII and George VI all deplored the prospect of another Anglo-German war, which, given their ancestry, they all had reason to regard as something akin to an internecine conflict: the fist threatened to "wave a red flag" in Trafalgar Square, if that was what it took to avoid a war; the second certainly expressed an admiration for the Nazi regime, and after his abdication met Hitler; but only the last (George VI) actually offered positive support for appeasement".

The romance between the Duke (*formerly* King Edward VIII) and the Duchess of Windsor (*formerly* Mrs Wallis Simpson) has been called the greatest love story of the twentieth century. Mrs Simpson, an illegitimate American child born of a Baltimore family who rose to become the mistress of the King of England and brought about his abdication, has recently been shown, by newly released FBI files and the research of several biographical authorities such as Charles Higham), to have been involved in espionage activities for the Nazis. It is said that in her rather turbulent personal past, the future Duchess of Windsor had learnt stimulating loving and sexual tecniques in China and was even reputed to have been working in a high-class brothel in the 1920s. She embarked upon a reckless and sustained love affair with William Bullitt, the wealthy US Ambassador to France both before and during the early part of the Second World War and with whom she conspired against Britain, in the interests of Hitler, to keep America out of the war and to help the Nazis defeat the Soviets. She would most certainly have risked losing her power and status once married to the heir to the British throne.

Prime Minister Neville Chamberlain, whose father Joseph Chamberlain had defended the Aryan-Saxon Connection, and had met Karl Haushofer (probably at the University of Cambridge, in 1899), a key figure in the Rudolf Hess case in England, was certainly not alone. Sir Samuel Hoare, another right-wing Tory and a Quaker, had already become involved in peace talks with Mussolini, when Italian troops, under the megalomaniac ambition of their *Duce* who wanted another 'Roman Empire', had invaded Abyssinia (*now* Ethiopia).

Winston Churchill and Sir Samuel Hoare were often bitter political rivals, although in private they enjoyed a cordial relationship that resulted in Churchill placing a great deal of trust in Hoare, posting him to Madrid as 'Ambassador Extraordinaire'. There, Samuel Hoare played a 'friendly role', with General Franco, to avoid the entrance of Spain into the War, even when Franco, in 1940, was so sure of Hitler's victory that he offered the Axis all his help. Hoare was not much liked by Sir Alexander Cadogan, the permanent Under-secretary to the foreign office, and a key figure in the

SO1 (Special Operations 1) who plotted the 'Hess Deception'. Sir Alexander wrote about Samuel Hoare and his wife, in 1940: 'The sooner we get them out of the country, the better. I'd rather send them to a Penal Colony. He'll be the Quisling of England when Germany conquers us and I'm dead'.

It has also been stated that the very popular 'Queen Mother', mother of her Majesty, the present Queen Elizabeth II, was also in favour of appeasement, and a fervent supporter of both Neville Chamberlain and Lord Halifax.

The last big reception and banquet attended at Blenheim Palace by British authorities and German, or pro-German guests, was probably the one described by 'Chip' Channon, the socialite Conservative MP, on 7 July 1939. By then, the Spanish Civil War had been won by Franco, the first and only successful ally of both Hitler and Mussolini – while the British were 'looking elsewhere' or vaguely excusing themselves for 'appeasement politics', a course bound to lead to disaster. 'The palace was floodlit – explains 'Chip' Channon – and its grand baroque beauty could be seen for miles…', while Austrian Tyroleans were happily dancing, and 'literally rivers of champagne' were flowing …'

By 1939, my paternal grand-father, Miguel Hernández, a loyal Republican Sergeant at the North African Spanish Garrison and city of Ceuta, had been shot by Military Fascist rebels, who had risen against the democratically elected Spanish Government, on a beach across from Gibraltar on St. Michael's day 1936. By then, my maternal grand-father, Antonio Bronchud, was sent to the dungeon of a medieval castle near Teruel, my 'Secret Castle', for being a member of the Spanish Socialist Party (PSOE), which, like the British Labour Party, is one of the most ancient democratic centre-left political parties in Europe.

British Prime Minister Baldwin's view in 1936 that 'Germany would strike east not west', and that to him 'a confrontation between Nazis and Bolsheviks was not a cause for concern', probably condemned my grand-parents and my whole family to the role of 'vanquished'.

Churchill's reaction to Baldwin, unleashed during a Commons debate on 12 November 1936, descended to basics: 'He is no better than an epileptic corpse'.

The presence of Churchill's views on History, and on Europe in particular, are still very much alive today.

Selected Bibliography

59. John Lukacs, *Churchill: Visionary, Statesman and Historian* (Yale University Press, New Haven and London, 2002).

60. Dominique Enright, *Winston Churchill: The Greatest Briton* (Michael O'Mara Books Ltd, London 2003).

61. Hugh Thomas, *An unfinished History of the World* (Hamish Hamilton, London 1979).

62. Robert Anderson, *Elgar and Chivalry* (Elgar Editions, Herts, UK, 2002).

63. Ian Kershaw, *Making friends with Hitler. Lord Londondery and Britain's road to war* (Allen Lane, Penguin Books, London 2004).

64. John Toland, *Hitler* (Wordsworth Military Library, 1997).

65. Charles Higham, *Mrs Simpson: Secret lives of the Duchess of Windsor* (Pan Books, Sidgwick & Jackson, 2004).

66. Vernon Bogdanor, Professor of Government at Oxford University has very recently (2006) discussed Sir Winston Churchill's attitudes to Europe: 'During Churchill's youth, at the end of the nineteenth century, people frequently spoke of the unity of European civilization. After 1914, however, that unity was destroyed by two totalitarian ideologies, Communism and National Socialism. It took almost the whole of the twentiethth century to overcome that tragic division. Churchill, oddly enough, saw what was to happen. He told his Private Secretary, Sir John Colville, in the early 1950s, that if he, Colville, lived to his 'natural span', he would see the end of Communism in Europe, since the Communists would be unable to digest what they had swallowed. Colville died in 1987, just two years before the fall of the Berlin wall.'

Chapter Two

The Spanish Civil War: Treason in North Africa

The distance between Blenheim Palace and Oxford is short. The distance between victory and defeat can also be short.

In my last year at the University I travelled up to Blenheim on my 'Vespa', the small Italian motor-scooter made famous by 1960s Italians, and particularly by brilliant movie directors like Fellini, Pasolini or De Sica.

In my spare time, there was another Oxford place I enjoyed the most: the Cherwell River. Punting or rowing up and down the river, were not my 'speciality', but walking along the river banks, and across the fields, while watching others punt or row was very relaxing, and at times really entertaining.

My favourite walks (1980-83) were in the company of Professor Raymond Carr, Professor of Spanish History at the University, and Fellow of St. Antony's College, his wife Sarah and their two hound dogs, whose names I am afraid I have completely forgotten. I have never understood why the colloquial word 'hound' is often used in English to mean a 'wretched' or 'contemptible fellow', for I can scarcely think of more friendly, vivacious and intelligent dogs.

Professor Carr, who died in 2015, was an extraordinary man. I must acknowledge his hospitality, friendship and support, given without the asking. He had a 'passion for Spain', and an insight into the nature of Spain, and Spanishness, without ever losing his English and Oxford 'don' approach or point of view. It is by itself rather curious that the word 'don', meaning 'a teaching member of a University staff', is taken directly from the Spanish, meaning 'gentleman'. Sir Raymond was a gentleman, and I am sure a great British patriot. I remember him as a tall, thin, attractive man, with small eyes, reasonably thick spectacles but very penetrating eyesight. His wife Sarah was friendly, highly intelligent and charming. They had no reason whatsoever for being friendly to me, as I was a Medical student, not an Historian, and a member of another College, Wolfson College. Perhaps, the only thing we really had in common at the beginning was a 'passion' for Spain. Professor Carr enjoyed high regard in my home country.

It has long been suspected that besides being a scholar he collaborated with the British Intelligence Services at a particularly high level. One such example was Manuel Fraga Iribarne, a key minister under the 1960s Spanish Government, then still under General Franco's rule.

I actually met my wife indirectly because of Fraga – a fact which he probably ignored. The reason is that in my last year at Cambridge (1979-80) I became the Treasurer of the Students Association known as the 'Young European Democrats', and I invited Fraga, then Spanish Ambassador in London, to give a talk in Cambridge under the auspices of the association and King's College (with Professor Colin Smith, editor of the Collins 'Spanish-English Dictionary').

Other friends and pupils of Professor Carr, more to the left of the political spectrum, included Maravall, Minister of Education under Prime Minister Felipe Gonzalez, in the first Socialist Government of Spain following Franco's death; or Juan Pablo Fusi, with whom Carr published several books and essays on Spain, and who later became the Director of the 'National Library' (*Biblioteca Nacional*) in Madrid. But we all suspected that Professor Carr's contacts reached much higher, perhaps even up to the King, don Juan Carlos himself.

As an example, while I was at Oxford, Spain suffered the most serious attack on our young Democracy, the famous 'coup' by Colonel Tejero . The short and fat Guardia Civil, with a three-horned hat and a huge moustache, who took the *Cortes* (the Spanish 'House of Commons') by surprise on 23 February 1981, claiming a sudden end to the 'Democratic Experiment', shooting wildly, but fortunately not killing anybody, and 'waiting from orders from unknown superiors' that fortunately never arrived, while tanks had been sent around Valencia by a rebel General and military garrisons the length and breadth of Spain were in a state of great alarm.

That night, I could not sleep at all, until, in the early hours of the morning, the radio I kept in my college room announced that King Juan Carlos was going to speak to the Nation, and ask the military rebels to stop their 'coup attempt' at once, which they did. I cannot forget the faces of amusement and even the laughs of some of my college students while watching the BBC News in the College TV room. To the extent, that at first I though that what was on the screen, Colonel Tejero shouting and shooting, was just some kind of British Comedy, or a Soap Opera. But when I realised what was really happening, a chill went through my heart, bringing back tragic memories of our Spanish Civil War, and the events that almost destroyed my family and taught me what it means to be 'vanquished' and to grow in a country without freedom.

In fact, as a doctor, I can definitely say that there at least two crucial human values that are not given enough credit until they have been lost or are under threat: personal health and freedom!

The day after the 'coup', Sir Raymond Carr phoned me. We had already met a few times, and I had been their guest for dinner on more than one occasion. He invited me to a 'special and secret' meeting with some very particular guests a few days later. The main guest was no other than Mr Felipe Gonzalez, leader of the Spanish Socialist Party (PSOE), then in the Opposition, who had just survived the ordeal of the massive 'hostage crisis' at the *Cortes*. He was accompanied by Javier Solana, not yet famous at the time, but well known for being the 'scientific mind' of the PSOE, he was by training a Physicist, and for his support for the then prevailing views in left-wing parties against the entry of Spain into NATO (entry which was clearly a silenced pre-condition for entering into the European Common Market, now the European Union). Ironically, many years later I visited Javier Solana's office when he was Secretary General of the North Atlantic Treaty Organization (NATO), in Brussels, before he became the first ever Mr PESC of the EU (the chief of International Politics and External Relations of the European Union).

Professor Carr had invited these distinguished guests to a meeting where, at most, I counted a dozen people present, whose names I shall not mention not only for the sake of discretion, but above all because I did not even know (and still do not know), who they were. I could tell that some of the gentlemen present – strangely, perhaps, there were no ladies – were American, because of their accents. This American presence served to placate Spanish 'nerves' prevalent both during and immediately after the 1981 'coup' as top American officials, including the Secretary of State, suggested a 'non-intervention' policy by the USA, on the grounds that it was just an 'internal Spanish affair'…

The main reason for the meeting, and its timing, was to give the Opposition's leaders (Mr Felipe Gonzalez and Mr Javier Solana) a chance to explain themselves freely as to what had really happened in Spain, and how to make Spanish Democracy once and for all a stable reality. Mr Gonzalez spoke, without any written papers in front of him, at great length, perhaps for three hours, but it all went rather quickly, and obviously some sort of understanding and agreement was achieved.

I felt proud to have attended such a meeting, and my gratitude goes entirely to Professor Carr for having given me the opportunity. Perhaps he thought at the time that I might have been tempted to embark on a political career myself, and I am truly sorry for having disappointed him in that. But I am a vocational doctor and cancer researcher. Not a politician.

A few days later, while walking his dogs by the Cherwell, in a 'minefield of cowshit' – as he put it, he asked me several questions, such as:

a) Why did I think that Spain was still largely an 'unmapped region' by modern historical scholars? To which I replied that I simply did not know the reasons.

b) Why did I think Spain had remained 'isolated for so long', to the extent that even the French used to say that 'Africa starts at the Pyrenees'? To which I answered that the 'isolation' was largely self-imposed, to keep the Spanish people separate from the processes of enlightenment and democratic reform in Europe, and to maintain them in the 'Traditional Order' of the Spanish ruling classes. For example, in 1901, the Spain, which had existed as a 'State' since the 1490s, counted on some eighteen million inhabitants, of which only half a million had any money at all, and who constituted the ruling and educated classes. But they no longer ruled over their erstwhile larger Empire that had once included more than half of Europe, the Americas (North and South), and parts of Asia. They only ruled over their large and under-performing portions of land, while in those days, only around ten to twenty percent of Spanish soil was well irrigated and fertile.

As for the rest – 17.5 million – were poor people working in underdeveloped agricultural areas or in the over-exploited industrial areas of Catalonia and the Basque region. The majority were largely illiterate, and were taught what was good or bad directly from the pulpit, conveniently placed above their heads, in Catholic churches. Only the clergyman, especially when praying or when listening to a confession, had the 'authority' to distinguish 'Good from Evil'.

'Are you, therefore saying' – Sir Raymond asked me, with a characteristic smile on his face – '...that Spain is "anachronistic"and out of date?' 'Yes, of course it is', I replied. 'This is precisely why I came here to study and be educated'.

'But', continued Sir Raymond, 'most young people in Britain regard Tory politicians who shoot grouse in Scotland as dreadfully anachronistic... not to mention "fox hunting" ' It has to be said that Professor Carr was very keen on 'fox hunting', while I have to confess I am not at all keen on bull-fighting.

In the past three hundred years, Professor Carr explained to me, although I do not remember his exact words, that the history of Spain had been a great 'disaster', a 'fundamental political failure'. Domestic divisions were the rule rather than the exception, lack of social and economic evolution meant endless revolutions, military coups and *pronunciamientos*. This is another key Spanish invention, like '*guerrillas*', '*fiestas*', '*tapas*', '*tortillas*', and Spanish *Flamenco*. A *pronunciamiento* meant that whenever a military man of the eighteenth and nineteenth centuries, with personal ambition and charisma felt that there was 'anarchy and rebellion' in the country, he felt legally and ethically entitled to conspire against whatever regime was in Government, be it military, monarchy or a democracy. Why did he feel that time had come to take power? To 're-establish order' and 'bring peace and prosperity' to the nation.

Even freemasons were distinguished by their domestic divisions, like all other Spanish social forces and political parties. Perhaps, only the Catholic Church preserved a certain Unity, although it was probably because of their ancient strict hierarchical system, their ultimate dependence upon Rome, and their traditionally dogmatic policies that translated as 'heretical' any ideological deviation from standard doctrine.

Every single institution on earth has a 'Black Legend': the Church (Catholic or Protestant), Freemasonry, virtually every empire or dominating power, whether it be the Americans, the Jews, the Muslims, the Japanese, the Chinese, and so on. There is probably a modicum of truth in all of these 'Black Legends', but they are all intended to make large-scale and often spiteful and pernicious generalizations on the nature of things, institutions and peoples. In other words, they are all manipulative attempts to imprint and perpetuate 'prejudice and resentment'.

The 'Spanish Inquisition' is part of the 'Black Legend' of Spain, but it is certainly not a recent invention by comedians like the Pythons (remember their threat of the 'softy chair' as means of torture). The Spanish Inquisition was an effective, and at times extremely cruel method of dictating 'Truth' and 'Moral Behaviour' to the people. Unfortunately it lasted longer in Spain than anywhere else – from the thirteenth century, when it was introduced into the Kingdom of Aragon, as we shall later see, by the Dominicans, to control the Cathar Heresy but remaining up until the nineteenth century. The Dominicans take their name from *Domini Canes*, literally meaning 'the hounds of the Lord', to symbolize their duty to 'protect God's lambs' from heresy, like good sheep-dogs.

In fact, if one considers the mechanisms and basic rules of repression and cultural control during the forty year long Dictatorship of General Franco, (1936-75), one might perhaps conclude that the Spanish Inquisition only truly ended in 1978, with the approval of the present Democratic Constitution.

Raymond Carr was especially amused by invention of the so-called 'negative *pronunciamientos*'. In this context, a certain charismatic leader, often a second rate politician or military man, declared in a formal and enthusiastic manner a 'Rebellion' against whatever government was currently in power, which was backed by the 'refusal of the army to support the government'. One of the most surrealistic examples happened in Spain in 1820. A single man, Major Riego, delivered a much needed programme of Liberal Revolution by declaration, on 1 January 1820, acting on individual impulse and without consulting civilians – the Liberal Constitution of 1812 (so liberal that it was neither understood by most pro-liberals in Spain nor abroad). In other words, Riego attempted to insert a liberalism into the constitution that was to destroy it. Professor Carr, like many others, believed that the real reason why the troops did not immediately destroy Riego's movement, was because most of them did not want to be sent to Latin America to fight against the 'insurgents' who eventually declared the independence of most of Central and South America.

A similar type of denial of support (negative *pronunciamiento*) drove Maria Cristina to abdicate as Regent in 1840, and Alfonso XIII to withdraw from Spain in 1931, leading to the establishment of the Second Republic.

This long history of repression and lack of democratic experience is still to some extent alive today, and therefore still a threat to peaceful coexistence and social progress , but more in the historical or subconscious memory than in the minds of most modern Spaniards. In the past, it has led to a number of revolutionary movements, including the Anarchists. The anarchist-dominated Regional Federation of Spanish Workers, broken by repression after 1884, led to a wave of murderous terrorists bombs which reached their peak in the 1890s and included the *Liceo* (the Barcelona Opera House in *Las Ramblas*) bombing which killed twenty-one theatre goers, and the killings at the *Corpus Christi* Procession which the anarchists claimed was a 'symbol of corrupt bourgeois life'.

A few years after these atrocities, the genius of Catalan Architecture and Modernism, Antoni Gaudí, built a little Chapel (still visible) in the emerging, and still unfinished *Sagrada Familia* in Barcelona, the last of the great Cathedrals of the World. In this little Chapel, he depicts the horrors of the Anarchists bombing. Long suspected to be a Mason, or Rosicrucian, Gaudi was both a firm believer in God and a fervent Catholic, although with a possible Gnostic element. He was fiercely in favour of Freedom of Speech, Creativity and Liberty, but clearly against absurd crimes committed in the name of 'Anarchy' and 'Atheism'.

At one of the dinners we shared together, Professor Carr asked me a very important question, which he posed in one of his most celebrated books although in different words:

'Was the Spanish Civil War part of a social revolution, set off prematurely by the generals' revolt which could not be defeated by the sacrifice of that same revolution because of the chaotic mix of committee-rule, the militia columns, collectivization and the internal divisions among Communists and Anarchists? Or was it really a war to defend an advanced form of democracy, a war whose successful prosecution was incompatible with radical social revolution?"

My answer was that, based on the experience of my grand-parents and on what I had learnt at home, and considering that I was born a member of the 'vanquished' in the Spanish Civil War, the correct answer to his question was the latter. The Spanish Civil War was 'in origin' a war to defend an advanced form of democracy, that unfortunately became 'part of a social revolution', with Anarchists and Communists fighting each other, and with Stalin exercising his military muscles, only when the 'friendly and fraternal' Democracies of the West decided out of cowardice and selfish interests not to intervene in favour of the Democratic Spanish Government, thereby betraying it.

In other words, considering its 'genesis', the Spanish Civil War was not, as the victors claimed, a war of liberation or a religious crusade, but an unjust war against an infant democracy at a very difficult time in the history of the world. This should be the final and objective verdict of History, without denying the sad truth that atrocities were indeed committed on both sides.

Franco was a shrewd opportunist, ruthless and devoid of any political message. He was not a politician like Mussolini, Hitler or Stalin. He was an 'illuminated military man', or – as Raymond Carr points out in his book *Spain:1808-1975,* he was an 'accidentalist'; he cared little for political forms provided they maintained 'order'.

The Western democracies failed Republican Spain. True, the young Spanish Republic made several early political 'mistakes in 1934 – a good example of which was the unwise unilateral declaration of independence of Catalonia (within an imaginary Iberian Federation) by President Lluis Companys and the practically simultaneous revolutionary uprising of miners in Asturia (backed by PSOE). Both traumatic events weakened the Republic.

Fear of a general war, Chamberlain's desire for appeasement with Germany and Italian friendship, the Conservative Party distaste for 'Red Spain', even if the presence of Communists in the Spanish Republican Government was absolutely minimal and without power, committed Britain to non-intervention, and brought pressure on the French Prime Minister Blum, sympathetic to Republican Spain, to adopt a similar course. In the early months the Labour leaders, tending to wards ideological support of the French Blum, raised pleas for the supply of arms to Republican and Democratic Spain.

Blum was himself embarrassed by his impotence in helping Spain, once it was apparent that non-intervention worked against the Republic, and only helped Stalin to mingle in the international arena for the first time. French arms deliveries only took place in the early days and, to the shame of all true democrats and true freemasons, the crucial French frontier was closed when the Fascist/Nationalist blockade left the Pyrenean route the only safe passage for Russian arms. Eventually, just across the Pyrenees, in south-east France, a number of refugee camps, which later morphed into Concentration Camps, under the Vichy/Nazi rule, were filled with thousands of Republican soldiers and politicians, as well as civilians escaping from Franco's repression.

At the end of the Spanish Civil War, a number of brave Spanish republican soldiers became key fighters against the Nazis under the French Flag (1940-45) Many joined the few remaining Free French forces in Northern Africa, and fought with the French General Jacques-Philippe Leclerc in Chad and Libya, defeating the Italians at the small but symbolical battle of Murzuch. Many Spaniards entered Paris on Liberation Day waving French and Spanish Republican flags – but to little avail: Franco was to remain in power until his natural death, in 1975 after ruthless repression of some two million Spanish citizens.

True, the Anarcho-Syndicalists and the various factions of Communists took full advantage of the chaotic situation, and abhorrent crimes such as the killing of between 500 and 5000 clergymen and nuns, took place in 'Republican' territory. The anger and fear felt in the Republican territories, the absence of support from Western Democracies and the loss of political control by the moderates on the Spanish democratic side, facilitated the vile assassination of land-owners, right-wing (although innocent) politicians, and many clergymen by Republican militias.

Churches were burnt and a totally absurd anti-clericalism led to outspoken defence of the Spanish Catholic Church by Franco and the other military rebels and a consequent declaration of a 'Crusade' against the Republic. In return for their blessing, the Fascists/Nationalists gave the Church all of their traditional privileges, and above all the control of 'education and the mind' at schools and universities. The Jesuits were re-admitted in 1938 and General Franco was paraded 'under Palio' with the bishops in post-war Spain (*see* Figure 31).

The Military Revolt against Spanish Democracy had been 'cooking for a long time'. Manuel Azaña, a Spanish freemason and Minister of War later to become President of the Spanish Republic, was a moderate man who clearly believed in a more progressive and democratic Spain. One of his first mistakes, however, was two-fold. Firstly he ordered the closure of the Military Academy of Zaragoza which many years later trained the future King Juan Carlos, soon after the start of the first Republican Government in 1931. The reason for the closure, probably true, is that Zaragoza was a Military Academy controlled by forces opposed to Democratic Government, although they were perhaps at the time more pro-Monarchy (King Alfonso XIII had exiled himself in fascist Rome), than pro-Fascist. In any case, General Franco was most upset by this because he was the military Director of the Academy.

The second political blunder committed by Azaña, is that he did not denounce with rigour the open criticism by Franco, and his refusal to accept the democratically elected Republican Army.

Not surprisingly, young General Franco started to plot against Azaña and his Government, together with his friend and colleague from the Spanish-Moroccan Wars (1923-1926), General Luis Orgaz, who later signed the death sentence of my own paternal grand-father, Miguel Hernández Morales, also a military man in North Africa since the 1920s, in one of the very early repressions and executions of 1936.

As an unexpected finding of my research on the events leading to the closure of the Military Academy of Zaragoza in 1931, I found out that the Supreme Commander of Aragon (*Capitán General*) in 1931 was none other than don Jorge Fernández de Heredia, a descendent of the Grand Master of the Order of St. John, don Juan Fernández de Heredia, whose secret castle and esoteric knowledge we shall examine in the following chapters. Jorge Fernández de Heredia was a 'staunch defender' of Traditional Order based on the power of the Church, the monarchy and the army, in Spain and he had signed many death sentences during and after the first attempt to establish a Republican Government in Spain in December 1930.

Probably because of that the Anarchists and Communists later destroyed, at the beginning of the Spanish Civil War in 1936, a true beauty of Renaissance Spain: the beautiful and unique Crypt and Tombstone, at the small Aragonese town of Caspe, where his ancestor, don Juan Fernández de Heredia, Grand Master of St. John, had lain buried since 1396.

Left alone by Western Democracies, and internally divided by

Revolutionary forces, the Moderates of the Republicans, those who know that it is wrong 'turning to the right nor the left from the strict path of virtue', neither 'bending towards avarice, injustice, malice, revenge, envy and contempt', were literally in the hands of the radicals and revolutionaries. But the Plot of the Conspirators was meant to lead to a *pronunciamiento*, or at least to a rapid 'coup'. Only because Spanish infant democracy had already more roots and support than the rebels had thought, the coup failed in all major cities, and what could have been a minor disaster ended up in a long and cruel Civil War.

According to Professor Carr, ' During the critical early days (17-23 July 1936) neither side acted with decision: if the army had been able to rise all over Spain on 18 July, as planned, the old recipe of a *pronunciamiento* might have been once more effective as an instrument of political change, and the Civil War might have been avoided. Similarly, if the Republican Government had issued orders to arm the workers, as some leading politicians had demanded on the 17 July, when the plot was discovered in North Africa (the city of Melilla), instead of two days later, the rebellion might have been more effectively crushed.

Hans Beimler, a German Communist, killed fighting with the volunteers of the International Brigade on the Madrid front, among whose members there were also several young Cambridge and Oxford students who gave their lives in a foreign country for their non-Communist and anti-Fascist ideals, '... the only way we can get back to a free Germany is through Madrid.' One young Cambridge man, Kim Philby, who was in fact a communist and a Soviet secret agent, actually served as war journalist on Franco's side. He was seriously injured near Teruel by Republican fire, ironically probably by soviet bombs, and was paradoxically decorated as a war hero by none other than Franco himself.

When it had already become apparent that the 'coup' had failed, and Spain was heading for a long and bloody civil war, on 27 July in Tetuan the American journalist, Allen, asked Franco: 'Do you mean to say that you are prepared to kill half of Spain?' (The *News Chronicle*, 29 July-1 August 1936), Franco replied with a triumphant smile: 'I shall repeat it for you, at any price we shall win this war'.

Another American journalist, Lawrence A. Fernsworth, who later published such works as *Dictators and Democrats* (1941) and *Spain's struggle for freedom* (1957), gave a personal account of what happened in July 1936. I reproduce part of his typewritten letter (dated October 1936) that I have found in the National Archives of Catalonia (*Sant Cugat*, Barcelona):

'My ears still repeat the echoes of roaring cannon and exploding bombs, of the intermittent putting of machine guns and the crackling detonations of rifles firing in continuous volleys, of horses hoofs, of bugle calls, of men shouting and other men screaming in anguish, of terror-stricken and screeching flocks of swallows flying back and forth in a frenzy as bullets whistle among them, of all the deafening cacophony of warfare by which, on the morning of July 19, rebellion was unleashed in Barcelona and elsewhere on the mainland of Spain'.

This young American author declares, among other things: 'The land is drenched in blood and the end is not yet in sight … Overnight, literally so, the course of Spanish history has been changed and perhaps the course of western history as well. Either some form of communism shall have invaded the West or fascism in one guise or another shall have acquired a third European front, shall be encircling France. Notwithstanding – he adds – the constitutional government is bravely fighting with its back to the wall, hoping to save the Republic as against both fascism and proletariat rule, but with heavy odds against it …'

Fernsworth explained that the rebellion against the Republic was the work of 'mutual forces united in a well understood mutual pact'. The 'forces' in question were 'the privileged and propertied classes, the army and the church'. He cited a letter by a certain Mr Edwin Henson, rector of the 'English College of Valladolid', and made public by the Catholic Archbishop of London himself attacking the democratic government. For example, one paragraph says: 'The news on the English radio has been very misleading. They speak always of the "government forces" and "the rebels". They should say "the rabble" and "the forces of Christian Law and Order".'

Thus, the Catholic Church gave General Franco a easy explanation for the war: it was to be seen as a fight between the forces of Christianity and Communism. This is the picture that emerges by perusing several of the documents in the Churchill Archives Centre, Churchill College, at the University of Cambridge.

The only 'real government' in Spain, according to this peculiar source, was that of General Cabanellas, in the small city of Burgos, who was a member of a military Masonic lodge and was later totally eclipsed by Franco. This interpretation of the war also found allies from among the Anglican Church. Among them, the Protestant Lecturer J. Norris who on July 2 1938 (when the pro-Soviets had already gained control in most of the weak Spanish Republican army because no other democracy came to help) wrote a hand-written letter to Prime Minister Neville Chamberlain (a letter deposited in the Churchill Archives Centre at Churchill College, Cambridge), stating that the war in Spain was entirely due to 'Russian plotting and planning' and that the Soviets had ordered the Communist Party in Britain to do the same thing: to start a great civil war.

Mr Norris' challenge to hold a public debate was officially accepted by the Hayes Labour Party and the debate indeed took place at Botwell Common, Hayes, on 10 September 1938. Norris's defence was on behalf of 'a United Christian Front'. He was not alone. A certain Mr Henry S. Lunn published a letter in *The Times* on 23 July 1937 entitled: 'Civil strife in Spain: a United Christian Front', stating that his mission was to unite all Christians in the war against the Anti Christ. He directly accused the British media of having misled the public into accepting the myth of a military rising against a democratic government'.

People like Norris and Lunn give credence and strength to the idea that Franco was a champion of Christianity, and would therefore become a 'good dictator'. This was also the view defended by none other than Randolph Churchill in an interview with General Franco for the *Daily Mail*, praising his 'sensitive policies'. The notion of a 'good dictator' was, of course, not new, but it can hardly fit the historical facts before, during or after the Spanish Civil War.

In his 1936 manuscript, in the National Archives of Catalonia (*Sant Cugat*, Barcelona), Lawrence Fernsworth, concludes, after a detailed analysis of the whole Republican period a number of interesting facts:

1. Never in Spanish history had the army been so well provided for, financially and materially, as in the first Republican budget.

2. Popular uprising against the Church was due to centuries of oppression, corruption, abuses and political entanglements. True, that some perhaps too hurried and unwise anti-clerical laws were passed by the democratic Spanish Parliament. For example, a special law dissolved the Jesuit order and confiscated its property. Another special law, known as the 'religious congregations law', suppressed exclusively religious schools, and limited the activities of religious orders. Finally, most controversial of all: the nationalization of Church property, but this did not mean its 'confiscation'. It meant that all patrimony of the Church in Spain became patrimony of the State, which was specifically charged with its protection and upkeep, and was exempt from taxation.

3. By prudent and moderate patience, by recourse to true 'Christian values' the Church would soon have recovered social prestige, except among the most radical who were, initially, only a small minority.

4. At the moment when the constitutional government, with its back to the wall, was bravely fighting to save Democracy in Spain both from the onslaughts of its enemies of the right and from the excessive demands of

revolutionaries of the kind commonly called 'red', the privileged classes, the army, the church, to protect their own interests, 'deliberately made common cause in an attack upon the government, deliberately unleashed a reign of terror in which both sides have since had an equal share of guilt, deliberately opened the gates to the revolution of the masses bent upon wiping out democratic government and establishing proletarian domination'.

Even people at the top in British political affairs received contradictory reports on what was really going on in Spain. For example, contrary to what Mr Norris and Mr Lunn had said, a personal lady friend of sir Winston Churchill, a certain 'Katharine A.', from Eastwood (Dunkeld), wrote a long and charming hand-written letter to the future Prime Minister (also to be found in the Churchill Archives Centre), asking him to carefully read the speech by Manuel Azaña, President of the Spanish Republic, on the first anniversary of the outburst of the civil war in Spain (July 1937). She makes it very clear to the future Prime Minister that the war in Spain was the 'result of a long prepared Nazi conspiracy' prepared by the Nazis and their supporters. She also warns Churchill that thanks to Hitler and Mussolini there were potent guns near Gibraltar, on Spanish-Moroccan soil, pointing towards the Rock and with the threatening capacity of firing over the Strait.

On 25 May 1937, Churchill delivered an impressive speech on the 'New Commonwealth Society', partly published in his 'Complete Speeches', containing the following: 'We are one of the few Peace Societies that advocates use of force, nothing whatever in common with abject school of Pacifists who seek submission to tyranny or wrong doing' and 'We cannot afford to turn our back upon Europe. Such doctrines are ignominious even if we were separated by 2000 miles of ocean from the European continent'. He added at one point:

'I cannot recognise on either side in Spain qualities which entitle them to carry standards of world causes. Frantic combatants should be separated by concert of Europe, and a political regime which is neither Bolshevik nor Nazi, set up, until Spanish people can regain natural poise and self-possession.'

'In a hundred years, from 1812 to 1914, we, in this island – explained Churchill – actually fought on the side of France and against France; on the side of Russia and against Russia, on the side of Germany and against Germany; even on the side of the United States and against them. Herr Hitler has stated a profound truth when he observed that in spite of all wars in recent centuries, great nations have all preserved their characteristic identities …'

General Franco too, like Mussolini, Hitler or Stalin, was possessed by an inner 'messianic' force, that made him truly believe that he had been chosen by God to lead a Crusade against the New Spain, and to rule with Absolute and Supreme Power. He proclaimed himself *Caudillo de España por la Gracia de Dios*: 'The Leader (the same as 'Duce' or 'Führer') of Spain by the Grace of God.' This type of **irrational** belief is the origin of much human suffering throughout history.

Figure 31
General Franco (with sun glasses, on the right of the Bishop) was paraded under *Palio* with the Bishops until his old age. Picture taken from the Spanish magazine *Historia* (Number 16, August 1976), but there is no author quoted.

The key to the war in Spain was in many ways the victory of Franco in North of Africa in the summer of 1936. The rest was easier than crossing the Strait.

In other words, the Nationalist/Fascist Military coup succeeded because General Franco managed to cross the Strait of Gibraltar with the North African Army, and the feared and cruel Moroccan Mercenary Forces, securing for himself the absolute leadership of the military rebels, and the unconditional military support, first of Hitler first and later Mussolini.

This occurred in great part because of the passive but shameful betrayal of the democratic Republican Government of Spain by western democracies, and in particular the British politicians in power at the time. They were more concerned with preserving peace at all costs, than with preventing war, as Winston Churchill pointed out several times. I honestly believe that not enough critical historical research on *mea culpa* factors and circumstances has yet been done in this Spanish context by British historians and military experts, including those associated with the Secret Services. There can be little doubt that initial 'non-intervention' and even 'supportive policies' by top English politicians to the right of the political spectrum, were in favour of the military rebels and, perhaps surprisingly, General Franco in particular. There was considerable tacit support for fascists ideas among the powerful classes of the United Kingdom at the time. A lot of political pressure, for example, was put on France, the only democracy with direct borders with Spain across the Pyrenees, to stop sending arms to the Spanish Republic.

The story goes as follows, according to two of the most prestigious and personally admired British historians: Hugh Thomas and Paul Preston.

Incredible though it may seem, the Spanish conspirators hired an English aeroplane which was to bring Franco to Morocco, where the 'alarm' would be given and the revolt started. In fact it appears that General Mola, the pro-Monarchist leader who later died in a mysterious air accident as did General Sanjurjo and who had been chosen initially as the future Dictator, had persuaded Francisco Herrera, a personal friend of the Conservative Spanish politician Gil Robles (who was later to be totally eclipsed and left out by General Franco), to speak to the Mallorcan millionaire Juan March, who had met Franco in 1933 , and to ask him for substantial amounts of money to finance the 'coup'.

I have mixed feelings about the person of Juan March. On the one hand, he had been jailed during the Republic for demonstrable Black Market Practices in North Africa including cheating Tax Inspectors. On the other, it just happens that he was later revealed to have been a bright and shrewd 'double agent' employed by both the British and Nazi German Secret Services during much of World War II. He is also a distant relative of my ex-wife!

In fact, *his* wife, Carmen Delgado (now deceased), was my ex-wife's grand-mother's cousin. I therefore have some familial, albeit distant, knowledge of what March really was and I am fairly sure that he was not a Fascist. He was a ruthless business man, who made a huge fortune and was regarded as one of the wealthiest men on earth.

It also appears, that by the early 1940s March's sympathies for Franco had evaporated as he came to realise Franco's true colours and his intentions as a totalitarian dictator. As rumour has it (and I believe on a very sound basis), by this late stage Juan March had even tried to support the early return of the Monarchy under don Juan de Borbón, father of the present King of Spain and son of King Alfonso XIII, who had died prematurely in Rome.

In any event, Juan March, who was too intelligent to be a Fascist, gave the money to Luca de Tena, owner of the conservative and pro-Monarchist Madrid Newspaper *ABC*, who in turn ended up contacting Juan de la Cierva, an aeronautical expert in London exiled for his right-wing ideas, to rent an aeroplane and an English crew to fly Franco in secret from Tenerife in the the Canary Islands to Las Palmas, and then to Spanish Morocco. A Dragon Rapide plane was hired in Sussex and flew from Croydon, piloted by an English Captain William Henry Webb, a veteran of the Royal Air Force recruited to do the 'dirty job'.

That trip was to change the History of Spain, leading to the worst, longest and most repressive dictatorship in Western Europe.

I have a very high opinion of British Intelligence, and I find it virtually impossible to believe that the British Secret Services were totally unaware of what was going on in Croydon and in Spain. As this Intelligence 'slip' later meant the torture and death of my own grand-father, I cannot, on this occasion, feel very proud of British democracy and the English tradition of freedom.

A book recently published by a young Spanish Historian from Ceuta, Francisco Sánchez Montoya, throws some light on what happened afterwards in North Africa.

On 29 May 1936, the senior General Sanjurjo, in Pamplona, had already accepted General Emilio Mola as the 'director' of the coup or *pronunciamiento*. In the Spanish Casino of Tetuan, then under the Spanish dominion in Morocco, young and not so young Spanish military officers had been heard talking about a possible coup in July. In the early afternoon of 17 July the coup started prematurely in Melilla, a Spanish city and military enclave in Morocco. My grand-father, Miguel Hernández-Morales, was a Sergeant in the Spanish Artillery in the nearby city of Ceuta. He was thirty-five years of age, and already had four children. My father was only five years old when this happened.

Several of the Top military men in the Army, and most of the Navy and Spanish Air-force in North Africa, did not join the 'coup', despite being under pressure from lower ranking military staff who were clearly in favour of preserving peace and democracy and desirous of giving another chance to the young Spanish Republican Government.

Figure 32
The Two Columns of the Strait of Gibraltar (the Rock and Atlas), with the arms of Emperor Charles V of Germany (Charles I of Spain). *Aci et Plus Outre* means 'Here and Beyond', for it was under this Emperor that it became evident that Christopher Columbus had not, as he thought until his own death, discovered just a few islands off the coast of India, but in fact a huge New Continent, eventually called 'America', that by then had become part of the Great Spanish Empire.

The Straits of Gibraltar have always been part of the Spanish Coat of Arms, and they are represented by the Two Columns (the Rock and the Atlas) that separate Africa from Europe. Even in the times of Emperor Charles V (Charles I of Spain), the Hapsburg monarch, the Two Columns (and the inscription *Plus Ultra*) were part of Spanish Symbolism (*see* Figure 32).

Figure 33
Key elements at the entrance of a Masonic lodge: the two Pillars and the All-seeing Eye. (picture taken from a nineteenth century Spanish Masonic manual of unknown authorship)

According to Greek mythology, Hercules was the hero whose mighty strength effected the separation of the two continents and thereby the creation of the Mediterranean, however, 'two columns' also contain a fundamental symbolism in Freemasonry (*see* Figure 33), and may still be found in most Masonic lodges as well as many old Cathedrals. When the Temple at Jerusalem was completed by King Solomon, there was nothing that more particularly struck the attention of the visitors than the two great pillars which were placed at the porchway entrance. They were formed hollow, to better serve as archives to Masonry, for therein were deposited the constitutional rolls. This tradition is almost certainly derived from Judaism, as the Scrolls of the Torah are also safely deposited in a hollow structure in most Synagogues.

The two pillars were made of molten brass, and were beautifully adorned with chapiters enriched with net-work, lily-work, and pomegranates. Network from the connection of its meshes, denoting Unity; lily-work, from its whiteness, denoting Peace; and pomegranates, from the exuberance of their seed denoting prosperity and plenty.

On that fateful day –17 July 1936 – the local Air Force Commander-in-Chief, De la Puente Bahamonde, first cousin to General Franco himself (whose full name was actually Francisco Franco Bahamonde), was promised rapid troop reinforcements from Madrid by the then Prime Minister, Casares Quiroga. For reasons that are still unclear, those reinforcements never arrived. Commander Bahamonde, loyal to the Republic and unable to send his forces into battle from a shortage of both pilots and fuel, gave orders to his men to destroy their own military aircraft rather than have them fall into the hands of the rebel Fascist forces. He was later executed by Franco's troops.

Initially, the military rebels took many prisoners and shot many members of left-wing and republican political forces, as well as many military freemasons. Freemasonry had always been liked by the Military, because, among other things, it taught discipline and orderly behaviour. General Franco's brother, a famous pilot called Ramon Franco, was himself a Mason, but Franco, throughout his life, displayed a virulent and obsessive hatred towards the Craft and all Masons.

My grand-father was a modest but upright man. As an artillery sergeant he had fought in the Spanish-Moroccan War in the 1920s, and in times of peace he ran the local main military depot. He also helped the local football team in the City of Ceuta, in the Strait, just across from the Rock of Gibraltar. That made him very popular and he had won much support among local people – politicians and Masons alike. I am unsure as to whether he was a Mason himself but he was certainly not happy with the military coup. Ironically, he was jailed because of 'adhesion to the rebellion' – a particularly perverse accusation considering that the 'rebels' were in fact those who had joined Franco in the military coup.

According to the Historian Francisco Sánchez Montoya, in late July, my grand-father became the leader of a secret plot to free the military companions and army officers who had been jailed in the Fortress of Hacho. The appointed day of action was 15 August 1936. Unfortunately the plotters, my grand-father among them, were betrayed, captured, almost certainly tortured to reveal the details of the plot and subsequently executed on St Michael's Day, 1936. As a matter of fact, the official time of execution was promulgated as 1 AM on 30 September neatly avoiding the *actual* St. Michael's day. Michael was my name day (Miguel). The name day is celebrated in Spain in a manner almost equivalent to a birthday.

Thanks to Francisco Sánchez Montoya, I have been able to read the full Court Martial proceedings. The Fascist Rebels deliberately wanted to represent themselves as the 'legitimate' party, and the reading of the rulings by the Military Tribunal on my poor grand-father make me feel ashamed of being a Spaniard. There was no proof whatsoever of any wrong-doing. They spoke of him as being 'dangerous and in contact with the Intelligence Committee of Madrid', but no evidence is given for that. He was not a political activist, but was ironically accused of being a 'Promoter of Military Sedition' when in fact the traitors and conspirators were those who killed him. He was jailed on 7 August and executed by firing squad on the beach across from the Rock on St. Michael's day.

To add insult to injury, it turns out from subsequent examination of the full proceedings of my grand-father's Court Martial, that the President and two other members out of the five military officers who took part in the Tribunal, did not agree with the 'death sentence' and were in fact prepared to change the sentence to 'six years in jail'. The person who had the last word, wrote and signed my grand-father's death sentence (and I have a copy of the original handwritten document), was none other than General Luis Orgaz, the same man who signed the death sentence of De la Puente Bahamonte (Franco's cousin), on the same day of the execution (29 September 1936). It appears that General Luis Orgaz had flown the day before (on 28 September), to a secret but crucial meeting near Salamanca, north west of Madrid, where the leaders of the coup (the *Junta de Defensa Nacional,*) had met to decide who was going to be the Supreme Commander in Chief of the Rebels, or 'Liberators' as they preferred to call themselves, and to plan a new global war strategy.

The Chief of this National Defence Council was General Cabanellas, the most senior of them all, who was himself a freemason and had formerly been a Liberal politician. He was a monarchist like so many others present and what they really wanted was the return of the King, Alfonso XIII. Franco, however, won the vote (even though he cheated by actually voting himself).

General Cabanellas (according to Paul Preston) later said: 'You do not know what you have done, gentlemen. For you do not know Franco as well as I do. I had him under my command when he was much younger in North Africa, and now that you have decided to confide the care of Spain to him, he will truly believe that Spain belongs to him, and to him alone.'

Prophetically, Cabanellas, who was later betrayed and abandoned by Franco, added ' He will not leave power, during the war nor after, until his death'.

General Luis Orgaz, Head of the Rebel Forces in Morocco was also there, but supported Franco who was given the titles of *Generalissimo* and 'Head of State'. He then took a plane back from Salamanca to Tetuan, and comfortably sat down to sign my my grand-father's death sentence.

On 30 September, the same day that my grand-mother and her four young children were allowed to see the dead body of my grand-father, riddled with bullets, the Bishop of Salamanca, the most famous of Spanish Universities, delivered a speech proclaiming the 'Last Crusade' against Republican Forces. He even quoted St Agustine, to separate the 'City of Hatred and Anarchy' (Republican Spain) from the 'City of Love and God' (Fascist Spain). In fact, Fascist Rebel forces called themselves the Nationals or *Nacionales*.

This was again a parody of truth, for they only referred to that Nation of Spain, *Una, Grande y Libre* (meaning 'One, Great and Free') which had been the result of Castilian domination and the end of the more 'pluralistic' Hapsburg's 'Nation of Nations', that was and still is the real Spain.

Professor Josep Trueta, who exiled himself to England following the end of the Spanish Civil War, becoming Professor of Orthopaedic Surgery at the famous 'Nuffield Department' of the University of Oxford, taught all that he knew about the surgical treatment of war wounds and fractures to the British Military Doctors and thereby gained a high reputation among his peers. He published, a wonderful little book in 1946 called *The Spirit of Catalonia (L'Esperit de Catalunya)* It is full of nostalgia for his native Catalonia and the pluralist vision of Spain. He dedicated this book to his Catalan friend and fellow exiled genius, the great cellist Pablo Casals. He concludes by saying that in science when the result of an experiment is always the same, it means that the real 'causal factors' are also the same. According to this prestigious physician, if Democracy and Freedom in Spain are always threatened whenever the 'Unitarian', and Castilian, vision of Spain are under threat, it is because the latter is by nature 'Totalitarian', and implies an unwillingness to respect the plural nature and historical rights of the different nationalities of the real Spain.

The 'United Kingdoms of Spain' include other ancient but deep-rooted peoples – two well known examples being the Basques and the Catalans, for example. Why may we not, therefore, embrace the political formula enshrined in the United states of America – *E Pluribus Unum* ('Out of Many, One').

It is true to say that Catalonia has never been an independent state. Over a thousand years ago, Catalan speaking people inhabited the southern-eastern parts of what is now France and across the Pyrenees into the north-eastern part of what is now Spain. They had been politically part of the medieval feudal system subject to the Holy Roman Emperor since the time of Charlemagne. In the twelfth century those fertile and culturally active regions became part of the Crown of Aragon by marriage between the Count of Barcelona Ramon Berenguer IV and a very young Peronella, princess of the Kingdom of Aragon, in 1137. Following the early eighteenth century War of the Spanish Succession (1701-14) the new King Philip of Anjou (grandson of Louis' XIV of France) imposed the dissolution of the Crown of Aragon and the disappearance (under this originally French Bourbon dynasty) of the local *Fueros*, – independent legal systems of the individual parts of the ancient Crown (Catalonia, Aragon, Valencia, Mallorca and Sardinia). Spain ceased to be a confederation of different Kingdoms and became a centralised political system predominantly ruled by a Castilian elite based in Madrid.

Some Catalan and, more especially, Basque clergymen did not support the 'Spanish Crusade' against the Democratic Republic, even though they were devoted Christians and Catholics but most clergymen did in fact support Franco. This 'root problem' of 'Nationalities' has not been solved even after forty years of repression and totalitarianism. Even today it has to be seen as the main subject of concern to the Kingdom of Spain. The rivalry between two famous football teams, Real Madrid and Barcelona Football Club, is not just a sports rivalry, but has its true basis in this mutual feeling of distrust and lack of understanding between two different visions of Spain, the 'Unitarian' and the 'Plural but One', that can only be reconciled by democratic and peaceful negotiations, but also by respect for Truth and comprehension of History.

It also appears that the military, loyal to the Republic, once it had become evident that the *pronunciamiento* had failed, were waiting for help from the Navy, faithful to the Republic, and the Air Force, but the British closed their port of Gibraltar to damaged Republican Spanish Ships, and made it very difficult for them to cross the Strait or attempt any landing on the beaches of Ceuta and Melilla. As we say in Spain, 'With friends like these, who needs enemies?'

I can imagine my grand-father, tortured in his jail at the Fortress, listening to the bombs and fighting from the Strait and hoping for a rescue operation by Democratic forces, to no avail. I can imagine him sobbing in the little Chapel where he was kept before his execution, and where he wrote an absolutely beautiful, but obviously dramatic, letter of farewell to my Grand-mother and his four children (the eldest was nine and the youngest two years old).

In his handwritten and agonizing letter, which my father showed me for the first time only a few years ago, he starts with a '*Catalina, amiga mia, perdóname…*' (Catalina- or Catherine- was my grand-mother's name): this means 'Catherine, my friend, forgive me…' Forgive him for what? Obviously for leaving her alone in North Africa, with four orphaned children, no money and the fear of more repression and prosecution. How could British Forces in Gibraltar simply fold their arms thereby helping the Fascist Rebels directly or indirectly?

Franco knew that to win the war he had to cross the Strait of Gibraltar as soon as possible with his loyal African Troops and his infamous *Guardia Mora* (Mercenaries from Morocco, ready to kill, rape and cut the throat of anybody at Franco's command). But the Republican Navy made things difficult for them, and even tried to damage the garrison and Fortress at Ceuta from the sea. The bombs hit the Fortress, where my grand-father was a prisoner, and a later survivor said that they were struck by panic but also overjoyed by the thought and hope that the war had not yet been lost by Democratic Spain.

On 5 August, the Republican warship *Lepanto* (named after the naval battle of 7 October 1571, which halted the expansion of the Ottoman Empire in the Mediterranean), was badly damaged by the Fascist Troops. *Lepanto*, that glorious battle for Christendom won by the 'Armada of the Holy League', that included Spanish as well as Venetian ships, and the brave Knights of St. John and Malta, was the site where the Crescent of Islamic Turkey was defeated by the Cross of Christian forces in the last great naval battle between fleets of galleys in the history of Europe but even the glorious name of *Lepanto*, failed to inspire British compassion. Franco asked the leader of his Air Force, General Kindelan, to telephone the British at Gibraltar and ask them not give aid and refuge to the damaged Republican warship. The British amazingly 'obeyed Franco's orders', and only the dead and wounded were allowed to disembark.

Crossing the Strait – the real *Rubicon* of the war, required Franco to seek foreign help. He first approached Mussolini, on 22 July, asking for at least twelve aeroplanes, bombers or aircraft for civil transportation. What he did not know was that General Mola, who had gained more credibility with Mussolini had already asked for help. Mussolini, simply wrote 'NO' in the telegram containing Franco's request.

It was only after General Sanjurjo died, in a mysterious air accident, a fate yet to be shared by several other of Franco's potential adversaries or competitors and further conversations between Franco's aid, Bolín and Mussolini's new Foreign Minister, Count Galeazzo Ciano, that Mussolini himself started to take Franco's requests and possible future role more seriously.

Franco was getting desperate, stuck with his troops in North Africa, while my grand-father and many other military staff were being taken prisoners or executed for not joining the 'Glorious National Movement', as they called it. So he approached Hitler himself. The story makes interesting reading. Franco, with the help of two Nazi business men in Spanish Morocco, Johannes E.F. Bernhardt, an active member of the Nazi Party and friend of General Mola, and Adolf Langenheim, managed to contact none other than Ernst Wilhelm Bohle, the head of the global *Auslandorganisation*' (the AO), and it was Bohle who procured a contact with the Deputy-Führer Rudolf Hess. According to recent research, this same Ernst Bohle should have been Hitler's emissary five years later (in May 1941) to negotiate a secret peace deal with the British , and he should have flown to Britain instead of Rudolf Hess, a situation which will be examined further.

We may take it that Ernst W. Bohle may be seen as the missing link between Franco and Hitler in 1936, and was probably set to occupy a similar role, in 1940-41, between Hitler and the British prior to the Nazis attack on the Soviet Union during the Second World War.

When I first came across the name of Ernst Bohle during my investigations, I must confess that it meant almost nothing to me. It turned out that he was probably the key link between General Franco and Hitler in the critical days of July and August 1936 as well as a key protagonist of the Rudolf Hess 'flight for peace' that took place in May 1941.

Ernst Wilhelm Bohle (1903-1960) was born on 28 July 1903 in Bradford, England in what was then peaceful and beautiful English countryside. Brought up in England, he was educated in Cape-Town, South Africa, and later studied in Germany (Cologne and Berlin), graduating in commerce and business administration in 1923. From 1931 onwards he became increasingly active in the Nazi party (NSDAP), becoming a full member in 1932 and, in May 1933, Director of the *Auslandsorganization* (AO), which had been created to promote Nazi ideas and propaganda abroad among all German expatriates as well as those of German descent.

In November 1933 Bohle became a full member of the Reichstag. He strongly believed in National Socialism, and worked very hard for the AO, travelling around the globe and creating some 230 subsidiaries or AO-offices across Europe, the USA and Latin America, as well as in Australia, Africa, India and East Asia, including Japan. He was thoroughly supported by Rudolf Hess, to whom Bohle reported. Neither of them felt 'anti-British'. Reliable evidence has both of them as being anti-semitic and, of course, Nazis but neither anti-British nor anti-American.

The AO units abroad were clearly designed for propaganda purposes, political and financial deals, and achieving 'miniature mirror images' of the Third Reich. Unlike the Rotary Club, which, like Freemasonry, had been outlawed and forbidden by the Nazis, and contrary to what Bohle stated on a number of different occasions, the AO *did* interfere in the internal political affairs of other countries on behalf of German national socialism. For example, it was through their office in Spanish Morocco that General Franco succeeded in getting the military and financial support from Hitler that he so badly needed to cross the Straits of Gibraltar, with his troops, and invade Spain.

In January 1937, Bohle was promoted to 'Chief' of the *Auslandorganisation* in the Nazi Foreign Ministry, and in July 1939 he became SS-*Obergruppenführer*. Bohle's personal power diminished considerably after the start of WWII, and especially after the fiasco of Rudolf Hess's flight to Scotland in May 1941, about which Bohle had confessed to Hitler of knowing beforehand. As will be seen, Hitler may well have been so informed but probably would have preferred Bohle, rather than his friend and closest personal ally Rudolf Hess, to be on the risky and eventually useless 'secret peace mission' between Germany and Britain.

In a personal letter by Bohle dated september 1937, slightly over one year after the outbreak of the Spanish Civil War, to Winston Churchill (also to be found at the Churchill Archives Centre in Cambridge), he presented his compliments to the Right Honourable Winston Churchill and sent him a copy of the speech which he would deliver to the German Colony in London on 1 October 1937, on the occasion of the traditional 'Harvest Thanksgiving Festival'. The letter was meant to reassure the future Prime Minister of the 'peaceful intentions' of the AO, and to open the gates of a future direct negotiation. Unsurprisingly, Churchill asked for all relevant information on Bohle, and from documents available in the Cambridge Archives, one may read the following:

'Bohle remained a British subject until a few weeks ago – the report was written in 1937 – when by due process of law, though this was not publicly known, he made a declaration repudiating his British nationality and adopted German nationality. There is, however, nothing known of his activities while he was legally a British subject which would render him liable to prosecution, however morally undesirable some of his actions or beliefs'.

Churchill had previously received an anonymous letter from a German non- Nazi national resident in the United Kingdom at that time, 1937, warning him against any 'friendly contacts' with Bohle, because of the Nazi threat through the seemingly harmless AO to Germans resident in the UK who were 'happy to live under the free air of this blessed country'.

Another document says:

'It is believed that just before the First World War (in 1913) – Bohle and his German parents emigrated from the UK to South Africa, where he 'was badly bullied at school for his German name and origins ... but this does not appear to have made him anti-British'. 'He has never professed anything but great friendship for this country ...'

In fact, during Bohle's address to the German colony in London in 1937, he makes it perfectly clear that England was his native country, and that he had spent the whole of his youth within the British Empire. He added: 'I have always had an inner understanding for Great Britain and the British people ... it is something that is a part of my inner nature. The same kind of natural insight could hardly be acquired by objective study'. In some sort of way, Bohle said in public that he really felt that he fully understood the 'British mentality', it being a part of himself, and that he could be trusted by the British people and politicians.

Yet, in his 1937 speech in London, Bohle makes it clear that for him and for the AO Hitler was the true *Führer* and had transformed Germany so that the terms 'Nazi' and 'German' were 'synonymous'. According to him, all good Germans should take an oath of personal allegiance to Hitler, and were 'duty bound to carry out any orders that they may receive'. 'To be National Socialist and to be German means exactly one and the same thing', he stated categorically.

Nazi Party members at the time were estimated to be around 300, but the estimated German 'contacts' around two thousand. Ernst Bohle evidently lied when he said that 'the National Socialists abroad are strictly forbidden to interfere in any way in the internal politics of foreign countries'. For that is exactly what he had done himself in the fateful summer of 1936, helping Franco to cross the Strait of Gibraltar with his troops. Similar lies became evident during his interrogation as witness to Rudolf Hess during the 1945 Nuremburg Tribunal.

By a struck of luck (and it must be pointed out that Franco was a 'lucky man), when Rudolf Hess, previously contacted by Ernst Bohle from Spanish Morocco, approached Hitler in July 1936 at Franco's request, Hitler was in a very good mood, having just attended Wagner's Opera *Siegfried* in Bayreuth.

The intense vibrations of Wagner's music, must have helped to inspire a positive response, in spite of Hitler's natural distrust for others, and for Franco in particular. He decided to support Franco, by sending twenty bombers, Junkers Ju-52/3Ms, together with weapons, money, supplies and experts. In fact, a secret operation was mounted by the Nazi admiral Canaris, head of the *Abwehr* (the German Secret Service) at the time, based on two 'disguised' commercial companies: HISMA and ROWAK.

Franco was not just reassured. He was enthusiastic and was almost literally 'over the moon'. He sent an urgent telegram to the other key conspirator, General Mola, stating: '*Somos los amos. Viva España*', meaning 'We are the bosses. Long live Spain'.

There is something perverse and terribly persuasive in Wagner's intense music, and his works were so much enjoyed by the Nazis that Wagner's romantic musical ideas on Power, Love, Magic, German Nationalism and Chivalry permeated the very souls of the key Nazi leaders. An Opera by Wagner was almost like undergoing an initiation No one, I suggest, can blame the Nazis for that. Wagner was a genius, and even Elgar, the greatest British composer of modern times, was prepared to accept that.

Elgar's admiration for and debt to Wagner have been well documented, and his favourite works were *Tristan* and *Die Meistersinger*. The vocal score of *Tristan* was given to him by Alice Elgar for his birthday in 1893, and bears his inscription at the start of the prelude: 'This book contains the Height, the Depth, the Breadth, the Sweetness, the Sorrow, the Best and the whole of the Best of This world and the Next'.

For some peculiar reason, there was probably little that Franco feared more than Freemasonry. As part of his overall campaign against it, he had a Masonic 'pseudo-lodge' constructed in Salamanca (*see* Figure 34), complete with 'three hooded black manikins' occupying the chairs in the East, to illustrate the supposed evils of the movements in three-dimensional form. So thus, paradoxically, although he hated Freemasonry he had a lodge built for himself.

The manikins were hooded, like Ku-Klux Klan activists, to reinforce the general opinion that members of Freemasonry never show their faces, hiding their true identities even to their brethren. This is an obvious lie for, as all true freemasons know the only time a candidate is temporarily blind-

Figure 34
A view of the East in the pseudo-masonic lodge that Franco created in Salamanca to show the evils of the Order. It is still there. Picture by Matthew Scanlan.

The last straw was the signing of the so-called Munich Agreement between Chamberlain and Hitler (*see* Figure 35).

Chamberlain was so naive as to say: 'We regard the agreement signed last night with Hitler as symbolic of the desire of our two peoples never to go to war with one another again. Churchill however, attacked him bitterly in Parliament: 'You were given the choice between war and dishonour. You chose dishonour and you will have war'.

According to Ian Kershaw , for the millions in Great Britain who had rejoiced when Neville Chamberlain returned home from Munich at the beginning of October 1938, thinking peace had been secured, the following six months would shatter all illusions. On 27 February 1939, he officially recognised Franco's Government. on behalf of the British Nation. The fact that he had overlooked, ignored or swallowed the shameful and humiliating price that had been paid, by again allowing Hitler to take over and invade the Sudetenland, (the German-speaking part of Czechoslovakia), was obviously interpreted as a sign of weakness and on 15 March, Hitler, who had been telling Nazi leaders throughout that he had long decided to smash what remained of the Czech state, occupied Prague. Too late, Hitler's real intentions were becoming clear. At least Chamberlain had the guts to say that 'Britain need feel no moral obligation over Czechoslovakia', and that 'he would go on with his policy of appeasement'. The then Under-Secretary at the Foreign Office, Sir Alexander Cadogan, noted in his diary on hearing this: FATAL .

The Spanish Republican government meanwhile had retreated north to Barcelona, but following the Munich agreement and with Stalin preparing for other things, the war was lost. Total and unconditionally lost to General Franco and his Fascist Colleagues. Rivers of champagne must have flowed at the Italian Fascist and German Nazi camps to celebrate this victory. However the war was not over for Franco. He wanted total repression of the two million Spanish citizens who sided with the Democratic Republic, most of whom had not fired a single shot. In March 1940, while at the same time making clear and public his support for Hitler in the Second World War, he issued a decree simultaneously banning 'Freemasonry and Communism'.

A special Tribunal was established in Salamanca to enforce the Law. Masons of the 18th degree and above were deemed guilty of aggravating circumstances, and usually faced the death penalty. According to some reports, between six and eight thousand freemasons lost their lives in and after the war, including the former Catalan President, from ERC (*Esquerra Republicana de Catalunya*) who was arrested by the Gestapo in occupied Paris, where he had exiled himself. He was sent back to Spain to be executed by firing squad at the Castle of Montjuich, where the Barcelona Olympics of 1992 took place and had things been otherwise, the 1936 Olympic Games should have taken place rather than in Nazi Berlin.

General Franco's hatred for Freemasonry was such that in 1952, long after the war had ended, he published a 334 page book entitled *Masoneria* under the pseudonym of a non-existent 'Jakim Boor'. In this anti-masonic pamphlet, he accuses freemasons of all sorts of acts of treason, among them the collapse of the Spanish Empire, and of being archaic enemies of the Catholic Church, and a mere instrument of Jewish and anglo-saxon domination of the world.

To give further publicity to this book, Franco's press office released the false news that the dictator had received the famous writer and celebrated historian 'Jakim Boor' in 'private audience'.In other words – he had received 'himself'.

My grandfather was not a Communist, completely the opposite. Neither was he an atheist. In his last letter to his family, probably written in a hot and sticky little military Chapel in the midst of the African summer, the very night before his execution by firing squad, he mentions God innumerable times, as he mentions his children and proclaims his innocence.

He commends his children, my father and his three brothers, and his wife to God. In his writing, he is so honourable and gentlemanly that he blames no-one in particular for his betrayal and death, except evil (*La Maldad*), and the fact that it was happening on St. Michael's day. The Archangel who defeated Satan was unable to help him.

Hijos mios, papá se muere…en el cielo nos encontraremos, were his last words in his agonizing letter : 'My dear children, daddy is dying. We shall meet again in Heaven …' Since then, it has been a tradition at home to light a candle by my grand-father's portrait on St. Michael's Eve, a tradition which I would like my children to continue, and that I dedicate to all people who have unjustly perished because of their love for freedom and peace in this our human world.

Figure 35
The Munich agreement of 1938 between British Prime Minister Chamberlain and
Hitler. (Picture from Manuel Aznar's book, ref. 94, by an unkown author)

Selected Bibliography

75   Raymond Carr., 'Spain: 1808-1975' in *Oxford History of Modern Europe* (Clarendon Press, Oxford, Second Edition, 1982).

76   Hugh Thomas, *The Spanish Civil War* (Pelican Edition, London, 1965).

77   Paul Preston, *Franco, A Biography* (Harper Collins Publishers, London, 1993).

78   Churchill Archives Centre: documents quoted from CHAR 2/397; CHAR 2/298; CHAR 2/295; CHAR 9/125.

79   Francisco Sánchez-Montoya, *Ceuta y el Norte de Africa. República, Guerra y Represión 1931-1944 (Editorial Nativota,* Granada, 2004).

80   Martín Corrales E., *Ceuta en los siglos XIX y XX,* IV *Jornadas de Historia de Ceuta. Instituto de Estudios Ceuties,* (Ceuta, 2004),p. 259.

81   Josep Trueta, *L'Esperit de Catalunya* (Fourth Edition [Catalan], *Editorial Selecta,* 1977).

82   Churchill Archives Centre: documents on Ernst Bohle quoted from CHAR 2/307.

83   Matthew Scanlan, *Freemasonry and the Spanish Civil War* 'Part II: Franco's Masonic obsession', In: *Freemasonry Today(* issue 30, 2004), pp. 32-34.

Chapter Three

The Battle of Teruel
and
the eventual defeat of the Nazis

In the complex multicultural historical context of Teruel, reviewed in Part I, Chapter 4, portraying Christians – Catholic and Heretic, Jews and *Marranos*, Muslims and *Moriscos*, hard by the Mediterranean shore of the *Meseta* in the fictional Land of Don Quixote's chivalry and real land Land of the Knights Templar and of St John, still known today as the *Maestrazgo*, the Spanish Civil War proved dramatic and tragic in equal measure. Hemingway's *For whom the bell tolls* could well have been written here.

My grand-father, Antonio Bronchud, was an unwilling participant in the famous Battle of Teruel during the Spanish Civil War, which cost him seven years liberty (1939-46) during which he experienced forced labour in Franco's Quarries. As so often happens in times of violent conflict and demagogical flux, the situation of Democratic and Republican Spain rapidly polarized with the moderates being pushed aside and the extremists gaining the upper hand. On 15 May 1937, Largo Caballero, a freemason and socialist leader of the PSOE (*Partido Socialista Obrero Español*) was forced to resign as Prime Minister, and Dr Juan Negrin, a physician who, though not a Mason, was considerably more radical, became the Prime Minister of Republican Spain until 31 March 1939, and whose Government was dominated by Communists.

Teruel was the only Provincial Capital that the Republican Army had reconquered by military force from the Fascist/Nationalists. General Franco was not going to let one victory spoil his Crusade, and therefore determined to recapture it 'with the help of God' and at whatever price. Moreover, since the times of the *Reconquista* and King Jaime I, it had been axiomatic that whoever conquered the highlands and *Meseta* of Teruel could control the pass to the Mediterranean, Valencia and Barcelona. Fierce fighting broke out on the fateful 18 July 1936 near the village of Sarrión, in the province of Teruel, where my maternal grand-father, Antonio Bronchud, was born and lived with his wife and two children, including my mother Nuria, who was only four years old when the Spanish Civil War broke out.

My grand-father Antonio was the grand-son of the local Judge and for reasons unclear to us, had decided that , in spite of his training and education, it was better to remain illiterate than to be able 'to read books'. 'Books can poison your mind' – he used to say to his children. It is much healthier to work in the fields and collect the harvest, than to read books or go to University. My grand-father did not agree, and in his early twenties he moved to Barcelona, to work as a miner in the Underground or Metro, as it is called locally.

Since hearing this story, I have always been keen on underground trains, and I love the 'Tube' in London, the 'Subway' in New York, and the Metros of Paris, Moscow and Barcelona. It certainly took skill and guts to drill through the bowels of these major cities, several hundred feet below, ground in order to establish one of the most efficient methods of transportation. I even find 'Undergrounds' romantic, and iconic symbols of their cities.

In the Barcelona of the 1920s, my grand-father Antonio Bronchud learnt how to read and write, and became a member of the Socialist Trade Union (UGT) and the Spanish Socialist Workers Party (PSOE), which is the equivalent of the Labour Party in the United Kingdom). He was a moderate socialist, who believed in the 'evolution of society', rather than the 'revolution' promoted by the various Communist Organizations in those days (not all of them pro-Soviet), and certainly not by the popular Anarcho- Syndicalists of Catalonia, so well described by George Orwell in his historical novel *Homage to Catalonia*', written after his traumatic experiences as a volunteer in the International Brigade – an idealistic anti-fascist who fought with the Spanish Republican forces.

'Justice' in post-war Spain simply meant 'repression', both physical and psychological. In this, General Franco was, virtually until his death in 1975, always ready to inflict pain on anone who disagreed with him, displaying a total lack of regard for their suffering. My grand-father Antonio, who had fled with his family to Valencia, the last big city to fall to Franco, was forced to return to his native to Sarrión because the victorious Falangists (Spanish Fascists) had taken his own father prisoner. He was arrested and imprisoned, initially in the dungeons of the medieval castle of Mora de Rubielos, from May 1939 until Christmas 1945. During those six and a half tough years, during which many of his companions were executed, my mother effectively had the status of a widow, while my beloved grand-mother Amparo was treated even worse. She was constantly discriminated against and frequently humiliated in her native *pueblo* of Sarrión, as the wife of a *rojo* or 'red'.

My grand-father appeared before no judge until 24 May 1944, five years after his capture, and then with no defence lawyer at all. He was not accused of any 'blood crimes', but of 'supporting the rebels', meaning the troops loyal to the Spanish democratic government. He was even wrongly accused of being a member of the *Izquierda Republicana*, instead of his Spanish Socialist Workers Party (PSOE), now back in government in Spain since 2004) and of being a militant in the anarchists' Trade Unions (CNT), rather than his (UGT), the socialist *Unión General de Trabajadores*. Antonio Bronchud was never an anarchist nor a communist. He was sentenced to thirty years in prison, a sentence he might have served if Hitler, rather than the Allies, had won the war.

My grand-father Antonio was not a church-goer, but he was not anti-clerical. He was more an agnostic than a believer. He proudly identified himself with the 'working class', but spoke no evil of the capitalists. He used to wear a white shirt and a black tie, and would read as many books as possible. His socialism was not based on making the rich poorer, but on making the poor richer. With these ideals and affiliations he made the wrong decision by returning to his native village of Sarrión, near Teruel, just in time to get married for the second time to my dear grand-mother Amparo, his first wife having died very young, leaving him no children.

At home, he attracted considerable attention. He was handsome (fair hair and blue eyes, like his two children, and my son). He knew how to argue in favour of peasants and the working class in general, both convincingly and with reference to relevant books. He was not a revolutionary, and even the local large landowners and priest showed respect for him. The birth of the Second Spanish Republic in 1931 was, to him, a 'dream come true'. A dream that unfortunately turned itself into a nightmare.

The tasks of the new Republic were many, and it's political leaders have often been blamed for having underestimated the difficulties ahead of them, and for trying to achieve reforms too fast. They wanted a progressive and democratic society, more equality with no distinction between the rights of men and women, less power for the Church (who controlled public opinion and education), less power for the Army (who had given up their previous Imperial ideas but had certainly not forgotten their natural ambitions), and the *Caciques* – the traditional local despots who lived idly in luxury while others often starved, or the *Latifundistas*, large land-owners who still behaved as Medieval Landlords.

Sarrión was, and still 'is', a real *Pueblo*. As Raymond Carr knew well, 'a Spaniard's natural emotional loyalty is to his *pueblo*'. His *pueblo* is like 'his country', and even the nearby *pueblos* are rivals. The *pueblo* was a moral, economic, and governmental unit. The most powerful individuals were not the traditional 'landowners', often aristocratic and 'beyond Good and Evil', but the *Alcalde* (the Mayor, although often the *Cacique*), the Head of the *Guardia Civil*, the Priest and the local Doctor. The favourite pastime of *pueblos* was, and still is, 'gossip', or, in any case, the *tertulias*, that are typically long and endless discussions on politics and sports at the local bars or cafeterias.

As a child and adolescent, from the age of three to the age of seventeen (1960-74), I spent all of my summer holidays in Sarrión. From 1975 onwards, the year that Franco died, I spent them in London, working as a laboratory technician in the famous Institute for Cancer Research (ICR), known as 'The Chester Beatty', by the Royal Marsden Hospital in Fulham Road. The Institute was named after the American millionaire 'Chester Beatty' who gave much of his money to Cancer Research, as well as a generous donation to revamp the British Secret Services until it was found that part of this money had come from several good business that he had himself established in the 1930s with the Nazis!

The Sarrión that I remember so well from my childhood, was a classic example of a Spanish *Pueblo* in the real under-developed Spain. It is is perched on a hill on the Aragonese *Meseta*, at some 1200 meters above sea level, like a quiet white dromedary enjoying a siesta. At the top, the tower of the church, like the minaret of a mosque, is visible for miles and miles and in the middle of the pueblo, the dome of the church, like the hump of a dromedary, has an interesting 'new-*mudejar*' pattern of coloured tiles as its roof. Next to the church is the *Ayuntamiento*, or City Hall, fronted by the 'Plaza', or central square. From this point, a number of medieval narrow streets descend in various directions towards what used to be the defensive walls of the once fortified little town. Not much remains of these walls in Sarrión, except for the Western Gate to the city, which led to the Teruel road. My grand-parents house is close to the opposite end of the village, or what used to be the Eastern Gate, leading to the road to Valencia.

Until 1970 the streets of the village were not paved, and were dry and dusty. There was no underground sanitation, and what little electricity there was depended on the local water fall which fed the electricity station near the old Windmill. Women above a certain age dressed in black, for most of them had at least one relative's death to mourn. There were sounds in the streets of children playing, swallows flying low and talking to each other, the repetitive and metallic sounds of the hammer and the anvil of the blacksmith, who was famous across the province of Teruel for his ironwork and his horseshoes, and who had once been the former fiancée of my grand-mother. At night, the sounds were different: the amorous singing of the frogs by the local pond, appropriately called the *Balsa de las Ranas* (frog's raft), and the little bells of the many goats who, when it got dark, returned, each one of them finding the right home, under the guidance of the village shepherd. There were almost as many mules and goats as inhabitants, about fifteen hundred in total. Ploughing and harvesting were still done in the traditional way, and the church bells called the people to prayers and to Mass as they had obviously done for many centuries.

This was probably the sort of Spain that one can still find, with local flavour and subtle differences, across many Latin American *pueblos*, in Central and South America but in Spain, the War arrived like Satan, and brother started fighting to the death against brother. Italian bombers bombarded Teruel and Sarrión, and several other key villages on the road from Zaragoza to Valencia. My grand-father used the skills he had learnt while working in the Barcelona Underground Stations to build an underground shelter for civilians. Even so, many were killed or injured.

Following the military coup or *levantamiento* of 18 July 1936, the province of Teruel had fallen under the rule of the military rebels, but Teruel was the only capital of Spain to be effectively rescued by the Republican army. This took Franco by surprise and disrupted his concentration upon Madrid in the winter of 1937, thereby altering the whole axis of the war. Air superiority had been supplied to Franco by the Germans and the Italians and the Basque Nationalists and Republicans had subsequently been defeated following the brutal massive bombings of civilians by the Nazis. The 'Condor Legion' of the *Luftwaffe* assisted by the Italian *Aviazione Legionaria* pulverized the Basque city of Guernica, whose destruction was immortalized in the truly impressive painting by Pablo Picasso. Madrid would soon have soon followed suit, as Franco had some 150 battalions prepared for a decisive battle, but the liberation of Teruel by Republican forces changed his plans and delayed the end of the Spanish Civil War.

The so-called 'Battle of Teruel' was fought at an enormous cost to human life with suffering on both sides and not least to civilians, including women and children. It was the last desperate attempt to defeat fascism in Spain, but the Republicans had little artillery and no air support and the troops were in bad shape and increasingly demoralized. Besides these military setbacks, the politics in Republican Spain, under the decisive influence of Stalin, were rapidly moving away from democracy and turning into chaos, anarchy, and communism.

Russian troops, sent in by Stalin together with the International Brigades fought together against Franco's troops, all through the hot summer and the very cold winter. It soon became evident that what should have been a war to defend an advanced form of democracy was turning into a chaotic social revolutionary 'guerrilla war', and was being used and manipulated by Stalin on the one hand and by Mussolini and Hitler on the other, to test new weapons, develop new military strategies and, in every sense of the word, 'rehearse' for what was going to come: the Second World War.

The defeat of the Spanish Republican forces at the Battle of Teruel, meant victory for General Franco. This gave impetus to all three of the European dictators who fought in the Spanish Civil War: Hitler, Mussolini and Stalin. They realized that the use of military force could really change the geopolitical map of Europe, and their thirst for imperial power was considerably reinforced by the weakness of the western democracies. Ironically, in another proof of the 'chaos theory' of human History, it was the non-agression pact between Stalin and Hitler (the Ribbentrop-Molotov Pact) that eventually led Europe and the rest of the world into a global conflict (1939-46) that cost some 50 million deaths.

Back in 1938 the Communist forces, driven by the military success of General Lister, had started to infiltrate and take control of the political structure of the Republic, now enfeebled and abandoned by the 'friendly democracies' of the west. The Republic's Minister of Defence, Prieto, had a number of fierce arguments with the Communist faction until he was forced to resign. The pro-Soviet Communists were so afraid of a victory at Teruel, because it would strengthen Prieto's position, that they 'set out to torpedo Prieto at the cost of losing Teruel'. This they did causing great pain to my grand-father, who was forced to flee Sarrión with his family and children and take temporary refuge in Republican Valencia, the last large city to fall under Franco.

Hitler and Mussolini never stopped their support for Franco. Even towards the end of 1938, in the final and decisive 'Battle of the Ebro' (the river that separates Catalonia and much of Aragon from the rest of Spain, and that probably gave name to the Ibers). Hitler sent enough fighter planes (ME 109s C1 and E2) and support aircraft (Fieseler Fi 156s, Heinkel 111s, Junkers Ju 87s, etc.) to keep the 'Condor Legion' actively engaged and, with a singular lack of scruple, bombarded the civil populations of Barcelona and every Republican defensive position along the river Ebro. The German air strikes were often orchestrated from their base in the Balearic islands

(AS/88). The German Ambassador to Franco's Spain, Eberhard von Stohrer (1883-1944), was not only decisive in achieving these ends, but cleverly intervened at the end of the Spanish War to save General Franco some 163 million marks claimed by Nazi regime to pay for their substantial war effort on Franco's side. General Franco got away with it, and paid nothing back, except for some minerals and raw materials.

The British did not just abandon the Spanish Republic. In some instances, they clearly supported Franco. For example, on 1 November 1938, they warned the battle ship *Nadir* (launched as *Ciudad de Valencia* in 1931, but confiscated by Franco) that the Republican merchant ship *Cantabria* (allegedly carrying supplies and possibly weapons for the Republican side) was sailing from Gravesend in the Thames estuary. It was an easy target for the *Nadir* who sank it close to Happisburg (Norfolk).

When the war was over, it was time for 'revenge', and Franco's war never really ended until his death in November 1975. Only a few months before he died (of natural causes), Franco still signed several death sentences by the terrible traditional method of the *Garrote Vil*, the garrotte or 'neck tourniquet'.

When my grand-father Antonio returned to Sarrión, his father, who had also been a member of the PSOE, was still in jail. Antonio Bronchud was taken to the Castle of Mora de Rubielos were he was severely punished, beaten in the medieval dungeons, and sentenced to forced labour. He spent seven years in jail, working in Franco's Quarries, and producing building stones for the Pyramid that Franco constructed to honour himself and his dead: *El Valle de los Caidos*, meaning the 'Valley of the Fallen', built by the forced labour of political prisoners in the Sierras North of Madrid, on the way to Segovia and Avila. It was built to honour those who fell on the Fascist/Nationalist side of the war. No memorial, however, was built for those who fell defending the properly elected Democratic Second Republic of Spain.

Franco's sepulchre is still there, next to a Huge Cross that dominates the landscape of North of Madrid, and which can be easily spotted from miles away.

This explains why the first time I saw the Castle at Mora de Rubielos, about 1967, my grand-father turned me away, whispering something like *Este es un Castillo Maldito. El Diablo lo habita*. 'This is a wretched Castle. The devil inhabits it'.

It was by this time no longer a military or political prison, but now the Headquarters of the local *Guardia Civil*. The *Guardia Civil*, with their characteristic little tricorn black hats, were and still are a para-military force, in that they are regarded as part of the armed forces, but in practice fulfil more civil and police duties than strictly speaking those of the military.

Although at the outbreak of the Civil War many *Guardia Civiles* remained faithful to the Republic as they did in Barcelona, in other parts of Spain, such as Andalusia, they turned to Franco, and some were more than likely involved in the vile assassination of the great Spanish poet Garcia Lorca , intimate friend of the genius film-maker Luis Buñuel, and the extravagant artist and painter Salvador Dalí.

The second time I got close to the Castle, close enough to see the strange carvings and stone marks that later captured my imagination, I was in the company of my mother. She told me how painful it was for her, in 1970, to see the castle where my grand-father had been beaten and imprisoned. For he had done nothing wrong , but tried to defend his *pueblo* and his ideals of freedom and progress. She told me how vividly she remembered, and still does to this very day, the anxiety and distress she shared with her brother and her mother when they tried, without success, to give some food to my grand-father, but the guards would not let them through the gates. She did not see him for seven years. She was effectively 'widowed' for seven years, but, at least, unlike my father, she had hopes that one day, they would see him again alive, which they did – but not until 1946.

My grand-father and his political comrades in prison hoped and prayed for a victory of the Allies but in the end were truly disappointed by the behaviour and political conduct of the eventual winners of the Second World War.

My grand-father could not understand how the British had allowed Franco's 'coup' and 'victory', without any support for, or tutoring of, the young and inexperienced Spanish Democracy. He did not understand how, after the 1941 fatal German attack on the Soviet Union, the British had tolerated and quickly forgotten that Franco, always on Hitler's side, sent, early in July 1941, the Spanish 'Blue Division' of 18,694 men, largely Falangist and Fascist volunteers, to fight on the Russian front together with the Nazis against what had become the key and much welcomed ally of Great Britain: the Soviet Union. In February 1942, Franco, while he was still sure of Hitler's victory, promised 'a million Spaniards' for Berlin, should they be needed to stop the Russians. On 17 November 1943, however, the Spanish Blue Division was heavily defeated, leaving some four thousand dead in Russia.

What might have happened had the Nazis reached an Armistice with Britain in 1941, as Rudolf Hess had wished, no-one will ever know.

Following the Rudolf Hess fiasco and, as we now know, 'deception' by the British Secret Services in May 1941, while my grand-father Antonio was still working in Franco's Quarries, unaware of what was going on in the rest of the world, Hitler had not only lost a faithful friend, the 'Quiet Nazi' as Hess was known, but also a certain 'stability of judgment' in his day-today decisions. Perhaps, Rudolf Hess was more important, emotionally and psychologically, to Hitler than previously has been thought. Perhaps with his quiet and almost mystic approach to things, Rudolf Hess gave Adolf Hitler that 'peace of spirit' and self-confidence that he lost from May 1941.

It was, after all, Rudolf Hess who saved Hitler's life in the famous Munich Beer Hall Putsch. It was he who helped him write *Mein Kampf* in prison, perhaps typing and correcting it. It was he who knew and shared his most intimate secrets, fears and desires, and he knew how unashamedly poor Hitler had been. Hitler too knew poverty and distress. He had 'gotten into the habit of passing the hours before dawn watching the droll little mice in his cell room chasing around after crusts of bread and leftovers'. According to Hitler himself: 'I had known so much poverty in my life that I was well able to imagine the hunger, and hence also the pleasure, of the little creatures. And yet, this apparently compassionate man, who like Rudolf Hess and even Himmler was austere and vegetarian for 'moral reasons', became one of the greatest monsters in Human History. A man who had felt compassion of hungry little mice eventually showed no compassion at all not only for Jews, but also for his own German people.

Heroes or Villains? That is the question. Hitler is now obviously regarded a 'villain' by most people, but he was not in Nazi Germany, where he was regarded as a 'hero', as he was in Franco's re-conquered Spain. In a 1941 book by Manuel Aznar, the grandfather of José Maria Aznar, Spain's latest Prime Minister until the 2004 March General Election which took place after the tragic Islamic terrorist bombings in Madrid on 11 March 2004. This distinguished journalist and diplomat, ideologically very close to General Franco, makes of Hitler a hero of the German and European Nations. He explains how he came to power, and why he did what he did up to 1941. He finds no blame in him at all, but directly accuses western democracies of corruption and treason. Of course, most of the blame was laid on Freemasonry, and especially the 'League of Nations', precursor of the United Nations,which in those days met in Geneva (Switzerland).

According to Aznar, Freemasonry ruled Geneva throughout the period between the two world wars. In his words: 'The Great Community of Jews of the World', both the public and visible one and the semi-occult and hidden behind the mask of Freemasonry, truly believed that they had at last found, in Geneva, their new "Sion".' He was rather harsh on the League of Nations, when in 1937 – still in the middle of the Spanish Civil War, they had prudently refused recognition of Franco's Government.

Aznar said that Sir Anthony Eden, then British Foreign Minister and one of the 'idols of the sectarian world', betrayed civilization and Europe. The only objectives of the English politicians, he added, 'was to use the "League of Nations" in Geneva as an instrument to keep all continental countries and nations permanently divided and quarrelling among themselves, and to corrupt those most poor and in need'.

Aznar, in a triumphant sort of way adds:

En el día de hoy, cautivo y desarmado el ejército rojo, nuestras tropas han alcanzado los últimos objetivos militares. La guerra ha terminado.

This was Franco's declaration, on 1 April 1939, that the Spanish Civil War had ended, with his victory and the total defeat of the Red Army (*cautivo y desarmado el ejército rojo*).

Aznar makes a final comment, that he must presumably have repented of in the following few years:

'Democracies have therefore just suffered another of their unforgettable failures … Defeated in their first great battle ('the Spanish Civil War'), and blind before what was happening, they would soon lose everything in a very short time'.

Fortunately, this last 'prophecy' by Manuel Aznar – written late in 1940 or early in 1941, never came true.

The 'inquisition' promoted by General Franco against any intellectual freedom was unprecedented even in Spain. One of the main targets was books. Regarded as dangerous 'weapons', books were confiscated and destroyed, or sent to the Archives of Salamanca, a beautiful University City northwest of Madrid, that might be compared both in history and in beauty, but I am afraid not always in intellectual achievements, to either Oxford or Cambridge. In 1938, even before the end of the Spanish Civil war, Franco created the DERD (*Delegación del Estado para la Recuperación de Documentos*). When his troops occupied Catalonia (or in the more ironic words of his troops, 'liberated Catalonia') seventy-five per cent of all libraries were closed and 160 tons of books and documents were sent to Salamanca between 1939 and 1940. In Spain, at least 800 tons of paper were confiscated by DERD, and three million people were catalogued as 'political enemies', and either shot, imprisoned or pursued for the rest of their lives by Franco's police. My grandfather Antonio, after being freed in 1945, had to report periodically to the Barcelona police until 1975 when Franco died from old age and probable medical malpractice.

The DERD, which in 1944 was renamed *Delegación Nacional de Servicios Documentales*, did not disappear until 1977, and the documents expropriated from the Catalan Republican Government (*Generalitat*) and archived in Salamanca, were not returned until January/February 2006, in a rather surrealistic police operation, under the orders of the Spanish Government but against the opposition of the local Salamanca right-wing politicians. The original documents were removed from their archives in a surprise operation, in the middle of the night under police protection on 20 January 2006, and were substituted by copies in the Salamanca Archives. Even so, these right-wing politicians have managed to keep these documents confiscated in Madrid, rather than having them returned to Catalonia (to the National Archives of Catalonia in Sant Cugat), by using deliberate legal tricks and absurd delaying practices.

What about Sir Winston Churchill? Or Stalin? Well, my views are clear, Churchill, albeit human and as such certainly not infallible, was a 'hero', and Stalin, whose period of power and totalitarian rule in the Soviet Union is estimated to have cost some twenty million lives, was definitely a 'villain'.

Churchill saved the world from what he had himself said would happen under Nazi Domination:

> 'Not a return to the Middle Ages but a lurch into a New Dark Age. If Hitler wins and we fall, then the whole world, including the United States, including all that we have known and cared for, will sink into the abyss of a New Dark Age, made more sinister, and perhaps more protracted, by the lights of perverted science'.

But, again, there were those who disagree.

As John Lukacs points out in his book *Churchill: Visionary. Statesman. Historian*, Churchill thought that Stalin was not really trying to impose upon others a new Credo or Religion, that of 'International Communism'. That would have been a most serious threat for western democracies.

Churchill correctly guessed that Stalin was, above all, a Russian Imperialist, and a good if cynical statesman. Until the last moment, hoped against all evidence, that Hitler would not be so stupid as to attack him but, following Rudolf Hess's fiasco and with no hope of an Armistice with Britain, Hitler, under pressure as well as extremely angry and upset, finally decided to invade Russia on Sunday 22 June 1941.

In early September, Stalin sent a desperate message to Churchill: 'The Soviet Union is in a position of mortal peril', which indeed it was, with the Germans rapidly advancing on Russian soil and capturing millions of Russian prisoners.

In December 1941, came the turning point of the entire war. The Russians stopped and turned back the German advance near Moscow, while the Japanese, who had been fighting their own imperialistic wars in China and Manchuria, finally attacked the American Pacific Fleet in Pearl Harbour which propelled the United States into the war.

America, it should be remembered, was not at that time prepared for a war of such magnitude. When the Philippine Isalnds were lost to the invading Japanese forces, General Douglas MacArthur, head of the U.S. military in those islands, blamed President Franklin D. Roosevelt, the American Chief of Staff Gen. George C. Marshall, and Dwight D. Eisenhower, soon to become the Supreme Commander of the British and American troops who formed the victorious Allied Expeditionay Force, as '... the men responsible for the American debacle in the Philippine islands', that some fifty years before had been taken by the Americans from Spanish dominion.

Eisenhower, a name of German descent, was no ordinary man. After spending almost ten years with MacArthur in the Philippines, Eisenhower found in General Marshall his 'ideal boss'. In October 1942, according to Stephen E. Ambrose (one of his main biographers) Eisenhower told an assistant: 'I wouldn't trade one Marshall for fifty MacArthurs'. He thought a second, then blurted out: 'My God! That would be a lousy deal. What would I do with fifty MacArthurs?'

John Lukacs, who has studied Churchill's psychology in depth, thinks that he had respect and some sort of cautious or even 'romantic' fascination for Stalin, althought certainly not for Communism. On the other hand, Churchill detested Hitler, and probably 'disliked' Germany (actually more based on his impressions of Prussia than Bavaria).

So, was Stalin 'good' or 'bad'? To people like my grandparents, who lost the Spanish Civil War, Stalin was not 'good' because he was a 'Communist Imperialist', and neither of them, Miguel or Antonio, was a Communist. To them, Stalin, having failed to help, Britain and France, were the only international powers to offer real military help to Spanish Republican forces. For this and other ideological reasons, most of the British establishment definitely regarded Stalin as a 'bad' person, until the Soviet Union became a 'life-saving' ally in the war. Then, at least for a number of years, Stalin became in England a 'good' person. On at least one documented occasion, Churchill referred to Stalin as 'a great and good man'. Between the two was perpetrated one of the most surrealistic and contradictory events in the Second World War: the fate of Greece.

Following the failure by the Italian Fascist Forces to conquer Greece rapidly, the Germans successfully invaded.

By 1944-45 Civil War broke out in Greece, and Greek Partisan Communists with their guerrilla tactics, fiercely fought and defeated, the Nazis and local Fascists. The 'Percentages Agreement', often trotted out as an example of Churchill's cynicism, was the method proposed by him – while the war was still on-going but the fate of Nazi Germany was no longer questionable, to divide a 'Liberated Europe' among the future areas of influence and dominion by the winning Allies: the Americans, the British and the Russians.

It may sound crazy now, but literally 'around a table' the great leaders of WWII were playing a 'Monopoly Game' that involved exchanging countries, nations and millions of people. Churchill, whose position of negotiating strength was 'more moral than real' because of the military supremacy of the Soviets and the Americans, defended a ninety per cent, near-absolute, British predominance in Greece. Incidentally, I have often wondered what role in this peculiar affair, if any, was played by British Intelligence in the Balkans, and by Sir Steven Runciman in particular.

The 'Percentages Agreement' saved Greece from Russian domination, but not Poland, who had ironically been the 'prime cause' for starting the war. But five weeks after the agreement, a Partisan Communist insurrection was about to overwhelm Athens.

Churchill sent a considerable British force from Italy to totally suppress it, so that, paradoxically, British soldiers were ordered to shoot Greek patriots who had been courageously fighting Italian Fascists and German Nazis for years. And yet, Stalin said not a word. He did not try to help the Greek Communists. On the contrary, he communicated to them that 'he had nothing to do with them', while Churchill referred to these Greek Patriots as 'Trotskyists', rather than 'Communists'.

Churchill has been criticised for failing to see that his policies left half of Continental Europe to the Soviets, and the other half to the Americans. He has also been questioned by modern German historians, such as Andreas Hillgruber or Martin Bernd, for 'hating Germany a lot more than Hitler hated Britain', and Austria's potential right-wing Chancellor, Jörg Haider, even called Churchill 'a war criminal', presumably for the heavy British bombing of German cities during the war, notwithstanding the fact that Churchill had personally persuaded both President Roosevelt and Stalin, back in 1943, to declare Austria, as an independent country, once liberated.

Another strange example of this peculiar 'special relationship' between Churchill and Stalin came with the unconditional surrender of Nazi Germany.

It would seem that when it became evident that Nazi Germany was going to be defeated, many Germans felt their safety and future to be better under the British and American than under the Communist Russians. Stalin was upset by the easy and rapid surrender of German troops to the Allies in western Germany, while Germans fought bitterly and hard for every inch of terrain in Silesia, Prussia or Czech Bohemia. Roosevelt, the American President, died on 12 April, and Churchill felt that he was no longer the 'leader' of the Democratic side. The Americans were not going to let that happen. They were – and still are today- the real leaders of the 'Democratic World'.

The Russians kept fighting and soon occupied Vienna, Berlin and Prague. A few days before Hitler killed himself in the bunker, to the great disappointment of Russian troops who first arrived there, Heinrich Himmler offered the unconditional surrender of the Third Reich to the Western Allies, but not to the Soviet Union. Churchill rejected this, on the grounds that he was a man of his word' – the saying is that 'An Englishman's word is his bond'. Stalin's gratitude to Churchill's reaction was self-explanatory: 'Knowing you, Winston, I had no doubt that you would act in this way'.

Nevertheless, Churchill must have had his doubts about Stalin's intentions. In spite of the imminence of victory in 1945, for the first time he realized that Stalin's power and ambition were immense. He became painfully aware that the Soviets considered the territories they had 'liberated' as 'their own'. The chances of a free Poland were zero.

In his VE day speeches Churchill warned the British people that there could be 'more trials and challenges' ahead, and it is now accepted that he went so far, in his distrust of the Russians, to ask Montgomery and other British Military Commanders to collect all the arms they could in Germany, just in case they were required for a confrontation with Russians advancing further west than agreed.

Churchill must have remembered the meaning of Rudolf Hess's prophecy, when he realized that his peace and secret mission in Britain had failed, and had warned the British that unless there was peace between Germany and Britain, and if the Germans lost the war then there would be Communist troops across the English Channel, ready to invade and join their Communist comrades in Britain.

In conclusion, my grand-father Miguel Hernández died, in 1936, and my other grand-father Antonio Bronchud spent seven years in terrible prisons, 1939-46, for defending ideas that are part of our Western values of freedom and tolerance, while Europe and the civilized world were turned 'upside-down' by a series of essentially **Irrational** and **Violent** events.

Their personal sacrifice was useless in Spain, where a totalitarian and fascist State ruled the country for almost four decades. But I feel proud of what they did. And that is what matters most to me and to the rest of my family. They did not die or suffer in vain.

With the coming of the 'cold war', Franco's well publicised claim to be the best bastion against Communism started to gain political ground in the West. President Truman held off Congressional efforts to help Franco in 1950. But in 1953 came the agreement with the United States on the establishment of U.S. military bases in Spain in exchange for international recognition of Franco's regime, and a substantial economic loan. When, in 1959 (two years after I was born), Franco was embraced in Madrid by General Eisenhower, Franco is reported to have said 'Now I have won the Spanish war'.

It is certainly ironical that it was General Eisenhower, former Supreme Commander of the Allied Armies, and later President of the United States of America, a West Point graduate (1915), and a lover of freedom, who embraced General Francisco Franco, a sworn enemy of freedom, in 1959. Such is the perversion of politics, and such are the complex plans laid down by Satanael. The sarcastic but profound Italian Renaissance writer Machiavelli (1469-1527) comes back to mind: placing expediency above political morality.

In his first direct combat experience in the north of Africa and southern Italy, from November 1942 to December 1943, Eisenhower had often been hesitant, even depressed and irritable, unsure of himself, defensive in both his mood and tactics. But he learnt from his mistakes, and matured both as a military man and as a politician. The only thing he shared with Franco was his hatred of Communism. It is even likely that Eisenhower had at some point of his life and career entered Freemasonry, like so many other American Presidents, since the time of George Washington. But General Franco represented in 1953 an ally against communism, the 'choice of the lesser evil' perhaps, and Spain was geographically an important landing area for American troops, the U.S. Navy or Airforce.

Franco had become the most powerful man in Spain's history. Not even the Emperors Philip II of Spain or Charles V had attained such degree of personal and totalitarian power. Yet, I can imagine his face when a then young American Chaplain of the USAF (American Air Force) based at Rota, a little Spanish town near Cadiz from where American planes could easily control the Strait of Gibraltar and is still used today, approached him on a secret visit in Madrid. His mission was simply to communicate to Franco that the Americans had opened the first lodge of freemasons in their base, on Spanish soil. The Chaplain's name was Reverend Dr. W. Armistead Boardman. There was nothing Franco could do. Freemasons were again back at work in Spain.

Perhaps, one of the main problems we have today, at the beginning of the twenty-first century, is the subconscious desire to leave behind for ever, and to completely forget the excesses committed in the name, and under the banner, of one or another ideology (to the left or to the right of the political spectrum) in the twentieth century.

This might help us to understand the 'absence of ideals', or the apparent lack of ideas, or of new enticing social and political projects for mankind. But no more revolution does not mean no more evolution of civilization.

Selected Bibliography

91.   Toland J., *Hitler* (Wordsworth Military Library, 1997).
92.   Raymond Carr, 'Spain: 1808-1975' In *Oxford History of Modern Europe* (Clarendon Press, Oxford, Second Edition, 1982).
93.   Edwards J. ,*The British Government and the Spanish Civil War 1936-39* (1979).
94.   Manuel Aznar. *Historia de la Segunda Guerra Mundial: Antecedentes Políticos y Declaración de Guerra*, Volume I (1939), (*Editorial Idea*, Madrid 1941).
95.   On the Nazi military aid to General Franco, there are several reference works: Ramon Garriga, *La Legión Condor*; Ramón Hidalgo, *La ayuda Alemana a España*; Meter Elstob, *La Legión Condor: España 1936-39*.
96.   Lukacs J., *Churchill: visionary, statesman and historian* (Yale University Press, New Haven and London, 2002).
97.   Ambrose S.E., *The victors: the men of World War II* (Pocket Books, London, 2004).

Chapter Four

My trip to Nuremburg:
The irrational beginnings of the Nazi Party

My first trip to Nuremburg was only recently. Germany, the largest and wealthiest country within the European Union, is a great mystery even for the Germans themselves. German unification as a state is a very recent phenomenon as it effectively took place in the second half of the nineteenth century. German reunification in 1989, following the fall of the Berlin Wall and the Soviet Empire, is of course an even more recent phenomenon.

Part One

Germany and Nuremburg: from the First to the Third Reich

Napoleon is partly responsible for the first unification, because following his invasion of eastern Europe and later his defeat, the 1,789 different autonomous or semi-autonomous German-speaking domains (principalities, city-states, small states) derived from sovereign little states of feudal origin were artificially clustered by Napoleon's victors (mainly the English, the Russian and the Austro-Hungarians) into some tnirty-nine larger 'domains'. Of these, Prussia , that as the name suggests probably had more to do with Russia/Poland/the Baltic States and Eastern Europe rather than with Western Germany, became the most powerful, and was soon able to challenge the other 'Germanic' states like the powerful Austro-Hungarian Empire, still under the Hapsburg dynasty), and Swabia (Schwaben), Saxony or Bavaria.

In the confusion after the collapse of the Western Roman Empire, it was probably 'Charlemagne' who in the year 800 A.D. became the first ruler of the 'Holy Roman Empire'. He cannot be regarded as German or French, for these nations and languages evolved later. But he was also known as the 'German Emperor', and a bastion of Christianity, stopping and fighting back the Islamic invasion of Europe.

After having been King of the Franks for some thirty-two years, Charlemagne was crowned by the Pope himself as Emperor of the Western Roman Empire, as opposed to the Eastern Christian Byzantine Empire. The emperor chose the small city of Aachen, or 'Aquisgrane', as his main residence and eventually his burial site. He asked a master mason named 'Master Odo' to direct the works of his palace and chapel. Whether 'Odo, was Frank or German, or Italian or even Jewish nobody knows. In those days, master masons did not erect large buildings just for a 'practical purpose'. They constructed them upon the basis of an idea.

The key to the building is the tall 'octagonal hall'. A huge and beautiful chandelier, donated by Emperor Barbarossa in 1165, hangs from the cupola of this octagonal hall.

The 'special relationship between the Pope and the Holy Roman Emperor' was not always easy. Friedrich I (Emperor 'Barbarossa' or 'red beard'), for example, at one point in the twelfth century invaded Italy, and the Pope excommunicated him in 1160. Barbarossa's initial response was the sacking of Rome itself, and the installation of his own 'anti-pope' (Paschal III). The emperor, eventually repented, kneeling and kissing the feet of the newly elected official Pope Alexander III. By 1184, however, he went again into open conflict with the newly elected pope, Urban III. Finally, in 1189, Friedrich died on his way to the Holy Land, as a Crusader, drowning while crossing a river in Turkey, before reaching the troops of his ally crusader King Richard I of England ('Coeur de Lion').

The 'Carolingian Octagon' at Aachen is a symbol of perfection, and it is a composite of a square, representing the earth with its four cardinal points, and the circle, representing infinity. The Royal Chapel of Charlemagne is an image of the 'New Jerusalem' predicted in the Book of Revelation by St. John the Evangelist: a new world was being created. And yet, Charlemagne's throne is unusually simple and rather humble. It can be visited in the upper level of the chapel, (*see* Figure 36), inside the hexadecagon, and has six steps, like the throne of King Solomon in the Old Testament.

Another, rather similar, Carolingian throne is to be found in the Cathedral of Girona, not far from the Jewish quarters of this ancient Catalan city in north-east Spain (*see* Figure 37). Though there is no evidence that Charlemagne himself ever sat on this throne in Girona, although one of his sons probably did when the city was taken back from Islam in the ninth century.

Figure 36
Carolingian Throne in the Royal Chapel at Aachen (Germany). Charlemagne and future emperors of the Holy Roman Empire sat on it to rule over their assembly of Knights and Noblemen.
(Picture by Alfred Carl)

In 2004 I was invited to give a talk at a scientific medical meeting celebrating the 150th birthday anniversary of Paul Ehrlich (1854-1915), the man who practically invented antibiotics and introduced the concepts of 'chemotherapy' and therapeutic 'magic bullets'. One of his correct intuitions was that the chemical dyes manufactured by the potent German chemical industry could be turned into effective anti-bacterial agents and life-saving medicines if they managed to selectively attack microbes. Several of these chemical dyes were proven to stain fairly selectively bacteria and yeasts, which were being described at the time by scientists like the French Pasteur or the German Koch, but for which there was no specific remedy. Paul Ehrlich speculated that, provided these dyes were 'bacteriostatic' (stopped the growth of bacteria) or 'bactericidal' (actually killed bacteria), without being unduly toxic or harmful to humans, they could be used as therapy for infections. In his great works he was often helped by his faithful fellow scientist, the Japanese Sahachiro Hata.

The Scientific Meeting to celebrate such eminent scientists was fascinating, but even more fascinating was the discovery of the beautiful city of Nuremburg itself, and the truly hair-rising experience of a visit to the 'Documentation Centre of the Nazi Party Rally Grounds".

Figure 37
Carolingian Throne in the Cathedral of Girona (Spain), that is still used today by the Bishop of Girona on special occasions. The first President of the *Generalitat*, autonomous government of Catalonia, was in fact the Bishop of Girona.

Nuremburg is a medieval city, founded in 1050 ('Norenberc'), under the German Emperor Heinrich III, but whose first glorious period came in 1140-1180 under the famous German Sacro-Romanic Emperor 'Federico Barbarossa', who became one of the symbols of the Nazis, and was known as the Greatest Leader of the I Reich. It is unfortunate for him that the 'secret operation' mounted by Adolf Hitler to invade Russia, which had been until 1941 an 'ally' of the Nazis, was in fact baptized 'Operation Barbarossa', and became a real disaster. Like Napoleon, but for different reasons, Hitler fell into the mortal 'Russian Trap'.

There are lots of interesting historical anecdotes about this operation, but here I shall mention just a few. According to Hitler, who was by birth Austrian until he was finally granted German nationality, the two main enemies of Germany were the Jews, and the lack of 'living space' for a Nation that needed 'space' to grow, like we need oxygen to survive. Neither of these two concepts were truly original.

Anti-semitism had unfortunately been part of European and German heritage for centuries. The same Charles IV, the Hapsburg Emperor of the First Reich whom we saw in Florence on the fresco by Buonaiuti at Santa Maria Novella, in the company of the Pope and Juan Fernández de Heredia, in 1349 had authorized the total demolition of the Jewish Quarter, where now stand the famous 'Central Market Place'in Nuremburg, next to the 'Church of the Virgin', also built in the fourteenth century by the architect and master mason Peter Parler. Next to it, the extremely original fountain called *Schönen Brunnen* was also built between 1385 and 1396, to commemorate forty heroes of the western world, including Alexander the Great, Julius Caesar, several Old Testament Prophets, Charlemagne (the first Sacro-Roman Emperor), King Arthur and Godefroy de Bouillon. Over five hundred of the 1500 Jewish inhabitants of these Jewish quarters were burnt to death in this first large 'Pogrom' on German soil. Even prior to the Great War, in 1913, Heinrich Class, president of the Pan-German League, claimed that: 'The Jewish race is the source of all dangers. The Jew and the German are like fire and water. They cannot mix'.

The notion of 'living space', *Lebensraum*, was popularised by General Karl Haushofer. He returned to Germany in 1911, after spending three years in Tokyo as military attaché, again another indication of the long-lasting friendly relationships between Germany and Japan. He not only spoke fluent Japanese and good English, but he was also married to the daughter of a Jewish merchant, and had a wide cultural and global vision of the world. However he blamed much of Germany's problems on a certain 'claustrophobic' situation, with a clear conviction that a nation's existence depended on the space it controlled. After the Treaty of Versailles, following the end of World War, I he became professor of 'Geopolitics', a subject which he more or less 'invented', at the University of Munich and counted among his most beloved students none other than Rudolf Hess. It was Rudolf Hess who later introduced him to Adolf Hitler. According to his ideas, the humiliated Germany, encircled and suffocated, was ready for an 'explosion', which indeed is exactly what happened in the decade 1932-1942. This explosion was – according to the founders of National-Socialism – going to lead Germany towards a Third Reich, which was to last at least a thousand years.

Rudolf Hess , the 'quiet Nazi', was born in Egypt, in the glorious city of 'Alexandria' where Alexander the Great is supposed to have been buried, though no traces have yet been found of such burial. I cannot hide a certain amount of sympathy and benevolent compassion for such a character.

In spite of his wrong ideas, for example about the Aryan race and anti-semitism, he was a man of courage and had a certain Quixotic element within himself, that eventually led him to perform one of the most extraordinary , and in my view decisive moves in the II World War: his solo trip to Scotland on a 'secret peace mission'.

He was the son of a German merchant, who was reasonably well off. Hess attended boarding school in Bad Godesberg before entering the prestigious and expensive *École Supérieure du Commerce* in Switzerland. He was an 'anglophile', and like Karl Haushofer or Prime Minister Chamberlain's father, who were good friends, he believed that the English were 'Aryan', like the Germans, because of their physical and genetic 'make-up' and their Saxon pre-Roman origins.

Hess should have gone to Oxford to study, but this was changed by the Great War (in 1914), and its tragic aftermath. Hess believed, like many Germans, that the nation required a 'leader' (*Führer*), in a similar sort of way as the Jews had been looking, and are still looking, for their Messiah. In short, Professor Karl Haushofer was his teacher, and Hitler his Messiah. Perhaps Rudolf Hess should have learnt what Plutarch had to say about 'Alexander the Great'.

Alexander the Great, like later Adolf Hitler, wanted to be a god. One of the differences between the two is that Alexander won the war, while Hitler lost it. Alexander's two real 'loyal pillars' were his horse Bucephalus, who died of old age in his Indian campaign which reached as far as the Ganges river, and to whom he dedicated a whole new city, and his personal friend (and probably homosexual) partner, Hephaestion. When the latter died, Alexander's grief over Hephaestion went beyond all reasonable bounds – he crucified the doctor who had treated him. He ordered all of the manes and tails of the animals in his army to be cut off as a sign of mourning, and he tore down the walls of the cities nearby. He banned all music. Then he went into the country of the Cossaeans and for no reason massacred the entire nation.

Neither Hitler nor Hess were homosexual, as far as we know but they certainly 'loved' each other. Besides being the most devoted and dedicated subordinate of Hitler, Hess had shared prison with him in 1923-24 (*see* Figure 38), and was his 'Knight', a modern Parsifal who conjured up the dream of a solitary flight to the enemy, which he did by flying alone and unarmed to Scotland on May 10 1941, convinced that he was carrying out the true will of his master, Adolf Hitler, and his teacher, Karl Haushofer, who had clearly taught both of them many times that Germany could not win the War while engaged simultaneously on two fronts: the west against Britain, and the east against Russia.

Why Rudolf Hess flew to Scotland personally, rather than sending the loyal and faithful Ernst Bohle will never be known until the full story is revealed by the only people who might have known more about this – the British Secret Services. In a brilliant war-operation they made Hess believe that the risk was worthy. Hess was keen to regain power with the Führer, in front of other more aggressive competitors, and to accomplish what Karl Haushofer had taught him: stop the war with Britain, and then attack the real enemy, meaning the Soviets.

To do what he did not only takes 'guts', and a certain degree of foolhardiness. The hypothesis that I find more believable is that Hess was somehow told that the King of England himself, George VI, or another member of the Royal family, wanted to meet him personally and secretly in Scotland, and was prepared to oust Churchill from Government, and immediately negotiate an armistice with Germany. As Hess was fond of esoteric knowledge and beliefs, and was rather keen on ancient legends of chivalry and the Teutonic Knights, as well as a full member of the secret Thule Society, it is even possible that he was lured into a non-existent secret meeting, of a possible ritual nature, with the King of England in his position as Past Grand Master of the Knights Templar – a position which George VI certainly held between 1937 and 1952.

When I requested the documents on Rudolf Hess, available at the Churchill Archives Centre in Cambridge, the person in charge, Ieuan Hopkins, found only two documents, and in his letter to me made the following comments: 'Surprisingly, these two documents appear to be the only ones which are found in the Churchill (personal) papers relating to Hess in 1941'. This *is* surprising because, at least in theory, these Archives contain all Churchill's personal correspondence and were part of his legacy when Churchill College Cambridge was founded. As it seems impossible that such a delicate issue as Rudolf Hess's case was only represented by two documents, one might infer that the rest of the relevant documents were concealed or destroyed for security or intelligence reasons.

One of the documents (CHAR 20/038/139-142) is a telegram, dated May 1941 soon after the landing of Hess in Scotland, from Churchill to Roosevelt, the American President, giving very brief information about Hess's comments during interview. Among them were the following:

> 'Hess seems in good health and not excited and no ordinary signs of insanity can be detected. He declares that this escapade is his own idea and that Hitler was unaware beforehand. If he is to be believed, he expected to contact members of a

'peace movement' in England whom he would help to oust present Government. If he is honest and if he is sane this is an encouraging sign of the ineptitude of the German Intelligence Service. He will not be ill-treated but it is desirable that the press should not romanticise him and his adventure. We must not forget that he shares responsibility for all Hitler's crimes and is a potential war criminal whose fate must ultimately depend upon the decision of the Allied Government'.

It is not of anecdotal interest that soon after his capture in Scotland in May 1941, Rudolf Hess was taken as prisoner of war under Churchill's instructions, rather than as Hitler's emissary on a peace negotiating mission. For some time the military person in charge of his supervision was called Captain 'Percival'. I am unsure whether this man's name was merely a coincidence, or the result of some rather subtle sense of humor.

Figure 38
Hitler, on the extreme left, with Hess, second from the right, in Landsberg prison (1923-1924).
They became intimate friends, and Hess played an important role in the writing of *Mein Kampf*,
Hitler's bestselling book. Picture taken from the Imperial War Museum (London)

Hitler really lost the war because he was moved more by his irrational forces, and particularly by his obsessive hatred for the Jews and for the Communists, than by his rational processes. It is however an interesting fact, if perhaps not analyzed in the depth that it merits, that Hitler mourned the loss of Rudolf Hess a lot more than might have been expected and his reaction to this loss, was in many respects 'pathological'. Again, as so often before, he felt alone and surrounded by people who worshipped him as a 'god' but whom he could never fully trust. His natural paranoid tendencies increased to even more dangerous levels.

'Oh, my God, my God! He has really flown to England' – said the *Führer* when he really found out that Hess had done what he had done. Anger developed into a rage, but underlying was the deep depression which he had suffered before for the loss of his friend and Deputy *Führer*. It must have played a role in some of his subsequent 'crazy' decisions such as the attack on Russia and we shall probably never know the real motives' for Rudolf Hess's solo flight to Britain on 10 May 1941, rational or otherwise, just when the War seemed more winnable than ever before.

We must now return to 'Operation Barbarossa'. There is the true but little known story that Hitler, acting on Haushofer's advice, and in spite of his hatred for Communism, was playing a dangerous 'friendly game' with Stalin, and had invited the Soviets, on 12 November 1940, to join the Tripartite Pact with Japan and Italy.

The foreign commissar Molotov, now more famous for the eponymous home made 'Molotov Cocktails' used in the 1968 'student revolution' in Paris (and elsewhere against the ghosts of the bourgeoisie), was invited to 'secret talks' to join the pact, thereby making it quadripartite, by none other than von Ribbentrop, later hanged after the Nuremburg Trials.

In spite of the insistence by Hitler that the pact offered security to the Soviets and granted them an expansion south into India, the wily Molotov claimed that Russia '... was more interested in Europe and the Dardanelles' than the Indian Ocean. He also questioned the quadripartite pact in that it did not seem to help the Soviets's interests in Swedish neutrality (i.e. that it was not occupied by the Germans), did not guarantee access to the Baltic Sea, or did not make explicit the fate of Romania, Hungary, Bulgaria, Yugoslavia and Greece.

Hitler was so upset that he did not attend the banquet at the Russian Embassy that evening, an occasion marred by the opportune appearance of British planes just as Molotov was proposing a friendly toast. Ribbentrop, who had retired with Molotov to the underground air-shelters, insisted that the Soviet Union should cooperate with Germany in the 'liquidation of the British Empire' and proclaimed that 'England was beaten but did not know it!'. To which Molotov wittily replied, to the accompanyment of the sound of exploding British bombs, 'If that is so, why are we sitting in this air-raid sheltervand whose bombs are those that are falling so close?'

In spite of warnings from many sources, including American and British, Stalin did not believe that Hitler was going to be so stupid as to attack Russia without first having reached an Armistice with Britain. By Sunday June 22 1941, at dawn, more than three million German men launched an attack on Russian soil. At 0300 hours exactly, on June 22, a year after the French had surrendered at Compiègne, German infantry moved forward under heavy artillery protection, and the Emperor Barbarossa saw the start of his Operation under the Nazi banners. Perhaps, Hitler might have been better recalling that it was on the same day, a hundred and twenty-nine years before, that Napoleon had launched his suicidal attack on Russia, when he crossed the Niemen river on his way to Moscow.

We know the eventual results – compounded by the similarly crazy attack of the Japanese Air Forces on the American Pacific Fleet in Pearl Harbour, a few months later in that fateful year of 1941. For the city of Nuremburg, which had become the main Grounds for the Nazi Party political Rallies, and the imperial symbol of the Third Reich which should have lasted a millennium, this was a huge disaster. By October 1945 there were fewer more desolate places on earth than Nuremburg.

Figure 39
**Hitler walking down the stairs in the company, to his left, of his two 'faithful pillars',
Hermann Göring and Rudolf Hess, all three of them extremely happy after he presented his
credentials to become delegate to the State of Brunswick in 1928, which gave him the much
desired German Nationality. (Picture from Manuel Aznar's book, by an unkown author)**

The young Austrian who had failed to graduate from high school, who was turned down by the Vienna Academy of Fine Arts, and who had merely survived in Vienna before enrolling for the Great War, had suddenly and 'democratically' become the Chancellor of Germany's re-birth on 30 January 1933. With the onslaught of Operation Barbarossa, the difficult, stormy but hopeful days for the Nazis from 1928 (*see* Figure 39) to 1933, when Hitler had become Chancellor of Germany, were definitely over.

It was in 1933 that Goebbels exclaimed: 'The New Reich has been born'. He was later to become Hitler's Chief of Nazi Propaganda and one of the 'brains' behind the Nazi Party Rallies in Nuremburg yet, by 1945, the war was lost, Hitler was dead, and Nuremburg was devastated and about to witness one of the most important trials in the history of International Law.

In the last month of the war, eleven major air raids by the Allies had literally destroyed more than ninety percent of the old city. Out of the original 130,000 houses, only 17,000 remained. There was no electricity, water or telephones. One can still see some of the pictures of the ancient Church of St. Sebald, whose building had commenced in 1230, as it looked following the air raids. What had been a jewel of the late Romanesque style of Gothic Architecture (particularly the Choir) had been so badly damaged by the bombing that the black and white pictures of the Church in 1945, which I saw on the walls, made me wonder what the real intention of such barbaric attacks by the civilized side of the war, had been. Poor old St Sebald – he became a Saint in 1425 after the Catholic Church at last recognised his 'healing powers', whatever they were? Until rebuilding, he was left alone and roofless in his ancient and beautiful sepulchre created in brass by Peter Vischer (1507-1519) and his children.

The city of Nuremburg was rebuilt after the war with great skill. Unlike England, where the old city walls have disappeared from most medieval towns, as a consequence of the lack of foreign invasions, many continental towns, like the ancient city of Avila in Spain or Nuremburg have retained an almost complete medieval town pattern. I enjoyed shopping in the many craft-shops and market-places in modern Nuremburg. Even children have a site of their own to exchange toys by the Church of the Virgin. While I wandered up and down the streets of this German city, the secret capital of Franconia, I found it hard to believe that just over sixty years before it had become the capital of a new Religion: Nazism.

Part Two

Nuremburg:
The Rome of a new paganism

Great importance was attributed by the Nazis to rituals. Hitler was aware of his charisma, and rhetorical abilities, but he knew that his voice, together with the right light and scenery could provoke fanatic devotion and totally brainwash his captive audiences. Startling visual effects – huge Swastika flags that flew from tall wooden towers, large German Imperial Eagles, electric organs, neon tube lighting (invented in 1935), huge avenues for the parades, and the mighty presence of military troops and weapons, electrified the environment and enabled the ordinary man to feel an important part of something sacred and powerful. Between 1927, the year that the Nazi Party (NSDAP) celebrated its first National Rally in the city and Nuremburg was transformed into the Rome of a new paganism. By1938, the event provided an exhibition of the ancient imperial treasures and was attended by one million visitors. In fact, between the Congress of 1927 and that of 1938 there was not only a steady increase of people attending but also an accompanying crescendo of militarism and anti-semitism.

Although it is true that by 1938 most Germans were truly fascinated by Hitler, and really believed that he was the messianic Führer who would restore their national pride, give them jobs and lead them towards a prosperous and glorious future, a minority had considerable doubts. It has been claimed by prestigious historians like Hoffman, in his works on the 'German Resistance', and more recently by Michael Baigent and Richard Leigh, that there were up to forty-six attempts on Hitler's life between 1921 and 1945. Two are worth mentioning. Following the annexation of Austria by Hitler, in March 1938, without bloodshed, the SS forces, initially meant as 'para-militaries' to protect the *Führer*, gained considerable power and influence. Some senior military men felt uneasy, to say the least and had devised a possible military coup to depose Hitler in case he continued his escalation of force and domination.

They alleged a plot by the SS to usurp military control of the whole country. On 15 September 1938 they expected Prime Minister Neville Chamberlain, to remain adamant over Hitler's aggressive demands on Czechoslovakia. Chamberlain however, unexpectedly gave way to Hitler, who wrongly inferred that he now had a free hand in Central Europe. Shaken by the heavy losses inflicted by the soviets and the Allied Anglo-American Forces, a second attempt on Hitler's life, coordinated by high-rank and aristocratic military men, among them, Claus von Stauffenberg, took place in August 1944.

Unfortunately the plot failed and the conspirators were rapidly judged before the Nazi's 'People's Court of Justice', and executed. Hitler was only slightly injured by a bomb blast, after which his criminal tendencies became even more pronounced.

From 1933 onward the Party Rallies were assigned a motto. Thus, in that year of 'electoral victory', the motto was the 'Party Rally of Victory', in 1934 the 'Party Rally of Unity and Strength', immortalized by Leni Riefenstahl's propaganda fim *Triumph of the Will*, in 1935 the 'Party Rally of Freedom'. This was especially ironic if one considers that during this Congress the Nazi Reichstag convened in Nuremberg and passed the racist 'Nuremburg Laws' that included the 'Reich Citizenship Law' and the 'Law for the Protection of German Blood and Honour'. They legitimised the segregation of the Jews and deprived them of civil rights, being degraded to 'second class citizens' along with homosexuals, mentally handicapped people, gypsies (Sinti and Roma), and non-whites. Using classical genetic charts although without any scientific foundation whatsoever, they drew geneaologies of families and kindred, and legally condemned mixed marriages, making a criminal offence of extramarital relationships. Although it was Hermann Göring who read the wording of these laws on 15 September 1935, Rudolf Hess took part directly and indirectly in their definition, even if he was never personally involved in 'race defilement' or 'blood crimes' of any sort, as far as it can be proven beyond reasonable doubt.

I was particularly impressed by my visit to the Nazi Party Rally Grounds, half an hour away from the city walls. When Hitler spoke in Nuremburg on 7 September 1937 about his building ambitions, he said '... these buildings are not intended for the year 1940, or for the year 2000, but, rather, they should reach out, like the cathedrals of our past, into the centuries of the future (*see* Figure 40).

The buildings were conceived to impress, but above all to intimidate. In 1934 Albert Speer, Hitler's favourite architect (but not his friend, unlike Dr Todt, builder of the Westwall and the famous Autobahn), was commissioned to draft the complex in a huge area in the south-east part of Nuremburg.

Figure 40
Hitler inspecting the Congress Hall model for the Nurenberg Nazi Party Rallies. (Picture taken from ref. 101, Nazi Party Rally Grounds, Nurenberg's Documentation Centre; unknown author)

The monumental dimensions of the buildings, which were never completed, were gigantic and pharaonic:

1.   The Congress Hall designed by the architects Ludwig and Franz Ruff had a façade reminiscent of the ancient Coliseum in Rome. A vast roof with no underpinning was to stretch over the interior court, in which over 50,000 people in-doors would assemble before the Führer.

2.   A granite stone tribune was built in the so-called 'Luitpold Arena', linked to the War Memorial erected in 1929, to be able to gather at least 150,000 people, all members of the SA and SS forces to honour their dead and promote a spirit of patriotic self-sacrifice.

3.   The 'Zeppelin Tribune', modelled by Albert Speer himself based on the ancient 'Pergamon Altar', with the famous central speakers' rostrum for the Führer, backed by a gigantic Nazi Swastika that was blown up by the

American troops soon after their arrival. The building could accommodate up to 100,000 people and was flanked by an impressive row of huge columns which were not demolished until as late as 1967.

4.   The German Stadium whose potential capacity of over 400,000 spectators is still the largest sports stadium in the world (the Maracaná Football Stadium,   in Rio de Janeiro, the largest in the world so far, accomodates some 200,000 people). The Stadium was reminiscent of the Ancient Stadium in Olympia (Greece), and all that was found by the Americans when they entered the city in 1945 was a huge hole excavated for the foundations of the building, that was deliberately filled up with ground water thereby forming the present placid 'Silbersee Lake'.

5.   Last, but not least, the 'Great Road'. I find this the most inspired work by Speer, in its plastic simplicity and emotional abstraction. Like a 'Path to the Future' from the 'Past', to convey the symbolic link between the Imperial Ancient City of Nurenmburg, with all its glorious History and Legends, within the Nazi Party Rally Grounds. To the north, this two kilometre long and sixty metre wide road paved with 60,000 granite slabs was cleverly aligned with the old city Castle and the Imperial Town. The Teutonic Knights had been present in Nuremburg since at least 1209, when Emperor Otto IV gave them the beautiful Chapel of St Elisabeth (St Elisabeth-Kirche), originally a gothic structure, replaced in 1785 by a new and larger building which maintained the secular traditions of this Germanic Military and Religious Order until 1809, when the order was dissolved under pressure from Napoleon. The church can still be seen in Jakobsplatz, next to the fourteenth century Church of St James (in Spanish, *Santiago*), or Jakobskirche, also used by the Teutonic Knights for their sacred rituals.

People marching south along this 'Great Road' would be walking 'against the sun' (*Cara al Sol*, as a Spanish Fascist Song would also say), backed by the 'Sacred Energy of the Inner Germany'. The impression on the individual must have been that he was participating in something major and significant, while at the same time conveying the impression of his own individual insignificance.

But what *was* this 'Sacred Energy of the Inner Germany'? I am now sure that this was the real **Irrational Force** that made the Third Reich of Nazi Germany possible. Immediately after my experience in Nuremburg I decided I must ponder the subject. Amazingly I later found out that a great deal of this 'Sacred Energy' came from the Runes and from the esoteric knowledge attributed to the Knights Templar and the Teutonic Knights.

Four historical characters, that not even the most imaginative film producer could have imagined, share the devious honour of exploiting and communicating such 'Secret Knowledge': Guido von List, who re-invented the Aryan race, Wotanism and Völkish Runes; Jörg Lanz von Liebenfels, founder of the 'Order of the New Templars', Rudolf John Gorsleben, founder of the 'Edda Society', and the intriguing and mysterious Rudolf von Sebottendorf, who was not only an Oriental Freemason and Founder of the 'Thule Society', but who could be regarded as the spiritual father of the Nazi Party (NSDAP).

I shall briefly summarise their biographical history, but first I would like to pay tribute to those 'Captive Masons', many of them freemasons, who were forced to work as prisoners of concentration camps in the infamous SS Quarries to allow these gigantic architectural exploits. Hitler, as the self-appointed 'Supreme Master Builder' of Germany, decided that five cities were going to be converted into *"Führer's* Cities": Nuremburg, Munich, Hamburg, Linz and, of course, Berlin, the future 'world capital named Germania'.

Figure 41
SS prisoners working under inhuman conditions at the Stone Quarry of Flossenbürg. Over 30,000 of the stonemasons died in this place alone. Hitler should have learnt from the Knights Templar that Masons should be free and protected, rather than abused and killed. (Picture taken from ref. 101, Nazi Party Rally Grounds, Nuremburg's Documentation Centre; unknown author)

I again regard myself as very fortunate to have met the Italian writer and chemist Primo Levi in my childhood and adolescent days in Turin. Primo Levi was born there in 1919, of a reasonably well-off Piedmontese Jewish family.

To be a Jew, for him, meant 'something vague' – he said – 'not really a problem: it meant an underlying consciousness of the extremely old history of his people, some sort of benevolent disbelief in religion, and a distinct tendency towards the world of books and of abstract discussions'.

After studying at the *Liceo Classico Massimo d'Azeglio* (where I also studied and was class-mate of his only son Renzo), he took a degree in chemistry at the University of Turin. During the war he helped to form what would have become an anti-Fascist partisan band, with the Anti-Mussolini Resistance Movement 'Justice and Liberty'. Unfortunately he, and a few others, were soon captured by the Fascist Militia on 13 December 1943. As a Jew, he was sent to Fossoli, near Modena, where over six hundred Italian Jews were soon gathered and finally handed over to a squad of the German SS.

They had learnt of their destination with relief: Auschwitz, '... a name without significance'. On arrival, the children, the old men and most of the women were sent to the gas chamber. The rest, judged capable of working efficiently for the Third Reich, entered the camps of Monowitz-Buna and Birkenau.

He was 'christened' *Häftling* 174517 and it was not easy to find the strength in himself to retain something of the old Primo Levi: 'Nothing belongs to us anymore; they have taken away our clothes, our shoes, even our hair; if we speak, they will not listen to us, and if they listen they will not understand. They will even take away our name ...'

Of over six hundred Jews sent to Auschwitz, only three made the return journey to Italy, through a totally devastated Europe, after their liberation by a Russian patrol on 27 January 1945. One of the three was Primo Levi. It is hardly surprising that his return to normal life was uneasy: 'I am in the *Lager* once more, and nothing is true outside the *Lager*. All the rest was a brief pause, a deception of the senses, a dream'.

He associates his anguish with the word *Wstavac*. It is the dawn command at Auschwitz pronounced by the night guard '... with the quiet and subdued voice of one who knows that the announcement will find all ears waiting, and will be heard and obeyed'.

But the author, in his great humanity, does not forget the faint glimmers of light that so seldom came in the desolation of the concentration camp. The simple humanity of his poem 'Singing', which I translated together with other poems from the Italian into English in 1980, is good evidence of that:

'Singing' *(3 January 1946)*

*'...But when then we started to sing
Our good nonsensical songs,
Then it happened that all the things
Were again as they had been.*

*One day was nothing but one day:
Seven make a week.
Killing seemed to us a bad thing
Dying, something distant.
And the months pass by quite swiftly,
But in front of us we have so many of them!
We were again just young people –
Not martyrs, not wretches, not saints.*

*All this and something else came to our minds
While we were continuing to sing,
But they were things like the clouds
And difficult to explain'.*

Primo Levi

Surprisingly, the person who probably stirred up esoteric emotions the most in the late nineteenth century in Austria and Germany, well before the Great War, was a woman. She was the Russian adventurer and occultist Madame Helena Petrovna Blavatsky (1831-91). In the Middle Ages she would have surely have been burnt at the stake as a witch or for heresy. In the nineteenth century she became famous worldwide.

She founded the Theosophical Society in New York in 1875, and in 1877 she published her book *Isis Unveiled*, using traditional esoteric sources, and even having recourse to plagiarism of others, to discredit the rationalist and materialistic culture of modern western civilization. At that time, she looked for 'True Knowledge' in the occult lore of ancient Egypt, and she was ironically inspired by many English authors, such as Sir Edward Bulwer-Lytton.

She decided later that 'True Knowledge' came from India, and in 1879 she moved to Madras with her most loyal followers. In her book *The Secret Doctrine* (1888), amidst pseudo-scholarly references and internal contradictions, she claims that:

1.   The instrument of the Omnipresent and Eternal God is *Fohat*, an electro-spiritual force which impresses the divine scheme upon the cosmic substance as the 'Laws of Nature'.

2.   All Creation is subject to an endless cycle of destruction and rebirth, which always terminates at a level spiritually superior to it's starting point. Humans are no exception, and she embraces the Hindu and Buddhist concept of 'Karma' whereby good acts earn their performer a superior reincarnation and bad acts an inferior reincarnation.

3.   There exists, in spite of appearances, a fundamental unity between all individual souls and the deity, between the microcosm and the macrocosm.

What made her really attractive was her charisma, and her subtle use of 'occult initiation practices', traditional Gnostic and Hermetic sources, lost apocryphal writings and great imagination. As a woman, she was unique in the nineteenth century inasmuch as she managed to restart what I would called **Schools of Irrational Intellectuals** in European and American circles.

Part Three

The Nazi Religion and Magic Runes

One of the schools, which ended up achieving great fame and influence, was founded in Vienna, the capital of Hapsburg Austria, by Guido von List. Born in 1848, he was a Roman Catholic until he visited the catacombs beneath St Stephen's Cathedral in Vienna, with his father. The dark and narrow vaults made such a strong impression on him that he later claimed that he had knelt before a ruined altar in the crypt and sworn to build a temple to Wotan, after the principal God in the pagan Germanic pantheon.

He was naturally attracted by anything 'esoteric', and also by Freemasonry, although there is no evidence whatsoever that he ever joined a lodge. There was however a significant Masonic architectural tradition in Vienna, still one of the most beautiful cities in the world. For example, the Emperor Charles VI (1711-40), who almost became Emperor of Spain and of the Hapsburg Austrian-Hungarian Empire as Charles V had done in the sixteenth century – already discussed in Chapter II ('Blenheim Palace Revisited') – vowed in 1713 to build a great church in Vienna dedicated to his Patron Saint, St Charles Borromeo, to deliver the city from the terrible Plague.

This *Karlskirche* (*see* Figure 42), as it is called, was built by the architect Fischer von Erlach, based on his vision of King Solomon's Temple in Jerusalem and almost certainly his knowledge of some of the illustrations of the famous *Code of Maimonides*, named after the historical rabbi and physician, born in Cordova in twelfth century Spain and who died in 1204 in Israel, being buried near Lake Tiberias.

In Vienna, Guido von List revived the pre-Roman myths of Germania, and claimed that the ancient Teutons had practised a Gnostic religion that he called 'Wotanism' after their principal God. This movement was soon to become very attractive to German nationalists who even before the First World War had felt a little 'uncomfortable' under the Hapsburgs because of their 'historical pluralism', amply demonstrated in Spain and which had accorded equal rights to the important 'Slav' part of the Empire.

Figure 42
Fischer von Erlach's 'Karlskirche' in Vienna, capital of the Hapsburg Empire, based on his vision of King Solomon's Temple in Jerusalem. The two columns at the entrance, Jachin and Boaz, are outstanding. Picture taken from Entwurff's 'Karlskirche' (Vienna), quoted by James S. Curl (104).

The German chauvinist mystique, the defence of Germandom against liberal, socialist and Jewish groups, the invention of the 'Aryan Race', that from a genetic and scientific point of view has never existed, and the Occultism derived by the Wisdom of the Runes, Mantic Sciences and Teutonic Astrology, Shamanic and Homeopathic Medicines eventually led to the foundation by List in the midsummer solstice of 1911 of a tiny inner ring of initiates called the HAO, which meant 'High Armanen-Order', with high-ranking members in Vienna, Berlin, Hamburg and Munich.

Guido von List (*see* Figure 43) took these few elect ones on 'esoteric pilgrimages' to visit certain places in the land of 'Ostara', where the spirit of 'Hari-Wotan' still reigned.

Typical sacred mottoes described by 'Germanic Runes' were: 'Know yourself, then you know everything', 'Do not fear death, for death cannot kill you', 'Man is one with God', 'Master the universe by mastering yourself'.

I wonder if some of the Runes found in the Castle at Mora de Rubielos (*see* Figure 44) meant similar sorts of things, which might have appealed to the Knights of the Temple, and the Knights of St John, as well as casting protective charms to defend the Castle from the forces of the Islamic enemy.

Figure 43
Guido von List, who preached 'Wotanism' and the power of Runes in Vienna (Hapsburg Empire) and Prussia before the Great War (1914-19). (Picture taken from Ref 103; *Österreichische Nationalbibliothek***, Vienna).**

According to Nicholas Goodrick-Clarke, a scholar and specialist on Nazi ideology who is currently a Research Fellow in the Western Esoteric Tradition at the University of Wales (Lampeter), this 'Armanen-Order', or *Armanenschaft*, borrowed concepts and structure from Rosicrucianism and from Freemasonry . The elite priesthood was divided into three grades, corresponding to the grades of Entered Apprentice, Fellow Craft and Master Mason in lodge hierarchy. Similarly, each grade has its own particular signs, grips and passwords.

List, characterized these secrets by such occult formulae as 'the unutterable name of God', the 'lost master word', or the 'philosopher's stone', culled from cabbalistic, Masonic and Alchemical sources. His own Gothic Motto was *Arehisosur* and was represented by runes called Swastikas.

Wotan was worshipped as the god of war and the lord of dead heroes in 'Valhalla', with obvious reference to the Pantheon of Scandinavian and other Northern European cultures (Vikings). In the *Havamal* myth, Wotan was wounded by a spear and hung upon a windswept tree without food or drink for nine nights. At the climax of his suffering he had a vision: an 'Understanding of the Magic Runes' suddenly came to him. He freed himself and related eighteen 'Runic Spells', which were typically concerned with the secret of immortality, mastery over the enemy, the ability to heal oneself, success in love, and the control of all the elements.

The 'Runes' found in my 'Secret Castle', carved in the stones by Masons and protected by the Knights of the Temple and the Knights of St. John, were again surfacing in all of their ancient esoteric powers in the germinal intellectual circles of Pan-German Nationalism, and later in Nazi Germany (*see* Figure 44).

Figure 44
Stone Marks found in the *Ex-Colegiata* (top: Church of St. Mary) and the Castle (bottom: *Castillo*) at Mora de Rubielos. Many of them are clearly runic elements. A Maltese Cross is also visible in the *Ex-Colegiata*.

Not only that, as I found out many of these Runes, and others not represented in the Castle or Church of Mora de Rubielos, were to be found in other parts of Spain and were part of the enigmatic written language of the Ibers.

I attatch the four Iberian Alphabets, (*see* Figure 45), as officially accepted by Spanish Academics. Professor Manuel Gomez Moreno was the first to publish these writings in 1922 and more fully in 1925, comparing inscriptions and stone carvings from archaeological sites in different parts of Spain. I have omitted the less pure and more 'Greek versions' of the Iberian ancient written language, used in some parts of Eastern and Mediterranean Spain because of their direct commercial and cultural contact with *Magna Grecia* (Greek Colonies in the fourth to second centuries BC) .

The four 'versions' of the Iberian written language are to be found in Figure 46. They represent the more authentic and original writing of the Ibers, who populated the inland area of ancient Spain between the river Ebro ('Iber', the largest in Spain), on the frontier between Aragon and Catalonia, and the central region of Teruel and Cuenca.

This land includes *El Maestrazgo*, or The Land of the Masters, where the Castle of don Juan Fernandez de Heredia and the Church of St Mary are located.

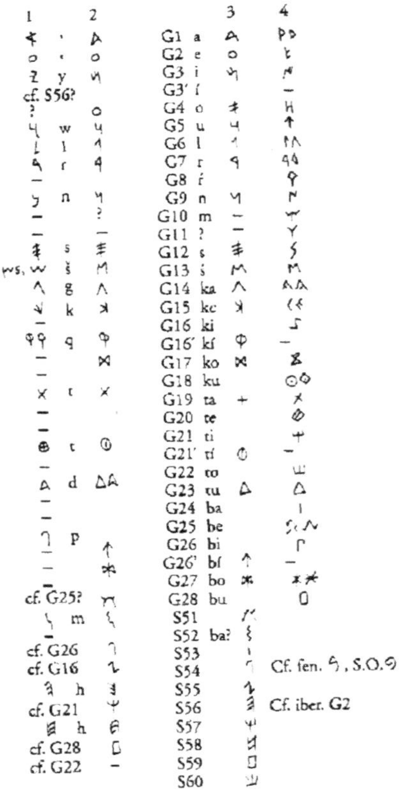

1	2	3	4
		G1 a	
		G2 e	
	y	G3 i	
cf. S56?		G3' i	
		G4 o	
	w	G5 u	
	l	G6 l	
	r	G7 r	
		G8 r̃	
	n	G9 n	
		G10 m	
		G11 ?	
	s	G12 s	
ws, w	ś	G13 ś	
	š	G14 ka	
	k	G15 ke	
		G16 ki	
	q	G16' ki	
		G17 ko	
		G18 ku	
	t	G19 ta	
		G20 te	
		G21 ti	
	t	G21' ti	
		G22 to	
	d	G23 tu	
		G24 ba	
		G25 be	
	P	G26 bi	
		G26' bi	
		G27 bo	
cf. G25?		G28 bu	
	m	S51	
		S52 ba?	
cf. G26		S53	
cf. G16		S54	Cf. fen.
	h	S55	
cf. G21		S56	Cf. iber. G2
	h	S57	
cf. G28		S58	
cf. G22		S59	
		S60	

Figure 45
'Paleo-Hispanic Iberian Languages' The equivalent 'phonetic sounds' are represented in Latin letters to the right of the 'classification groups' (G1 to G28; and S51 to S60). (Picture by Luis Michelena)

In Figure 46, modified from the original by Luis Michelena we find a summary of the four classic 'Models of Iberian Signs':

1. The so-called 'Phoenician' Model; the Phoenicians, originally from Carthage, had established several commercial colonies and cities along the coast of the Iberian Peninsula, and even past the Straits of Gibraltar in what is today's city of Cadiz.

2. The writings more often found in the South-East part of Spain (along what today is known as the Costa del Sol).

3. The written symbols more often used in the South and South West (Andalucia)

4. The symbols more often used in the Levante, that includes the present regions of Valencia, Catalonia and Aragon, and include Mora de Rubielos.

Some of them, for example 'G17', are found carved in what remains of the City Wall of Tarragona, which used to be inhabited by Ibers from the Levant, before the Romans conquered it. This symbol *is* identical to the rune called **DAGAZ** in Germanic or **DAEG** in Old English. It is the runic symbol of 'Hope'. Hope is a light that never fails, a flame burning in the darkest night, an energy **never to give up**. The Tarragona of the Ibers never surrendered. It was conquered and destroyed by Rome, but on the smouldering ruins of the ancient city the Romans built their main city in Spain: Imperial **Tarraco**, whose Temples and Amphitheatre and Aqueduct are still the pride of today's inhabitants of Modern Tarragona.

It is of interest that this very ancient culture (the 'Ibers') , whose language has not to this date been completely deciphered, mingled in central and North East Spain with Celtic peoples, creating the so-called 'Celt-iberian' culture. The Celts , as it is well known. were great sea-travellers, and populated vast parts of ancient Europe, including Ireland, Wales, parts of Scotland and North West France. They also exchanged products and goods with other Northern European Cultures, such as Germanic and Viking tribes, even before the more 'civilized' Romans appeared.

It should therefore not surprise us that Runes became cultivated in twentieth century Germany and Austria by other post-Great War Aryan Occultists, such as members of the Edda Society, started by Rudolf John Gorsleben (1883-1930), who was born in the beautiful region of Alsace-Lorraine, a French province which had been annexed by the German Second Reich in 1871, after its victory in the Franco-Prussian War. Gorsleben, who had fought in the First World War in a German unit attached to the Turkish Army in Arabia, fighting against the Bedouin tribes and their British supporters in Palestine, was regarded as a military hero (decorated with twelve military distinctions) and was arrested in April 1919 together with Dietrich Eckhart by communist insurgents during the Munich Soviet Republic Revolution. They escaped death by a miracle, and Gorsleben made an effort to develop the knowledge of Runes into a science.

Guido von List's ideal state was a 'male order' run by a special 'elite, whose power was run by a holy, absolute and mysterious 'Occult Chapter'. The similarities with the plans by Himmler and the SS are striking. In his book *'Himmler's Crusade' – The true story of the 1938 Nazi expedition into Tibet –* Christopher Hale explains how Heinrich Himmler was the man who 'built piece by piece and with a numbing attention to detail, the "bureaucracy of genocide".' Richard Breitman had already called him 'the architect of genocide'. In 1942-43 when the Nazis were no longer in control of the war, and there was a sudden and crazy rush to complete the 'Final Solution', Himmler was regarded, even by his fellow Nazis, as the incarnation of 'Hitler's Evil Spirit'. Cold, calculating, ambitious, cruel, and criminal he changed the plan on the Jewish problem from 'massive deportation to Madagascar' – it is not a bad joke and it was certainly contemplated by the Nazis – to the infernal killing machines of the concentration camps: trains full of people, hard labour, brutality, incredible medical experiments on live human subjects, gas chambers and death, followed by mass incineration of bodies.

What made him sinister was his capacity to concentrate on little things, his conscientiousness without a conscience, his hobbyist tendencies, his esoteric beliefs in the dark side of Astrology, Heraldry, Alchemy, the Holy Grail and Tibetan culture. In 1938 – in the middle of the Spanish Civil War, he sponsored an expedition to Tibet to confirm the myth that Aryans descended from the Himalayas. Five Germans, all of them officers in the SS (from *Schutzstaffeln* meaning 'protective squads'), arrived in Lhasa at the beginning of 1939, with two rather unusual flags strapped to poles.

One was a Swastika, an ancient rune, but also the 'Wheel of Life' in Tibet and since 1933 the national flag of Nazi Germany.

The other flag showed a double *Sieg* Rune, the unmistakable and chilling insignia of the SS. Both Runes were part of the Evil SS-Ring (called SS *Totenkopfring*), as seen in Figure 46.

The ring was at first presented to senior SS officers of the Old Guard (of which there were fewer than 5,000) who had displayed extraordinary valour and leadership skills but by 1939, disciplinary issues aside, this SS ring was available to any officer with three years service in the SS, and in second World War, virtually the entire SS leadership, including the *Waffen*-SS and the cruel *Gestapo*, had the ring. In October of 1944 production of the rings was cancelled due to the increasing economic stresses of the final stages of the war. 14,500 were made altogether.

The design of the ring is based on runes and reflects Himmler's interest in mythology and occultism, as well as 'black magic'. The skull (or *Totenkopf)* – literally 'death's head') was the traditional symbol of the SS, taken from other German and Prussian military units of the past, The two *Sieg* (victory) runes represent the lightning flash runes of the *Schutzstaffel*, while the *Hagall* rune represents the faith and camaraderie that was idealised by the leaders of the organisation. The swastika was originally a rune paradoxically meaning 'light and hope'. However, the SS liked to portray this as another influential symbol of the power of the Aryan race. SS men should sacrifice all for their brothers, as is emphasised by an SS motto 'Give death and take death'. The ring showed the name of the bearer, the date of presentation, and a facsimile of Himmler's signature, plus the abbreviations. M Lb. for *Meinem Lieben*' or 'my dear'.

The lunatic Nazi Expedition of the SS to Tibet in search of the real origins of the Aryan race was directed by Ernst Schäfer, who had become Himmler's preferred scientist and anthropologist in the same way that Albert Speer, who by the end of the war was Minister for Armaments and War Production, had become Adolf Hitler's protégée. Hitler flattered Speer by commissioning the colossal rebuilding of Berlin and Nuremburg, while Himmler made Schäfer the Director of his 'Institute for Central Asian Research'.

Himmler's sick mind went further. He felt a strange admiration for both the Jesuits, with himself as 'Ignatius of Loyola', and the Knights Templar. When he saw the North Tower of Wewelsburg Castle in 1933 (the year the Nazis came to full power in Germnay) at the heart of what had been the pagan empire of the Saxons and close to the Teutoberger Forest where Hermann (Arminius), had defeated the Roman Legions, he decided he would build his own 'Castle of Camelot'.

The SS School *Haus Wewelsburg* was for the *Reichsführer* both a monastery and a fortress – an SS Vatican. Sited on a tapering ridge overlooking the river, it is a narrow triangle in plan whose apex points due North. The North was the cardinal point from whence Evil Forces came, and indeed it is in the North that the main gate of the Castle of Mora de Rubielos, our 'Secret Castle', is located. And it is precisely in that North Gate of the Aragonese Castle where one can find the highest density of 'Protective Runes' in the building.

In 1933, Himmler had been immediately struck by this geometry and believed that it depicted the 'Spear of Destiny', an occult symbol. An immense round tower was built at the apex of the triangle, and inside it was Himmler's dark Camelot where the higher-ranked SS officers assembled to 'practise spiritual training and meditation', as had Ignatius of Loyola. Today only a *Sonnenrad*, a twelve-spoke sun wheel embedded in the marble floor, once lined with gold, remains in this North Tower. For Himmler it represented the 'Centre of the New World Order'.

Figure 46
Runic Symbols in the Evil SS-Ring of the Nazis (called *SS Totenkopfring*): one can see Runes that are also remarkably similar to some of the ancient written symbols used by the Ibers, in Aragon and Valencia, e.g. G12 (4), G16 (4) and G 27 (4) clearly visible in Figure 46. In addition, the 'Skull and Crossbones' symbol still used by many Secret Societies, is also visible at the bottom.

If Himmler was a dangerous criminal, long before he was famous the Occultist Germans produced a more bizarre and less dangerous, though still racist, character: Adolf Josef Lanz, who was born of middle-class parents, but soon added for himself an aristocratic 'von Liebenfels' to his name.

He was the founder of the 'Order of the New Templars' (ONT). His initial interest in the Knights Templar Order stemmed from reading the story of 'Parsifal and the Knights of the Grail', in great vogue because of the masterly operatic genius of Richard Wagner. Lanz's high regard for the Templars was probably because he had been a Cistercian himself, and it was St Bernard of Clairvaux, the Cistercian founder, who had composed the Templar Rules in 1128. With the help of rich Viennese friends he started publishing the Pan-German and Racist magazine *Ostara*, regularly read by Adolf Hitler in his poor days in Vienna before the Great War, and a small Castle, Burg Werfenstein, which was a romantic medieval ruin perched upon a sheer rock cliff above the

River Danube at the Village of Struden near Grein in Upper Austria.

Lanz celebrated Christmas Day 1907 by hoisting a Swastika flag upon the tower of Burg Werfenstein. Austrian scholars were the first to suggest that young Adolf Hitler read and admired Lanz von Liebenfels. But they had to wait until 1951 when Lanz finally admitted that Hitler had visited him at his home in Vienna, at the *Ostara* Office in 1908-1909. Lanz said that Hitler was interested in the racial theories of Lanz and wished to buy some back numbers in order to complete his collection of the *Ostara* Magazine. Lanz noticed that Hitler looked very poor and gave him the requested back numbers free, as well as two crowns for his return fare to the city centre.

According to the extravagant Neo-Manichean theories of Lanz, the earliest ancestors of the Aryans were the 'Atlanteans', who had lived on a continent situated in the northern part of the Atlantic Ocean. They were probably derived from then original divine *Theozoa* with electromagnetic sensory organs and superhuman powers. Catastrophic floods, perhaps a Tsunami, eventually submerged their continent in about 8000 B.C. and they migrated south and eastwards in two groups: some went to the British Isles, Scandinavia and Northern Germany; while others moved further south to Babylonia and Egypt.

He gave these ideas a new scientific name, though there was no real evidence for them whatsoever: 'Ariosophy'. The golden age of 'Ariosophy' for Lanz was the Middle Ages, because of the 'racist-chivalrous cult of the religious and military orders'. The suppression of the Templars in 1307 signalled the end of this era and the ascendancy of 'racial inferiors'. He claimed that the cryptic heritage of 'Ariosophy' was the 'Order of Christ', founded in 1319 by the King of Portugal and under whose flag and banners the world was mapped and Christianity grew oversees, and he further identified the two Hapsburg houses of Spain and Austria as the cryptic agents of a new 'ariosophical empire'.

Christopher Columbus, a native of Genoa in Italy according to most, but born in Mallorca according to others, a genius who changed the world, and who remains an enigma to the extent that we are still unsure of his exact burial site in the Cathedral of Seville (according to some) or in the Dominican Republic according to others, had a peculiar way of signing his documents (*see* Figure 47) basing his signature on three letters, X-M-Y, meaning according to official historians: Christ, Mary and Jesus or 'Yesu'. But virtually the same graphic forms are also found in the Iberian language (G19, G13 and G11 of the Levante's written language on column 4 of Figure 46). He also added his own 'Christogram': Chi-Rho , in Greek, and *Ferens* (meaning 'carrier' in Latin, or 'phorus' in Greek).

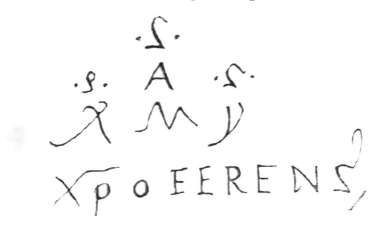

Figure 47
**Signature of Christophorus Columbus (*Archivo de Indias, Sevilla*), and rerpoduced in the first
edition of '*Cristobal Colon*', by Washington Irving, 1851 (*Gaspar y Roig Editores*, Madrid)**

The Christogram 'Chi-Rho' , as initial letters of 'Christos', became a magical and popular amulet at the time of the Roman Emperor Constantine, and later in the fourth century AD. It has been claimed by several authors that Christopher Columbus knew before his famous trip the exact route to the West Indies (which turned out to be the Americas) and that he had either learnt this from the Knights Templar's heirs in Portugal (including the famous Prince Henry the Navigator), or from some local friars in the Canary islands.

Lanz claimed that Charles V of Germany (Charles I of Spain) had plans to reconquer the East from the Turks, following the victory of Lepanto, with the help of the Maltese Knights of St. John but that it was a machination by the Jews and the Lutherans that had made this an impossible task.

The list of the **Irrational Intellectuals** cannot be complete without Baron Rudolf von Sebottendorf, who merits a small Chapter on his own.

Selected Bibliography

98.　Baigent M. and Leigh R. Secret Germany: Claus von Stauffenberg and the Mystical Crusade against Hitler. Jonathan Cape, London, 1994.

99.　Alfred Carl. Aachen and its cathedral. Notes on the city and a guide to its centre Einhard Publishers, Achen.

100.　Churchill Archives Centre, Churchill College, Cambridge: CHAR 20/036/005, Winston Churchill personal minutes for May 1941; CHAR 20/038/139-142:telegram from Sir Winston to Roosevelt, President of the U.S.A.

101.　George Mosse. Nazi Culture. London 1966.

102.　Visitors Guide. "Fascination and Terror"- Documentation Centre of the Nazi Party Rally Grounds. Museen der Stadt Nürnberg, 2004.

103.　Miguel Hernández-Bronchud. *Four Poems by Primo Levi*. Lycidas. Volume 9 (1980-81), Wolfson College, Oxford. Special Charter Edition.

104.　Nicholas Goodrick-Clarke. The Occult Roots of Nazism. Tauris Parke Paperbacks, London 2004.

105.　James S. Curl. *The Art and Architecture of Freemasonry. An introductory Study.* BT Batsford Publishers, London 1991.

106.　Monzon Royo J. *Historia de Mora de Rubielos. Segunda Edición*. Teruel, Ayuntamiento de Mora de Rubielos, 1992.

107.　Manuel Gómez-Moreno, 1925; '*Sobre los Iberos y su lengua*', In: *Homenaje a Menéndez Pidal, III*, pp. 475-99, (*Revista Misceláneas*, Madrid).

108.　Manuel Gómez-Moreno, 1949. '*Suplemento de Epigrafía Ibérica*', '*Misceláneas*', pp. 283-330.

109.　Luis Michelena, 1979. '*La langue ibère*', In: *Actas del II Coloquio sobre Lenguas*, pp. 23-39 (republished In: *Revista e historia*, pp. 341-56, Madrid, 1985).

110.　Christopher Hale, *Himmler's Crusade, The true story of the 1938 Nazi expedition into Tibet* (Bantam Books, 2003).

111.　Hurtado García J.A., *De cómo el Temple llegó a América antes del descubrimiento oficial*, Chapter XXI of *Codex Templi, Los misterios Templarios a la luz de la Historia y la Tradición* (*Templespaña, Ediciones Aguilar*, Madrid, 2005).

Chapter Five

Sir Steven Runciman and von Sebottendorf in Istanbul

This short Chapter does not pretend to bring forward anything new or important about the History of our twentieth century, nor about the so-called Rudolf Hess case, but it is certainly a good example of how reality often goes considerably beyond fiction, surpassing it in **unpredictable** and **unexplained** contents. In other words, one does not need to 'invent' anything at all. One simply, needs to explain the facts and point out the enigmas.

Sebottendorf is probably the most cosmopolitan and intelligent of the **German irrational intellectuals** involved in the birth and growth of Nazi Germany. According to the excellent review by Nicholas Goodrick-Clark in his recent book *The Occult Roots of Nazism'(see* previous chapter), 'his penchant for shady deals and espionage led him into subterfuges which also earned him the reputation of a trickster'. The son of a working-class Prussian family, Sebottendorf made an early break with his ordinary background by going to sea and working in the Middle East. He saturated himself with 'Occultist' ideas in Turkey, and one of the few surviving early texts by him, first published in 1924, recently re-edited in English (*The Practice of the Ancient Turkish Freemasons: the Key to the Understanding of Alchemy*) makes it clear that he was pro-Islamic, fascinated by Sufism and irregular Freemasonry in general, and Alchemy and Mysticism in particular. He says in this book:

'True mortification lies in sublimation, in unification, in the *Unio Mystica*, in becoming One with God'.

This is what he proclaims to be the real objectives and powers of Alchemy, rather than the mere transformation of Metals.

According to several of his official 'biographies', Rudolf von Sebottendorf was the alias of Adam Alfred Rudolf Glauer (9 November 1875 – 8 May 1945), who also occasionally used another alias, Erwin Torre. He was an important figure in the activities of the Thule Society, a post-World War I German political organization that was a precursor of the Nazi Party. He was a practitioner of Sufi meditation and astrology.

Glauer was born in Hoyerswerda, Germany, the son of an engine driver from Dresden. He used the alias Sebottendorf because he claimed that he had been adopted by the Sebottendorf family and had a claim to the title of count. After a career as a merchant seaman, Glauer settled in Turkey in 1901 and became the supervisor of a large estate there.

Glauer (Sebottendorf) visited the Cheops Pyramid in Egypt in Giza, in July 1900 and became attracted to the cosmological and numerological significance of the pyramids and ancient Gnostic theories. At Bursa he made the acquaintance of the Termudi family, who were Greek Jews from Salonica. The businessman Termudi, involved in banking and in the commercial exploitation of 'silkworm cocoons, had retired to devote himself to a study of the Kabbalah (*see* Figure 48), Alchemy and Rosicrucian texts.

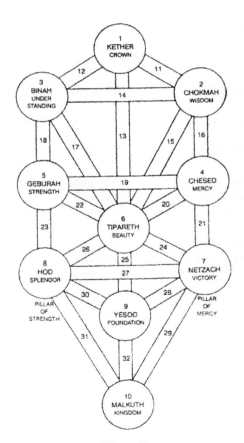

Figure 48
The '*Sephirotic* Tree' of the Cabbala, that contains the Map of 'Energy-Intelligence'.

It appears that the Termudis were freemasons in a lodge that may have been affiliated to the French Rite of Memphis, and Glauer was initiated into this Lodge around 1901.

The Termudis were also interested in the 'Davidic' geneaology, the descendents of King David, father of King Solomon. One of the unexplained mysteries of Jesus (is that, according to the prophets of the Old Testament, and to Isaiah in particular, Jesus as the Messiah had to be of Royal Blood and hence descend from King David himself. How could the people of Israel, or the High Priests of the Temple, know whether anybody was of royal Davidic blood?

According to Knight and Lomas, '... at the time before Jesus was born, the priests of the Temple of Jerusalem ran two schools: one for boys and one for girls. The priests were known by titles which were the names of angels, such as Michael, Mazaldek and Gabriel. This was the way in which they preserved the pure lines of Levi and David'. The same authors suggest that when each of the chosen girls had passed through puberty one of the priests would impregnate her with the seed of the holy bloodline and, once pregnant, she would be married off to a respectable man to bring up the child. It was the custom that when these children reached the age of seven years they were handed back to the Temple school to be educated by the priests.

Whatever the truth, Glauer inherited the occult library of the old Termudi, including the complete edition of *The Zohar* or Book of Splendour. In the splendid English version translated by Harry Sperling and Maurice Simon, we read that King David was singularly devoted to the Almighty. He would rise at midnight and sing songs of praise, for as soon as the North Wind began to blow at midnight he knew that the moment had come when God rose, as it were, to amuse and enjoy Himself with the righteous in the Garden of Eden. King David headed his prayers with 'Hallelujah', that literally means 'Praise ye the Lord'. This was the most excellent title, embracing as it does in one single word the name of God and the call to praise.

Nicholas Goodrick-Clark mentions in his book that the Masonic lodge which Glauer had joined in 1901 may have supported the 'Secret Society of Union and Progress', founded by Salonican Turks, to generate a pro-western and more liberal consciousness against the repressive and corrupt totalitarian reign of the Sultan.

According to some sources, an unlikely link between the secret Sufi Bektashi Sect and European Freemasonry was also established. Glauer was so 'integrated' into Turkish way of life that he took Turkish citizenship and fought with the Turks, receiving wounds, during the Second Balkan War in 1912. In fact, he claimed that he was naturalized as a Turkish citizen in 1911, and subsequently legally adopted by an expatriate Baron Heinrich von Sebottendorf under Turkish law.

Subsequently, armed with an aristocratic name and a Turkish passport, he returned to Germany and married his second wife, an extremely wealthy divorcee called Berta Anna Iffland.

This led to accusations of 'fortune-hunting', and other irregular dealings, as a result of which he and his new wife 'disappeared' for a while, until in 1916, in the middle of the First World War when they settled at Bad Aibling, an elegant Bavarian Spa. In September 1916, he visited Hermann Pohl, a leader of the *Germanen-orden* in Berlin, which summoned all fair-haired and blue-eyed Germans of pure Aryan descent to defend the **Inner Germania**. One of their common interests were the **Runes**, to the extent that Sebottendorf started publishing a monthly Order periodical called *Runen* in January 1918.

Glauer was deeply influenced by Sufi mysticism, other Eastern philosophies, and in particular, the writings of Madame Helena Petrovna Blavatsky. He used Blavatsky's *The Secret Doctrine* to launch his own recreation of ancient Germanic myth, positing a coming historical moment in which he theorized that the Aryan race would be restored to prior glories by the appearance of a Race of Supermen. Glauer eventually became the prime mover behind the Thule Society, which was one of the most important precursors of the Nazi Party, although the Nazi Party itself, once it had become ascendant, obliterated the Thule Society.

What happened next, like most things in Sebottendorf's life, is not altogether clear, but it appears that in 1918, during the Soviet Revolution which had significant effects on Germany, the Germanenorden was banned, and the term 'Thule Society' was adopted as a 'cover-name' to continue its right-wing political activities. One ought not to forget that the political project designed and defended by Karl Marx (himself a German Jewish intellectual exiled in London where he was later interred in Highgate Cemetry), was due to take place in Prussia, rather than in Russia.

The Thule Society, which espoused ideas of extreme nationalism, race mysticism, virulent anti-semitism, and the occult, was formed shortly after the end of World War I in Munich by Glauer. It attracted about 250 ardent followers in Munich and about 1500 in greater Bavaria. Members of the Thule Society included Rudolf Hess, Dietrich Eckart, and Alfred Rosenberg. Adolf Hitler however, was never a member of the Thule

Group, probably because of his impoverished background.

Thule agents infiltrated armed formations of the Communist Party in Munich and plotted to destroy the party, hatching plans to kidnap the party's leader, Kurt Eisner, and launching an attack against Munich's Communist government on 30 April 1919. The Thule Society also started its own newspaper, the *Münchener Beobachter*, in 1918, and eventually encouraged the organizer Anton Drexler to develop links between the Society and various extreme right workers' organizations in Munich.

Drexler was instrumental in merging the Thule Society with a workers' party with which he was involved. The merged organization became known as the *Deutscher Arbeiterpartei* (DAP). It was the DAP to which Adolf Hitler was introduced in 1919. By 1 April 1920, the DAP had been reconstituted as the Nazi Party (NSDAP – *NationalSozialistische Deutsche ArbeiterPartei*) and Sebottendorf, who was accused of negligence in allegedly allowing the names of several key Thule Society members to fall into the hands of the Communists, resulting in the execution of seven members after the attack on the Munich government in April 1919, had fled Germany for Switzerland and then for Turkey.

He returned to Germany in January 1933 but fled again in 1934. Several months after the Nazi seizure of power in 1933 , Sebottendorf published a book with the sensational title of *Before Hitler came: The early years of the Nazi movement*. This book was not well received by Hitler, who thought that Sebottendorf was claiming too much for himself and the Thule Society that he had created. Hitler wanted to be made clear to the German people that it was he, the Führer, who had created and fostered the Nazi party. Probably the only two other people that he would consider as co-authors were Rudolf Hess and Hermann Göring.

However, Sebottendorf's claim that he provided the early and crucial journalistic basis of the Nazi party is quite correct but he was forced to leave Nazi Germany and became an agent of the German military in Istanbul during the period 1942–1945 (while apparently also working as a double agent for the British military).

In that period, we find another old protagonist of this book living and teaching in Istanbul, probably while working for the British Secret Service – Sir Steven Runciman, the expert on the Christian Dualists and the Crusades.

When he died, the obituaries dedicated to Sir Steven Runciman which appeared in the two most traditional English newspapers, *The Times* and The *Daily Telegraph*, shared a fairly similar eccentric view of this character, whose picture I found at our 'Secret Castle' (Mora de Rubielos) in a poster in July 2001.

We read from the obituary in the The Times:

'Sir Steven Runciman Scholar, linguist and gossip, whose revisionist History of the Crusades and studies of Byzantium were massively researched and widely read Steven Runciman was famous for throwing light on some very dark ages, and attempting, as he said the historian must, "to record in one great sweeping sequence the greater events and movements that have swayed the destiny of man".'

As well as being the leading historian of the Crusades, he was a world traveller, the companion of royalty – at least four queens were said to have turned out for his eightieth birthday – and an aficionado of the foibles of the powerful, whether past or present. Details of forgotten personalities glint in all his writings, and he could discourse upon ancient genealogies, scandals and feuds, for hours on end. His most important work, the three-volume *History of the Crusades*, took a more sceptical line than had any previous Western historian and which was freshly informed by a reading of Islamic sources. Two hundred years earlier Gibbon had portrayed the Crusades as doomed romantic escapades, and wrote of "the triumph of barbarism and superstition" but in Runciman's eyes, the Crusaders were not a chivalrous host who captured but failed to keep the Holy Land, they were the final wave of the barbarian invaders who had destroyed the Roman Empire. They completed this work by destroying the real centre of medieval civilisation and the last bastion of antiquity, Constantinople and the Byzantine Empire. In charting the medieval phase of the endless struggle between East and West in the Middle East, Runciman's sympathies were unambiguously with Byzantium against the bigots and wreckers of the West. His final judgment of the whole enterprise set a standard of self-laceration which British historians have since struggled to surpass: "High ideals were besmirched by cruelty and greed, enterprise and endurance by a blind and narrow self-righteousness; and the Holy War itself was nothing more than a long act of intolerance in the name of God, which is a sin against the Holy Ghost.'

James Cochran Stevenson Runciman – which was his full name – was the second son of Walter Runciman, the first Viscount. His paternal grandfather was a 'Geordie' albeit of Scots descent who ran away to sea at age eleven, became a master mariner by twenty-one and founded a shipping line. His maternal grandfather ran a chemical works in Jarrow. His parents were both Liberal MPs – the first married couple to sit together in the House of Commons – thus he knew Winston Churchill since before the First World War. His best friend at Summerfields prep school was the son of Herbert Asquith and in 1991 he claimed to have known every Prime Minister of the century except Campbell Bannerman, who had died when he was three, and Bonar Law, 'whom nobody knew'. He was a linguist from the age of three, when his governess began to teach him French.

Latin followed at six, Greek at seven, and Russian at eleven. With these accomplishments and a budding interest in history, he was a King's Scholar at Eton, and from there he won a scholarship to Trinity College, Cambridge. His mother had taken a first in history at Girton, and he followed her example with a first in 1925. He soon became a fellow of Trinity and a university lecturer. His rooms in Nevile's Court were famous for their French 1820s grisaille wallpaper, depicting Cupid and Psyche, and his exquisite bric-a-brac. He kept a green parakeet called Benedict, which he use to spank with a pencil for misdemeanours. He was already immensely grand, and loved socialising. As well as books and pictures – including Edward Lear watercolours – he collected anecdotes and people, and the names in his gossip did not so much drop as float diaphanously. He was a broad-gauge gossip, ranging across the academic, literary, social and royal spheres with tales and tittle-tattle about many generations in many countries. A typical example was his story of the Queen of the Belgians who had one of the first facelifts, and was left with a permanent smile, so that when the King died she had to return to the clinic to have it let down again.

Through his Etonian friend Dadie Rylands, now a young don at King's, Runciman met John Maynard Keynes, and through Keynes's wife, Lydia Lopakova, he met Diaghilev. Rylands also introduced him to the Bloomsbury set around Virginia Woolf (for whom Runciman never much cared). Lytton Strachey's attacks on the then accepted greatness of the British Empire formed a precedent for Runciman's growing scepticism about much earlier attempts at conquest; and the enthusiasm of Roger Fry and Clive Bell helped to foster his interest in Byzantine art. As a bachelor don he was a guide, friend and teasing mentor to a number of undergraduates, including Guy Burgess and Noel Annan, whose affection he won for life.

He gave intimate lunches and dinners enlivened occasionally by telling the fortunes of his guests, including the odd king, by Tarot card. But his heart was in travel and research, and the historian George Trevelyan advised him to leave Cambridge if he wanted to write as a result of which in 1938, having come into a considerable fortune on his grandfather's death, he resigned his fellowship at Trinity (though the College made him an honorary fellow in 1965).

During the war he was a press attaché to the British legation in Sofia and then in Cairo, and from 1942 till 1945 was professor of Byzantine history and art at the University of Istanbul.

I do not wish to be 'repetitive', but to be fair also to The *Daily Telegraph* let us also reproduce part of their Obituary:

> 'Sir Steven Runciman, who has died aged ninety-seven, was the pre-eminent historian of the Byzantine Empire and of the Crusades; he was also a celebrated aesthete, gentleman scholar and repository of the civilised values of Edwardian times. His *magnum opus* was the three-volume *A History of the Crusades*, published between 1951 and 1954. In its preface Runciman set out his credo, one that derived from Gibbon, and stressed the claims of grand narrative over narrow analysis: "I believe that the supreme duty of the historian is to write history, that is to say, to attempt to record in one sweeping sequence the greater events and movements that have swayed the destinies of man".'

For Runciman, the Crusades were not romantic adventures but the last of the barbarian invasions. In fact, Sir Steven considered the Crusades a vast fiasco: 'The Crusades were launched to save Eastern Christendom from the Muslims. When they ended the whole Eastern Christendom was under Muslim rule. When Pope Urban preached his great sermon at Clermont the Turks seemed about to threaten the Bosphorus. When Pope Pius II preached the last Crusade, the Turks were crossing the Danube...'

His opinion was partly determined by his sympathy for the Byzantine Empire, often at odds with the Crusaders and an oasis of culture surrounded by unappreciative savages. It was a condition with which he identified. His prodigious work on a culture previously damned as effete was largely responsible for the blossoming of Byzantine studies in Britain. His view of the historian's task – and his belief that one writes to be read – demanded that he aim as much at a non-specialist audience as at fellow academics. His lucid style was admirably suited to this, with a simplicity and dispassion that had been the ideal of Byzantine iconographers. The popular success that his books enjoyed showed that others too came to enjoy the labyrinthine complexities of Levantine history. They had in Runciman a surefooted guide who could render the past visible and familiar, as in a memorable description of the messianic Peter the Hermit – 'his long, lean face horribly like that of the donkey he always rode'.

Steven's mother was the first woman to take a First in History at Cambridge and the first wife of an MP also to secure a seat in the Commons. Steven breathed a rich mixture of political gossip (he would go on to meet all but three of the twentieth century's Prime Ministers). One of his first memories was of waiting for suffragettes to carry out their vow to break the windows of the houses of Cabinet Ministers. With their afternoon walk imminent, Steven and his young sister inquired of the two burly ladies waiting outside when their protest would begin, since they were anxious not to miss the fun. The campaigners left in a huff, and the Runcimans' was the only house left undamaged that afternoon.

In 1916 he went to Eton as a King's Scholar; the future George Orwell was in the same election. In his first year, however, Runciman grew seven inches and his worried parents kept him at home for much of the remainder of his schooldays. He passed the time reading history books. Consequently, when he did see his teachers he thought them ill-informed. 'I wish this boy was kinder to me', read one master's report. In 1921, Runciman went up as a History scholar to Trinity College, Cambridge ... among those invited to take roseleaf jam in his rooms – home to a large green parakeet named Benedict – were two other beautiful young men, the aspiring arbiters of taste Stephen Tennant and Cecil Beaton.

Runciman took every opportunity to travel, visiting Istanbul for the first time in 1924. There he was told by a gypsy, correctly, that he would have several illnesses but live to a ripe old age. Runciman had a lifelong fascination with the supernatural (and the naturally superior); he later read the tarot for King Fuad of Egypt and became court fortune teller to King George II of the Hellenes.

On graduating in 1924, Runciman approached practically the only scholar then interested in Byzantine studies, J.B. Bury, and asked to be his pupil. Bury initially refused, relenting only when he learned that Runciman could read Russian; he promptly thrust articles in Bulgarian at him and told him to come back in two weeks. Later lessons proved difficult to arrange as Bury's overprotective wife took the precaution of burning all letters addressed to him. Runciman was reduced to waylaying Bury during his daily walk along the Backs.

His researches had, however, been interrupted by pleurisy, and in 1925 he recuperated by sailing to China. In Peking, he was summoned to play piano duets with the ex-Emperor, Henry Pu Yi, who told him that he had chosen his forename out of fondness for the Tudors; his chief concubine, whom he hated, was named Bloody Mary. When Runciman returned to Cambridge, he found that the college servant with whom he had boarded his parakeet refused to relinquish the bird, telling him sternly: 'Polly likes it here'.

Runciman taught at Cambridge until 1938 and was fondly regarded by his students, among them Noel Annan and Guy Burgess.

He also continued to travel widely, collecting people and places. His charm brought him friends that included George Seferis, Benjamin Britten and Edith Wharton, while his taste for exalted company brought encounters with, among others, the royal houses of Bulgaria, Romania, Siam and Spain. He saw much of the world before it subscribed to a uniform culture. In 1934 he visited Bulgaria, encountering the Istanbul-bound Patrick Leigh Fermor, and on the way back from Mount Athos, Greece, in 1937 helped to deliver a baby. It was, he said, '... a sight no innocent bachelor should see'. In Siam he saw a ghost, which dissolved before his eyes, but missed lunch with Bao Dai when the young ruler of Vietnam broke his leg playing football; 'not', thought Runciman, 'a suitable pastime for an Emperor'.

During the Holy Fire ceremony in Jerusalem at Easter, 1931, he and Princess Alice, who were seated in a gallery, amused themselves by dropping molten wax from their candles on to the bald patch below of the unpopular garrison commander; the irate soldier was the future Field-Marshal Montgomery.

When the Second World War broke out, he was recovering from severe dysentery and his health meant that he was only offered the untaxing job of censoring letters written by the Army's Cypriot muleteers. Burgess got him a job instead with the Ministry of Information and he was soon back in Bulgaria as press attache. Runciman always denied that he had in fact been a spy there, but in the records of the Italian Secret Service, which fell into British hands, he was rated *molto intelligente e molto pericoloso*.

In 1941 the Germans advanced on Sofia, and Runciman narrowly escaped death when a bomb exploded in the Istanbul hotel to which he had been evacuated. The device, concealed in the embassy luggage, had been set to explode aboard the train from Sofia; but the train reached Istanbul an hour early, and the bomb killed eight people in the lobby as Runciman was inspecting his room. In 1942 Runciman was appointed Professor of Byzantine Art and History at Istanbul University, at the Turkish government's request. There he researched his history of the Crusades. Having used his diplomatic contacts to smooth the accession of the young leader of the order, he was also made an honorary Whirling Dervish.

It turns out that Sir Steven Runciman and Rudolf von Sebottendorf knew each other, and secretly (or perhaps 'discreetely') met in Istanbul between 1942 and 1945. This should probably not surprise us if one considers their nature and their connections with both the British and the Nazi Secret Services.

There are, of course, no written records of these 'secret meetings' in Istanbul. I can only count on confidential accounts by a then young witness. Some of these meetings took place at the famous 'Pera Palace Hotel' in Istambul. Originally built in 1892 as a guest-house for the passangers of the luxurious

'Orient Express', the train that crossed Europe from London to Istanbul, it remains open to the public although not in the best of shape. Agatha Christie, that most famous of all mystery writers, hid herself in room 411 of this hotel in 1926 to plan her famous novel 'Murder on the Orient Express'. It is the Orient Bar of this hotel, however, which can pride itself on entertaining many other distinguished guests including such famous spies as Mata Hari or the aforementioned Kim Philby. Even the King of Italy, Vittorio Emmanuele III, and the Duke of Windsor, spent some of their time at this emblematic and charismatic hotel overlooking the Golden Horn and the Bosphorus.

Figure 49
Istambul's Blue Mosque. A beautiful building in one of the great cities of the world. Turkey managed to remain 'neutral' during the II WW, but a great deal of espionage and counter-espionage went on along its narrow streets and busy market places (bazaars).

Sir Steven and Rudolf met on several occasions, but I have no idea of what military or political information was ex-changed between the two. I also suspect that some of these meetings were purely of an 'informal nature'.

I further suspect that the first time that the two men met, Sir Steven did not particularly like the German Baron. Sebottendorf, after all, was not only a Nazi, he was also a shady character, dishonest and racist. Runciman however, was a man of such curiosity, open mindness and intelligence that he must have enjoyed getting to know Sebottendorf. Istanbul between 1942 and 1945 must have been an exciting place and the perfect setting for them both.

They must surely have talked at one time or another about historical subjects, like the Crusades and the Fall of Constantinople, while Runciman was reading Gibbon's description of it. Following the heroic death of the last true 'Roman Emperor' on 29 May 1453, the Turkish Sultan Mehmed entered the Church of Hagia Sophia, the first Vatican, later turned into a Mosque. He noticed among the dead bodies of women and children who had taken refuge there, a Turkish soldier hacking a piece of the wonderful marble pavement and asked why he was destroying the floor. 'For the sake of the Faith' – replied the soldier. Then the Sultan struck him with his sword and said: 'For you the treasures and the prisoners are enough. The buildings of the city belong to me'.

Sebottendorf was no longer an admirer of Hitler, whom he blamed for the disastrous attack on the Soviet Union and the Criminal Activities of the SS and Gestapo. But he remained fond of Rudolf Hess. He regarded Hess as one of his 'initiates' into the Thule group's activities and other esoteric secrets. He must have asked Sir Steven for whatever news on Hess he might have had.

We have already mentioned Rudolf Hess several times in this book. This is because he is an example of **Irrational** behaviour that is still very difficult to judge on an **Ethical** basis. His ideas, and particularly his racist and Anti-Jewish stand, were ethically wrong. His anti-communism was probably a little 'extreme', but who is now going to openly defend Stalin's Communism as having been ethically right? And who is going to claim that no nation has not been 'racist' at one time or another in its history?

Can the Americans, for example, say this with regards to their black minority? Can the Europeans claim it with regards to the Jews, or to the Gypsies? Can the Jews say it with regards to the Arabs, or the other way round? I do not think so. No nation is free from racism.

Selected Bibliography

112.   Baron Rudolf von Sebottendorf. *The Practice of the Ancient Turkish Freemasons: the Key to the Understanding of Alchemy* (First Published in 1934, Published in English by RÜNA-RAVEN Press, P.O. Box 557, Smithville, Texas 78957, 2000).

113.   Knight C. and Lomas R., *The Hiram Key* (Century, 1996).

114.   Harry Sperling and Maurice Simon. *The Zohar* (The Soncino Press, London & New York, Second Edition, 1984).

115.   Allen WS. *The Nazi seizure of power* (Quadrangle Books, Chicago, 1965).

116.   Bewley C., *Hermann Göring and the Third Reich* (Devin-Adair, 1962).

Appendix

I was born in Barcelona on St Patrick's Day (17 March 1957) when my personal history begins, but like everybody else I am a son of Chaos, having inherited all previous human horrors and glory. I bear witness to our time, and I confess my inability to tell what will happen to our species in the future.

I leave the power of prophecy to Nostradamus.

Perhaps more surprising than our inability to determine our future, is our inability to determine *our* past? This book is a good example of that. For my part, the most attractive, and until now relatively unknown character is the fourteenth century Grand Master of the Knights of St John – don Juan Fernández de Heredia. His long life (1306-96) and his prolific and vigorous activities are well documented. In the fields of diplomacy and politics he was personal advisor to several kings and popes during their exile in Avignon and their eventual return to Rome. In literature and philosophy he reintroduced classical autthors such as Plutarch into western culture and authored a recompilation of history up to his time which included an unusual interest in the Orient and the Tartar conqueror Ghengis Khan. He was an expert in medieval military architecture, rebuilding castles and new powerful city walls, not only in his native ancient Kingdom of Aragon but also in far away places such as Alghero/L'Alguer (in modern Sardinia, Italy) and in Avignon, Rome and Rhodes.

He lived, amongst other places, in Avignon (where he eventually died) and owned an extremely rich collection of writings (albeit before the invention of printing). Unfortunately most of them have now been lost, the important exceptions being held in collections at the *Biblioteca Nacional* in Madrid, or in the library of San Lorenzo del Escorial (near Madrid) or the Vatican libraries.

Several pieces of evidence strongly suggest that this learned, late medieval man, who might be seen as a precursor of the Renaissance, was considerably larger than his official or *exoteric* biography. Examine, for example, the winding staircase engravings and the equilateral stone triangle at his medieval castle in Mora de Rubielos (Teruel), or the strange persecution by an Ur-Spanish Inquisition (which extended to erasing his Maltese cross in the initial text letters of some of his best illustrated illustrated books). It is this intuitive *esoteric* side to don Juan's life and thought, together with his powerful connections, that most attracted my attention. He might have been said to belong to the *Who's Who* of European Power in the foutreenth century (in this context *see* Andrea Buonaiuti's beautiful frescoes in Florence), and his patronage of medieval operative stonemasons in his many architectural but preponderantly military Works.

He not only knew popes and kings well, including the King of England – who took him prisoner and later freed him (twice!) during the Hundred Years War in France – or the King of France or even the German Emperor Charles IV (famous for his bridge in Prague and 'finishing' the cathedral in consultation with the great Peter Parler, the German-Bohemian master builder). He was also familiar with key stonemasons and master builders from both continental Europe and England, including the little known Englishman Reynaldo Fonoll, or DesFonoll, who had been brought by Aragon's King Jaume II *circa* 1325 into Catalonia from England (in all likelihood from **Oxford**) to build the flamigerous gothic cloister of Santes Creus (near Tarragona) as well as many other impressive works.(*see From Stones to God*, by Miguel Hernández-Bronchud (2011), also available from Hamilton House Publishing Ltd., Rochester-upon-Medway, UK).

It is these surprising and unexpected sets of coincidences and still visible pieces of evidence, that prompted me to spend over a decade travelling across both modern Spain, France and many parts of the Mediterranean to the main sites visited by don Juan. From what I learned I therefore venture to propose the following hypothetical connection between don Juan Fernández de Heredia and the medieval (free)masons.

I have had the audacity to suggest that he was the 'missing link' between medieval 'speculative' stonemasons or lodges of operatives and the Knights Templar, some of whom he met personally, after their royal pardon and subsequent 'pensioning off', in his youth at Alfambra and Villel in Teruel *circa* 1320-30, or the Knights of St John (who inherited most Templar castles and properties in the ancient Kingdom of Aragon following the formal dissolution of the Templars by Pope Clement V in 1312 and the proclamation in that same year of their innocence by King Jaume II of the Aragonese Crown, at the magnificent *Corpus Christi* Capitular Hall of Tarragona's cathedral.

English speculative freemasons might like to have me share a version of my hypothesis with you on the possible medieval origins of our UGLE Coat of Arms and Don Juan Fernández de Heredia. Could he have been the link between the Knights Templar, the Knights of St John and the Medieval Guilds of Masons ?

Figure 50
The Coat of Arms of the United Grand Lodge of England.
(The Metropolitan Grand Lodge has the same quarterings on the shield.)
This window decoration is from the Grand Master's Robing Room,
Freemasons' Hall, Great Queen Street, London

Freemasonry has, since its formal inception with the uniting of four London based lodges in 1717, sought an answer for its roots in history. The speculations have been as varied as the Freemasons who have offered them. Among the speculations have been:

1). Masons of Ancient Egypt (incl Moses),
2). The Roman Building Guilds,
3). Solomon's workmen and a host of others.

The first so called 'histories' of Masonry are found in a series of mainly but not exclusively English documents stretching from the late 1300s to the mid-eighteenth century which are now collectively known as the 'Old Charges'. Some 120 versions have been traced of which over 100 are still in existence. Although
the versions have differences they have a common form: a history of Masonry followed by a series of charges giving the relationship between the duties of Masters, Fellows and Apprentices. This type of 'history', in the fashion of the times, is a combination of fact, Biblical stories and

pure legend, with a special emphasis on Geometry.

In 1723 the Revd Dr James Anderson, a Scots Presbyterian Minister in London, at the request of the premier Grand Lodge set up in four London pubs in 1717 reviewed the Old Charges and produced the first Masonic *Book of Constitutions*.

He prefaced the rules and regulations with the history from the 'Old Charges' bringing it down to the formation of Grand Lodge in 1717. In 1738 he produced a second edition of the *Book of Constitutions* in which he greatly expanded the historical introduction, introducing all manner of legendary, biblical and historical figures as Grand masters, Patrons or, simply, lovers of Masonry. He made no distinction between operative and speculative and that, combined with his claim that the events of 1717 were a revival caused by Sir Christopher Wren having neglected his duties as Grand master, gave birth to the idea that speculative Masonry was a natural outgrowth from the operative craft.

The theory of a direct descent states that as the medieval stone masons began to organise themselves they gathered in lodges as a means of protecting the craft. In the lodges they were divided into apprentices and fellows; developed simple entrance ceremonies; and had secret modes of recognition so that when stone masons moved from one building site to another they could prove that they were of the 'fellowship' and were worthy to be set to work. In the late 1500s and early 1600s these operative lodges began to admit non-operative or gentleman Masons and turned them into lodges of Free and Accepted or Speculative Masons.

From the early 1620s there is evidence in the account books of the London Masons Company of non-operatives and operatives being accepted into an inner circle, known today as the 'Acception'. It has been claimed that this is evidence of a transitional lodge in England but the accounts appear to show that both sorts were joining a separate group, not gentlemen joining the London Masons Company. The evidence is, to say the least, confusing. In 1646 Elias Ashmole, the antiquary and founder of the Ashmolean Museum at Oxford, records in his diary that on 6 October 1646 he was made a Freemason at his father-in-law's house at Warrington. Happily he recorded those present, none of whom had any connection with the operative craft.

We are left with the eternal question: where and when did ancient operative masons first develop speculative rituals and did they at any stage interact in a fraternal manner with warrior monks like the medieval Knights

Templar or the Knights of St John (known today as Knights of Malta) ?

I decided to approach the issue first from an analysis of the United Grand Lodge of Englands Coat of Arms.

In the Arms two cherubim stand one each side of a large shield whose border has lions on it (the lions were a nineteenth century addition by the British Royals). The 'quarterings on the shield itself are (a) on the left, three castles and a chevron. (▲) On the chevron is a pair of open compasses. On the right are the four quarterings of a lion, an ox, a man, and an eagle. Above the shield is the Ark of the Covenant with cherubim, and over the Ark is Hebrew lettering (honouring Adonai). At the foot of the whole is a scroll bearing a Latin motto. Its quarterings are derived partly from the Arms of the Premier Grand Lodge, that of the 'Moderns', and partly from the Arms of the Grand Lodge of the 'Antients'. The castles, chevron, and compasses are taken, with a certain amount of adaptation, from the original Arms that were granted to the London Company of Masons in either 1472 or 1473 and probably a century earlier to the London Guild of Masons. Originally the Company of Masons' Arms (*see* Fig. 51) carried the motto 'God is our Guide', altered by the time the 1677 engraving to 'In the Lord is all our Trust'; this, however, was changed back to the original motto late in the nineteenth century. Both of these mottos carry a great significance for the Initiate, who quite early in his career is required to affirm that he puts his trust in God.

GOD·IS·OUR·GUIDE

Figure 51
Arms of the Worshipful Company
of London

The Worshipful Company of Masons of London (1356; Worshipful Company's coat of arms accepted 1472/3) but what are the real origins of this coat of arms? We do not know for sure. After the union of 1813 the Arms of the two English Grand Lodges were combined.

1). 'The Moderns': the castles, chevron, and compasses represent all that survived of the Arms of the Premier Grand Lodge.

2). 'The Antients': had years before, adopted the *Tetramorphus* of the lion to represent strength; the ox, patience and assiduity; the man, intelligence and understanding; and the eagle, promptness and celerity – four emblems which reveal to us that to the 'Antients' the Royal Arch was an integral part of the Order.

Figure 52
A classical *Tetramorphus* mural which was hidden until very recently by a false wall in front of the altar in the village of Camañas near Teruel.

The classical *Tetramorphus* is a fairly common early medieval Christian image in Romanesque Catalan and Aragonese churches, across the Pyrenees, but it was not as well known in England or other parts of Europe. In the Kabbalah, there were four worlds of the Tree of Life. There are four creatures in Ezekiel's dream and in the Book of Revelations, four primary mental functions (Carl Jung), four Cardinal Points & four Dimensions in our universe.

In the year 1675 a Spanish Jew, Jacob Jehudah Leon, had exhibited in London a model of King Solomon's Temple which attracted considerable notice. Laurence Dermott, the alert Secretary of the 'Antients' Grand Lodge, examined this model about ninety years after its first exhibition, and in connection with it he saw at the same time a strange coat of arms, which he promptly appropriated to use as the achievement of arms of his Grand Lodge. The assumption is that it was the *Tetramorphus*.

Not a lot is said or explained about freemasons before 1717 in *The History of English Freemasonry* (1994) by John Hamill, ex Curator and Librarian of the UGLE. Unlike in Scotland, English records show no evidence of 'operative' lodges nor of secret modes or words of recognition but he admits that the guild system in London (the Worshipful Company of Masons) was the only one extant in England in the sixteenth and seventeenth centuries. The late C.J. Mandleberg (a Past Master of the *Quatuor Coronati* Lodge No. 2076, UGLE) in recent years confirmed the puzzling existence within the Worshipful Company of London masons of an influential 'inner circle', called the 'Acception', probably dedicated to speculative discussion and perhaps the true intellectual 'embryo' of modern Freemasonry.

In the early 1700s a new theory of Masonic history was presented in Europe which was that Freemasonry had begun in the medieval deserts of the Levant with the Crusaders and Knights Templar. The responsibility for this theory lies with two different men, Andrew Michael Ramsay (Ramsay's 'Oration' stresses links with the Knights of St John) and the German Baron Karl Von Hundt (the Order of the Strict Observance stresses links with the Knights Templar). The Chevalier Ramsay, was a Mason, a gentleman of much culture, and a tutor of the Second Pretender to the English throne, Charles Edward Stuart ('Bonnie' Prince Charlie). This distinguished exile, while in France, is said to have developed a Masonic system with a sixth degree, designated the Knight of the Temple and during one of his visits to Scotland, to have created Knights Templar there. With the Pretender's approval he attempted to use his Masonic connection to aid the exiled Stuarts return to the British throne. On 16 April 1746, the Jacobite troops of Charles Edward Stuart were completely defeated at the battle of Culloden after which The Chevalier Ramsay simply fades away…

Von Hund said he had been initiated as a Masonic Knight Templar in 1742 by unknown superiors and a mysterious *Eques a Penna Rubra* who was never never subsequently seen again. The mystery as to exactly what happened remains today.

On the other hand, in his book *The history of the Order of the Temple*, by Sir Patrick Colquhoun of London, England, published in 1878, the author stated that in 1769, Mother Kilwinning Lodge in Scotland issued a charter to

Kilwinning Masonic Lodge in Dublin, which authorized the conferring of the degree of Knight Templar therein, but it would appear that the Order was found in Dublin prior to that date in the possession of military organizations composed of the soldiers of Scotland and Ireland. It is probably by this same military source that the Order was introduced into the United States of America in Boston at about the same period. Hughan, the great English Masonic authority, makes the positive statement that the first authentic record of the conferring of the Order is found in the minutes of St. Andrews Royal Arch Lodge in Boston under the date 28 August 1769: 'the petition of Bro. William Davis coming before the lodge begging to have and receive the parts belonging to a Royal Arch Mason, which being read, was received and he unanimously voted in, and was accordingly made by receiving the four steps, that of Excellent, Super-Excellent, Royal Arch, and Knight Templar'.

Thus we are left with the question: did medieval operative masons and Knights Templar, or Knights of St John – who obviously collaborated very closely in the building of castles, fortresses, war-machines, churches, chapels, and cathedrals – also share fraternal relations, speculative rituals and symbols?

Several years ago, I came to a positive conclusion while investigating the life and works of don Juan Fernández de Heredia (1306-96), the fourteenth century Aragonese Grand Master of the Knights of St John (about a century before the political birth of modern Spain). I came across several unexpected findings in the remote Spanish region of Teruel called *El Maestrazgo* (literally, 'the land of the Masters'), which once was the fragile twelfth century frontier between the Christian kingdom of Aragon and the Islamic kingdom of Valencia.

These findings, explained and documented in my two books *The Secret Castle* (available in three editions) and *From Stones to God* – both books available on the web from Amazon and Apple Books – led me to understand that even if Scotland (between the fifteenth and sixteenth centuries) is often given credit as the birthplace of Freemasonry and its hypothetical link with the Templars, it was in Spain and Portugal where the Military and Religious Christian Orders won decisive and irreversible victories against Islam: a process known as *La Reconquista* (between the ninth and fifteenth centuries). Furthermore, it was in north-west Spain, where the *Camino de Santiago* comes to an end, that defined an intial Christian 'backbone' in Europe and its sure and certain protection by the Knights Templar.

The Scottish hypothesis was popularized by bestseller books such as : *The Holy Blood and The Holy Grail* (1982) by Michael Baigent, Richard Leigh and Henry Lincoln; or *The Temple and The Lodge* (1988) by the same authors (minus Lincoln). Their book was the first to argue (in great detail) that there was a link between Rosslyn Chapel in Scotland and Freemasonry. Interest in Rosslyn Chapel increased again with the publication of the novel: *The Da Vinci Code* by Dan Brown (2003). Unfortunately for their hypothesis, Rosslyn Chapel chapel did not exist at the time of historical Knights Templar – it was built 150 years after the dissolution of the Templar Order.

Serious doubt has also been cast on any connection between Freemasonry and Rosslyn by Robert Cooper, Curator of the Grand Lodge of Scotland Museum and Library and other authors, among other reasons because:

1). the St. Clairs, builders and owners of Rosslyn, had been enemies of the Knights Templar: the family testified against the Templars when that Order was put on trial in Edinburgh in 1309

2). 'Rosslyn Chapel bears no more resemblance to Solomon's or Herod's Temple than a house brick does to a paperback book' (according to Mark Oxbrow and Ian Robertson)

3). The famous carving in a Rosslyn capitol of a 'blindfolded man on his kneels with a rope around his neck and a book in his hand, and a knight behind', may have been produced in the 1860s when architect David Bryce, a known Scottish freemason, was asked to undertake restoration work on areas of the church including many of the carvings.

Notwithstanding the above observations, Rosslyn Chapel contains one small but fantastic piece of evidence. In it there is a carving of two men, side by side, showing a blindfolded man in medieval garb, kneeling and holding a book with a cross on the cover, in his right hand (presumably the Volume of the Sacred Law). Around this man's neck is a running noose, the end of which is held by the second man who is wearing a Templar robe. When this little carving, now thought to be the work of Scottish architect and freemason David Bryce (*circa* 1860), was found by Knight and Lomas, they were in the company of brother Edgar Harborne, an officer of the United Grand Lodge of England, and Worshipful Master of the 'Caius' Lodge who installed me in the chair of King Solomon in Cambridge, England, in 2002

In this appendix I have provided an alternative and innovative 'Templar/Masonic hypothesis' to that of Rosslyn, which may better fit the historical facts and dates without in any way questioning the sheer beauty, strong symbolical and mystical energies of Rosslyn. It is, for example, well documented that a later Sinclair – an eighteenth century descendant of William St Clair (builder of Rosslyn Chapel in the fifteenth century) and also his namesake), became the first appointed Grand Master of the (Masonic) Grand Lodge of Scotland. Needless to say, the above hypothesis requires further research and has no intention of questioning Scotland's long term Alliance with both the (historical) Knights Templar and Freemasonry. It places the ancient Kingdom of Aragon squarely on the map at the time of the medieval *Reconquista* from Islam and before modern Spain was created.

Our trip to Mora de Rubielos invites enquiry into a key issue: exactly when did these Masonic rituals and practices start to become speculative, rather than remaining purely operative? Our findings inevitably suggest that some speculative rituals and ceremonies were probably already in use at the time the Templars first (twelfth-thirteenth centuries) and the Hospitallers later (fourteenth-fifteenth centuries) dominated the Castle of Mora de Rubielos. To quote Keith Jackson: '... it is not unreasonable to estimate that commencing with the Entered Apprentice (degree) a zealous brother, possessing the requisite time, finance and ready acceptance, could conceivably advance through more than 110 degrees ... in England alone'. Freemasonry is, in its essence, a ceremonial method of approach to truth, and it is beyond dispute that most degrees have a distinct lesson to impart, with an inner meaning. It is in this context, and no other, that one must understand the modern chivalric degrees in Freemasonry, including the degrees of Knight Templar, Knight of St Paul or Mediterranean Pass, and finally Knight of St John of Jerusalem, Palestine, Rhodes and Malta.

Another interesting link between Freemasonry and operative stonemasons is, without any shadow of doubt, the so-called 'Mark Degree'. Many learned and influential freemasons believe earnestly that 'Choosing his Mark' was, in addition to being important as a part of the Fellowcrafts' Degree in England, an integral part of the qualifications for the degree of Mark Master Mason. The symbolism of this degree is based on the marks on the stone, on the meaning of some ancient Hebrew characters, with allegorical reference to the building of King Solomon's Temple, as well as on the beautiful Cedars of Lebanon, and the responsibility of another master builder – Adoniram. The lesson of this degree is that 'The stone which the builders refused is become the headstone of the corner'.

In the Kingdom of Aragon, as in England, Scotland, Portugal and elsewhere, the Knights Templar were not found guilty on all the charges brought against them by the Pope and the King of France. The National Archives of Catalonia are within walking distance from my home. They are in a modern fully equipped building by St. Cugat, near Barcelona. But the ancient Archives of the Crown of Aragon are still in Barcelona. They used to be close to the ancient Cathedral of Barcelona, in the *Barrio Gòtico* or Gothic Quarter, of this beautiful Mediterranean city. Possibly, some of the documents will return to the Gothic Quarter once their premises have been redecorated. They contain some of the most comprehensive documents regarding both the Knights of the Temple and the Knights of St. John of Jerusalem, but unfortunately these documents consist almost entirely of administrative and accounting information. There is virtually nothing, as one might expect following centuries of the Inquisition, on their secret practices or esoteric knowledge.

These unique ancient archives were first researched in depth by Joaquim Miret I Sans (Barcelona, 1858-1919), and later by many Catalan and foreign scholars, among whom I cite two whom I have met personally: Jesús Mestre i Godes, and Josep Maria Sans i Travé.

In brief, don Juan Fernández de Heredia was a soldier, a diplomat, a sailor, a humanist, a builder/architect, and a religious Grand Master. He became key advisor to several kings of Aragon, as well as to several Avignon Popes and anti-popes at the time of the Schism of the Catholic Church. He fought bravely at the battles of Crecy (1346) and Poitiers (1356), was taken prisoner by the English and pardoned by king Edward III. His initial coat of arms shows the same three castles (*see* Figure 53) as the Worshipful Company of Masons (only later did it show seven castles).

Figure 53
Original coat of arms of don Juan Fernández de Heredia in a strange wooden altarpiece at the museum of the Cistercian Monastery of Poblet (Tarragona), with artistic reference to the Holy Shroud and the Nativity of Jesus.

An elderly don Juan Fernández de Heredia, with his characteristic *barba bifurcata*, is shown within a capital letter in one of his many medieval manuscripts, holding his hands in a strange posture considerd to be of magical significance. His Maltese Cross was erased by the Spanish Inquisition.

Figure 54
The elderly don Juan Fernández de Heredia with *barba bifurcata*
and hands held in ritual posture

His origins are obscure. He was born either in 1306 or 1310, the illegitimate son of a nobleman from the ancient Kingdom of Aragon. Nobody knows who his mother was but nevertheless he became a Knight of the Hospitallers, a position usually reserved for aristocrats or the legitimate children of noble feudal lords. His first historical appearances link him to two castles in the province of Teruel previously owned by the Knights Templar, called Villel (1328) and Alfambra (1333). In Aragon the Knights Templar were neither found guilty of heresy nor other crimes (a resolution taken unanimously by the Council of Tarragona in 1312). When their order was abolished by pope Clement V, most of their properties in Aragon and Catalonia passed to their brethren, the Knights of St John – the Hospitallers. At the time don Juan was a Knight of St John in Teruel, there were still many former Knights Templar in the region and he lived with some of them in both Villel and Alfambra, near Mora de Aragón (now called Mora de Rubielos).

Not far from the castle of Alfambra, now totally devastated, and as an integral part of the same defensive Knights Templar positions around the city of Teruel (arab *Tirwal*), we find both the only original Knights Templar frescoes with a *Tetramorphus* (in the Templar chapel at the tiny village of Camañas) and the Castle of Mora de Aragón (now Mora de Rubielos) with an intriguing thirty-six step winding staircase leading three levels down from the exoteric chapel to an esoteric Temple, with a large Equilateral Triangle, with a missing apex, on the Eastern wall (twelfth to thirteenth centuries).

Figure 55
The esoteric Temple in the vault of the Castle at Mora de Rubielos
Note the large Equilateral Triangle with a missing apex, on the Eastern wall.

Figure 56
Mora de Rubielos castle's winding staircase with thirty-six steps (each with one Masonic carving except for the first three and the very last one); and an Equilateral Triangle on the East (unmistakably Masonic).

Besides these obvious monumental and artistic pieces of evidence, I gathered a significant amount of historical evidence to support my claims – quoted in my two books *The Secret Castle* (2008, 2010 and 2012), and *From Stones to God* (2011), and recent speeches (2012) in Barcelona (*Biblioteca Arús*) and Madrid, short of a specific document stating that don Juan was indeed a cryptic Templar Knight or (free)mason. The mere existence of such hypothetical document would, in any case, seem to be quite irrational and a *contra natura* expectation, given the absolute secrecy of the nature of these rituals and fraternal relations at the time.

Figure 57
Knights Templar Chapel (Ermita del Consuelo) in Camañas (Teruel), with wooden frescoes (depicting knights on horses in battle against Islam).

Other Works

By

Miguel Hernández-Bronchud

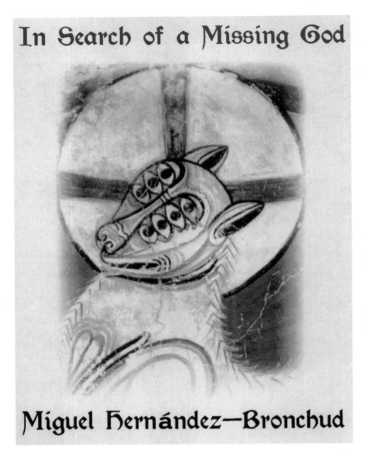

In Search of a Missing God

Miguel Hernández—Bronchud

The Search for God in a Secular Age

This book is a search. A search for meaning and for hope. A search, perhaps, for a God who will provide us with this meaning and this hope. A God who seems to have hidden Himself away, or whom we have lost. But where should we search? 'Seek me in the void', said God according to the prophet Isaiah (45,19). That is, seek me in silence, seek me in darkness, seek me on the darkest side of life, in illness and misfortune. Seek me also in the tiniest, most insignificant things. Like another prophet of Antiquity, Elijah, who did not find him in the mighty wind that 'rent the mountains and brake in pieces the rocks' but in a gentle, almost imperceptible breeze, in a 'still small voice' (1 Kings, 19, 11-12)

amazon

Available on Kindle or iBooks
ISBN 978-0-9550352-7-2

From the pen of Miguel H. Bronchud comes an originally researched e-book on the history of medieval art – particularly with regards XI to XIV centuries Romanesque and Gothic churches, cathedrals and monasteries in England, Spain (Aragon, Castile and the Pilgrim's Way to Santiago) and southern France. It is also a unique book which comprehends the artistic expressions and some of the secrets and hidden knowledge of the Knights Templar and their Brethren and successors the Knights of St John (Rhodes and Malta) in medieval and pre-Renaissance Europe, including their strange frescoes and idol Baphomet.

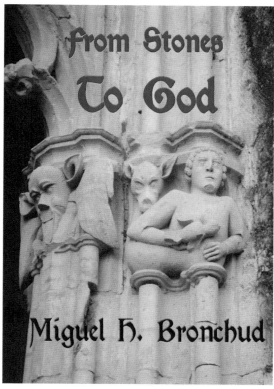

Readers will find accurate and fascinating accounts of the works and lives of three master builders and creative geniuses of the XIII (Reinard des Fonoll, who travelled from England to the ancient kingdom of Aragon to take the flamigerous Gothic with him to Spain), the XIV century (Don Juan Fernández de Heredia, Grand Master of the Knights of St John and advisor to several popes and anti-popes at the time of the Avignon Catholic Church crisis), and the modern architectural genius Antoni Gaudí, whose masterpiece *La Sagrada Familia* was recently consecrated by Pope Benedict XVI in Barcelona. The book suggests and outlines several specific cultural tours in England (its main cathedrals), Spain (Barcelona, Catalonia and Aragon, Castile, and the Pilgrim's Way to Santiago), Rhodes and parts of Italy (Florence) and southern France. After reading the book and enjoying its hundreds of different original photos, the reader will be able to plan short (3 or 4 days) or longer (1 to 2 weeks) trips to explore the mystical energies of Spanish Templar castles and churches, the light and darkness of Spanish and English cathedrals, the remains of city walls in Avignon, Rome and Rhodes, and the architectural wonders of Barcelona. Insights on the three main characters of the book will expand the reader's knowledge of medieval esoteric traditions, the true Christian origins of Freemasonry, the legacy of the Templars, and the all embracing but controversial concept of God both in the Middle Ages and Modern times.

Printed by Amazon Italia Logistica S.r.l.
Torrazza Piemonte (TO), Italy

65647799R00138